The Low Countries

Cover:
North Sea
© Derek Blyth

TLC

2015 The Low Countries

ARTS AND SOCIETY IN FLANDERS AND THE NETHERLANDS

23

**Published by
the Flemish-Dutch
cultural institution
Ons Erfdeel vzw**

Contents

Turning Tides

Chronicle

Next page and page 110 :

Kris Martin, *Altar*, 2014, Steel, 340 x 440 cm, Ostend

© Erwin Acke

Framing the Sea

Can one frame the sea? Kris Martin tried to, using the frame of the Ghent Altarpiece, a polyptych known also as the Adoration of the Mystic Lamb. *Voilà*.

The theme of this edition is the sea, water in all its forms, turning tides.

Everything is water, claimed Thales of Miletus round 600 BC. Some assert that that statement was the beginning of philosophy. Water is life. All life comes from the water. The land is what is left behind by the sea. The Low Countries, and the Netherlands in particular, know all about that. They have been won from the sea. But that victory is never definitive. Dikes and dams have to tame the sea and the rivers. Dredgers repair and maintain the coastline with additions of sand. And in the meantime climate change threatens to raise the waterline - of both the rivers and the oceans. Will the Low Countries still exist in five hundred years' time? Are the tides turning?

But we're nowhere near that point yet. The Low Countries border the North Sea. I readily admit that its countless different shades of grey are a more fascinating spectacle than the beautiful but monotonous blue of the Mediterranean Sea.

In this book, then, we take a closer look at water in all its forms, water which has been such a determining factor in the formation of the Low Countries.

You can travel the length of the Belgian coast by tram, from De Panne to Knokke. You can sail from Vlissingen to Texel. You'll find it all in this book.

We wonder whether the ports of Rotterdam and Antwerp could coordinate their activities, but perhaps, as far as China is concerned, Zeebrugge, Ghent-Terneuzen and Vlissingen are just hubs of one and the same mega port offering access to Europe.

There is a portfolio of pictures, too, showing what people do on the wide sandy beaches of the Low Countries in their summer hours of idleness. The great pirates of the past are also honoured: Piet Hein who captured the Spanish Silver Fleet near Cuba, and Jan Bart from Dunkirk, who fought not only for the Republic but for the French Sun King too - pirates go where the money is – without speaking a word of French. Today, Somali pirates raise the problem of the law of the sea. In his *Mare liberum* (1609) the Dutch jurist Hugo Grotius was the first to deal with the legal status of the open waters (the sea belongs to everyone; everyone may trade freely on it) but today we still need an international law of the sea, especially where pollution and overfishing are concerned. With regard to the latter, however, what food can we still obtain from our North Sea? And finally, there's no sea without seascapes and poems, of course, a flood of words to conjure up the roar of the surf, the eternal lapping of the waves.

And the tides? They keep on turning.

11

LUC DEVOLDERE | *Chief Editor*

Sleeping with the Enemy

The Netherlands and its Waters

[MAARTEN ASSCHER]

Every living being has its natural enemies, with the result that many species can exist in competitive balance with each other. Mosquitoes have their swallows, dinosaurs their meteorites, liberals their socialists, writers their critics. The same is true for countries: Switzerland has its avalanches and Japan its earthquakes. Likewise, the Netherlands has its water. The country has steadily battled its way out of the water over the last thousand years and one day – although hopefully it will take a while yet – it will eventually disappear into it again. In the meantime, a community of people has gathered on this sodden ground that has turned their greatest enemy into their right to exist. They have compromised in innumerable ways with the menacing water and, time after time, it has been a matter of pride for them to make a virtue out of a flood, preferably as a preventive measure, even before the worst comes to the worst. Is there a discernible pattern in this? Has it endowed the Dutch with a particular mentality? Is there a link between the watery geography of the country and the psychology of its inhabitants?

You will have to work out for yourself how it is in other countries but if you think about the Netherlands, you will quickly realise that there is one national theme running through the whole geological, political and social history of our country: water. There are few periods or events in Dutch history in which water has not in some way or other played a supporting or even decisive role. From Roman times, when the Old Rhine formed the boundary of the territory taken by the Romans, up to and including the German occupation, which was forced on the Netherlands in 1940 with the bombardment of the port city of Rotterdam and brought to an end in 1944/1945 after months of fighting for the bridges over the rivers of Gelderland and North Brabant. There is also the Dutch East India Company and its trade with the East, the *Watergeuzen* at Den Briel and the Napoleonic armies who simply marched into our country over the frozen rivers in 1795.

In short, our national history is a history of water. Just as Italian history is hewn from marble, French history is woven into Gobelins and British history is built in bricks, so Dutch history is a scene painted in watercolours, with an arrow-straight horizon separating the grey water from the grey sky or – with a bit of luck – the grassy green polder from the clear blue sky.

Ten sorts of water

A country's national theme manifests itself in all sorts of varieties, forms and gradations, and for every individual variation there is a separate name. The French with their 368 types of cheese, the Belgians with their reputed 1,100 sorts of beer, the Scots with their endless assortment of whiskies. Can we regard the Netherlands' water in the same way? I think we can, although obviously not all sorts of liquid are unique to the Netherlands alone. But against the background of our flat, watery ground surface every type of water in the Netherlands has its own specific significance. Let us, for the sake of convenience, limit ourselves to 10 sorts of liquid.

Blankenberge, Belgium

Sweat

Everyone sweats, but it looks very much as if the Dutch do so more often than others, or at least more than other Europeans. A glance at the meteorological statistics shows that the inhabitants of Portugal or Cyprus, for example, have twice as much opportunity to sit in the sun or rest in its shadow as the Dutch. Whereas the sun shines 1,521 hours a year in the Netherlands, it shines a good

3,037 hours and 3,381 hours respectively in the other two countries. Despite an unemployment rate of 7.7%, people work hard in the Netherlands and a comparatively high percentage of women participate in the employment process too (65.4%). In more or less all the bigger cities compulsory closing on the Day of the Lord has been abolished now and – even more significant – the Dutch state deliberately discourages its subjects from all having a day off at the same time: the Netherlands has the lowest number of national holidays of all the countries in Western Europe. There are only 8, while in Greece there are officially 12 public holidays a year and in Spain even 14.

Tears

If it is true that countries derive their national self-awareness particularly from overcoming disasters, foreign oppression and other collective tragedies, one might regard tears as the ultimate liquid of nationality. Over the centuries, many of these tragedies in the Netherlands had to do with water (floods due to storm tides, breaches in the dikes or extreme weather), but enough mass misery has also been caused by acts of war, persecution, explosions and airplane accidents. Have the Netherlands wept more than other countries during their history, or had more reason too? I doubt it, but it is interesting to note, for example, that the disastrous flood of 1953 (1,538 dead) was considered from the beginning to be a punishment from God that must be accepted in silence (the Minister responsible addressed the Lower House: 'Who can deflect the hand of the Lord?') The Dutch are not a people that like public sorrow or mourning too much, just as, in general, they keep any tears of joy till they're safely inside their own houses. Apart from football supporters, that is, but apparently they are beyond any laws.

Dew

The International Organisation for Dew Utilisation (or OPUR as it is known by its French acronym), is headquartered in Paris and has existed since 1999. The organisation tries to stimulate the use of dew in agriculture and the cultivation of all sorts of edible crops, in areas all over the world where there is a serious shortage of water. There is definitely no need for the organisation in the Netherlands. We do

Skipsea, UK

have dew, mainly in the spring, summer and early autumn, but dew in the Netherlands is a luxury phenomenon, Nature's delicate embellishment. Poets are the ones who are most aware of it: 'The dew hangs like pearls on branches and leaves' (J.H. Leopold), 'White and still hung the dew o'er the meadows' (J.A. der Mouw) and 'Two eyes and a woman's body / He lay, like her, stretched out on the dew' (Gorter). The rest of the population detests it. It is not without reason that the traditional early morning walk on Ascension Day, here in the Netherlands, is referred to as *dauwtrappen* or treading the dew. The poetic wetness is trampled energetically underfoot.

Holy water

These days there is a tendency to report on pretty well all subjects in terms of winning or losing. 'Dutch lead in leaving the church', wrote the church news website Kerknieuws.nl, on the publication of a report by Statistics Netherlands. At the start of the twenty-first century only one out of five people still goes to church, mosque or another house of prayer, whilst at the end of the nineteenth century 98% of people said they considered themselves to be religious. In the north of the country and in the Randstad there are now fewer believers than non-believers. In Catholic churches the holy water increasingly remains undisturbed and half of the still remaining Dutch RC Church buildings will have to be disposed of in the years to come. One church after another is being demolished, converted into shared business premises, an apartment complex or a concert hall. Is there anything to be done about it? The Taskforce on the Future of Church Buildings, which was founded in 2006, thinks there is, but it seems to me to be a case of 'One must let God's water flow over God's acre', to quote an old Dutch saying used as far back as the sixteenth century.

Groundwater

If you want to know how damp the Dutch soil is, you can stick your spade into the ground. Nine times out of ten - unless it is a bone dry summer or the soil is sandy - you will hear a slurping noise as you lever it backwards and forwards. Better still, take a bit of a distance and have a look at the whole of the Netherlands. The SMOS (Soil Moisture and Ocean Salinity) satellite was launched in 2009 for this purpose and has confirmed with observational data from space that the Netherlands is indeed the most sodden country in the whole of Europe. Countless types of water end up together in the Dutch soil: from above (rainwater), from the sides (river water) and even from below (groundwater). All that water needs to be regulated and must be able to be drawn on as a source of drinking water, for industrial use, irrigation, firefighting, etc. For that an enormous conglomeration of administrative bodies has been set up, district water boards, ministries, provinces, municipalities, waterworks and other institutions. If you want to know how the Netherlands functions administratively, you should disguise yourself as a drop of water and jump down out of a cloud, or slip in via the Rhine at Lobith. I guarantee you a rollercoaster ride past innumerable authorities, organisations and companies.

Swimming pools

According to the last count (2012) there are 1,537 swimming pools in the Netherlands. Two thirds of them completely or partially covered. Nearly half (45%) are open to the public. In the Netherlands there is a swimming pool for every 10,900 inhabitants. The average temperature of the water is 28 degrees Celsius. Two things can be deduced from these figures. First of all, that everything is documented in the Netherlands. Nothing escapes the notice of the statisticians. Secondly, that comparatively speaking the Netherlands has an awful lot of public swimming pools. France has 2,898 for a much larger population, and the United Kingdom 4,674. So what does this mean? Apparently all those Dutch rivers, lakes and canals are too dirty or too dangerous to swim in, and the average Dutchman considers the North Sea, the IJsselmeer and the Waddenzee too cold. In terms of the national psychology the explanation could be that people in the Netherlands are so distrustful of the sea and all the rest of the public water that in all those swimming pools they want at least to teach their small children not to drown. The Netherlands at its best: as a water welfare state.

Neeltje Jans, the Netherlands

Lakes

There are around 4,000 polders in the Netherlands. That is land that has been constructed artificially, by draining, diking or development. Yet by no means all the lakes have been lost to impoldering. Assuming that the definition of a lake is an enclosed still water surface of minimum 50 hectares, there are still 2,500 lakes left in the Netherlands. The largest of them all, the IJsselmeer, was actually added in 1932 with the construction of the Afsluitdijk. But a great many, like the Schermeer and the Beemstermeer, were drained and disappeared in the early seventeenth century. In the West of the Netherlands, especially, whole areas were surrounded with dikes and a ring canal and the water was pumped off by hundreds of windmills, stretching as far as the eye could see. Afterwards, too, the windmills continued to pump, making sure that the ground that had been drained remained dry. That carried on until the invention of the steam pumping station which, in the years 1849-1852, made it possible to drain even the big Haarlemmermeer, ground on which Schiphol Airport was built in the twentieth century. It is no exaggeration to suggest that the Netherlands owes its seventeenth-century prosperity to two wooden machines: the sailing ship with which riches were brought home from the colonies in the East and West, and the windmills with which prosperous and fertile land was made and kept safe for habitation - for the peaceful and unostentatious enjoyment of that wealth.

Rain

In 2014 the Netherlands' problems are mainly luxury problems. Not civil war, famine or earthquakes. That, in the best Calvinist tradition, is something to be thankful for, but one of the most irritating luxury problems is cycling in the rain against the wind. Since it rains on average 8 percent of the time in the Netherlands (an average total of 847 mm per year) and there is almost always wind (on average 8 km per hour, even 20 km per hour at the coast) you get a good soaking on your bike several times a year. On the other hand, the uncertainty of the weather conditions in this part of the world (varying from a record cold of -27.4 degrees to a record heat of 38.6 degrees, and a record rainfall of 148 mm in one day as opposed to 36 consecutive days without rain) does provide something to talk about with fellow countrymen with whom you have nothing else in common, like people in shops, in a waiting room or on public transport. What are people supposed to talk about in Malta or Cyprus, where for eight long months the weather is pretty much the same every day? In the Netherlands, a higher power has taken care of that problem.

Sea

The sea, which gave the Dutch trading nation a sphere of activity that stretched right around the world in the seventeenth century, has also betrayed the inhabitants of the Low Countries again and again since time immemorial. Long is the list of storm floods that have wiped out whole villages and driven the water right up into the streets of Amsterdam. Sometimes I think that it is mainly the surrounding sea, with all its accidents, shipwrecks and floods that has forced the Dutch to their knees, with all their sense of futility, before the almighty Calvinist God, since the start of the Golden Age. Only prayer and a combination of frugality and diligence could give them the hope that their predestined demise might be kept at bay for a while. Nowhere in the Netherlands can as many Protestant churches be found as along the coast of the North Sea and the banks of the former Zuiderzee, now the IJsselmeer. The Dutch Bible Belt still links the many port towns and fishing villages along the former Zuiderzee with the traditionally deeply religious province of Zeeland. In both places nothing but the dikes separate the roaring of the surf on the one side and the thunderous preaching of the Reformed Church minister on the other.

Rivers

When foreigners speak of the Netherlands as a land of water, they are referring primarily to the sea. But the majority of Dutchmen live nowhere near the sea and rarely go to it. The Netherlands is a country with an abundance of water because of the fact that two important European rivers, the Meuse and the Rhine, both flow through it. With the Scheldt, just south of the Dutch/Belgian border, these rivers and their innumerable tributaries are what make the Low Countries a delta. It is mainly thanks to the Meuse and the Rhine, which branches off into the Waal and the IJssel, that more than a sixth of Dutch territory consists of surface water. Most of the flooding that has affected the Netherlands over the past centuries was the result of rivers bursting their banks rather than the dikes being breached by the sea. The Netherlands' heroic struggle against the constantly threatening water is therefore not so much a war against a natural enemy from without as a never-relenting struggle against the most fundamental and ineradicable nature of the Dutch landscape itself. This inner struggle, this armed peace has given the Netherlands its taste for negotiation and compromise, and perhaps even its talent for a certain bluntness. Because usually there is no time to lose.

Uneasiness?

The Netherlands? You need only fly over it once by plane and you will understand the problem immediately, certainly if you are also aware that due to geological processes and ill-considered peat cutting about half of the land surface now lies below sea level. Just as his great-great-great grandfather first emerged from the waves of the North Sea and set foot on the beach at Scheveningen in 1813, to become King of the Netherlands two years later, our current monarch, Willem-Alexander, came to the throne from water management. That makes even the highest symbolic authority of our country subject to water, the one element that surrounds and flows through the entire surface of the Netherlands.

The Dutch definitely do not derive their sense of nationhood from the social, administrative or intellectual elite above them. Certainly not now, when populism, large-scale sporting events and an unprecedented dumbing-down of the media provide sensation day in day out and an unremitting stream of human interest. Perhaps – for instruction and enjoyment – the following question should be included sometime in one of the many public surveys carried out by those research bureaus that are always so well-informed about what concerns 'the people': 'Which is greater: your respect for the authorities or your uneasiness about the rising sea level?' You can guess the answer now: neither. ▪

© All photos by Carl De Keyzer.
From: *Moments before the Flood, Lannoo, Tielt, 2012.*

Translated by Lindsay Edwards

Along the Belgian Coast in a Streetcar Named Desire

[DEREK BLYTH]

Most people tell you the same thing. The Belgian coast is ugly. It is just a long line of apartment buildings. It has been ruined by property developers. It rains almost every day. The waiters are rude. The mussels have grit in the shells. The wind blows sand in your face. And so it goes on. No one has a good word to say about the Belgian coast and yet millions visit it every year. I am standing at De Panne station thinking about this paradox when the tram arrives.

I am setting off on the longest tram ride in the world, all the way along the Belgian coast from De Panne to Knokke. The route is 67 kilometres from beginning to end with 68 stops along the way. I could do the whole journey in two hours and thirty minutes, according to the timetable, but I have decided to get off along the way to take a look around. I want to find out if the coast is as bad as they say.

De Panne station. The doors close. We are off. Next stop Plopsaland. It is soon clear that the coast tram is not as quaint as you might hope. It speeds through the streets of De Panne like any other tram without offering even a brief glimpse of the sea. You might as well be on tram 94 in Brussels.

Sint Idesbald

The tram stops at Sint Idesbald. I get off here to visit the Paul Delvaux Museum. It is a long walk from the tram stop. I have time to think about the artist I have come to see. Delvaux was a quiet, reclusive painter who died 20 years ago at the age of 96. For most of his life, he painted Neo-Classical nude women in unsettling locations, like a third-class Belgian railway carriage or a deserted Brussels street.

The museum is dark and quiet. A skeleton stands in a glass cabinet along with a collection of skulls and paintbrushes. I sit on an old wooden seat salvaged from a railway carriage and contemplate a voluptuous naked woman with big brown eyes.

It is hard to know how to interpret these paintings. Fortunately the museum has put up a text by Delvaux. "One must first find the subject: an object, a landscape, a face in the street that touched and has captured your attention, a piece of music, even certain passages of a book," he writes in an essay titled The Birth of

a Painting. "One must now find the other elements that complete the ensemble and make it stable and efficient." I am not sure this makes his work any clearer.

Nieuwpoort

I am still thinking about Delvaux when the tram arrives. It rumbles through the streets of Nieuwpoort and emerges on the harbour front. I get off to take a short walk down to the beach. But then I notice a little ferry carrying people across the river estuary. What lies over there, I wonder. The ferry is crowded with families and cyclists. On the far side, I find a bird hide where you can sit in darkness watching rare species paddling around in the mudflats. It feels wild out there in the middle of the marshes, far from the crowds on the other side eating waffles and ice cream.

Middelkerke

The tram arrives in Middelkerke. It sounds dull. And looks dull. The tall apartment buildings have no charm. No anything. I contemplate catching the next tram that comes along. But then I discover one of the most romantic museums on the coast.

Kusthistories opened in 2009 in an old post office building. It is a museum of the coast. Here you can see a historic coast tram and an ancient go-kart, as well as a reconstructed hotel dining room and several creepy waxworks figures dressed in vintage swimming costumes. It is a sad, romantic place to wander around, like flicking through a childhood photo album, with its faded photographs of demolished Art Nouveau buildings and menus of hotels that vanished decades earlier.

I walk down to the sea to look at the old casino. It was built on the promenade in the romantic Anglo-Norman style. I sit inside in the Tavern on the Sea with a cup of coffee looking out on the grey sea that stretches all the way to Norway. It is only later that I learn of plans to demolish this quaint casino. It makes sense, I decide, if Middelkerke is to preserve the purity of its dullness.

Raversijde

The tram now runs along the sea. I can see tiny figures walking along the beach. People on horses. Little black dots that are dogs. On the other side of the tracks, huge menacing guns in the dunes point to the sky. They are relics of the great Atlantic Wall built in World War Two, a warren of dark concrete tunnels and abandoned bunkers that was meant to protect Nazi Europe from invasion. But the guns were pointing the wrong way when the Allies finally arrived here.

Oostende Marie-Joséplein

I step off into the light drizzle and see the warm lights of the Café du Parc across the street. This comfortable old Belgian place is just as I remember it. The old leather sofas, the brass coat hooks, the large mirrors. All still there. The retired couples reading La Libre Belgique. Still living comfortably on their pensions. The waiters in black uniforms. Polite but formal. The filter coffee dribbles into a glass cup. It is slow, but then no one is in much of a hurry here. I drink my coffee and wait. The tram is not due for another 15 minutes.

I walk down a long empty colonnade. It leads to an impressive statue in honour of King Leopold II. It was Leopold who commissioned the tramline, funded the grand hotels and built the first resorts. Without his money, the coast would be very different. He turned it into a summer playground for Europe's élite. Now he sits on his horse high above the beach huts, surrounded by bronze figures representing his adoring subjects.

Except no one adores Leopold any more. He is accused of ruthlessly exploiting the Congo for his own gain. Some say his agents cut off people's hands, which is why activists came here one night and hacked the hand off one of the bronze figures. The protestors say they will return it if Ostend apologises for Leopold's crimes.

I find myself later in the Langestraat looking for the city museum. It moved a few years ago into the old summer residence of the Belgian royal family. Its dusty rooms are filled with old ship models, seaside souvenirs and faded ferry posters.

I stand in a small room watching a short video in which an actress is dressed as Queen Louise-Marie. "This is where I lived at the end of my life," she says. A creaking staircase leads to the top of the building where a little observatory was built for Louise-Marie. When she became too sick to climb the steps, she was hoisted up here on a chair to enjoy the sea view. Now the sea view has gone.

I sit in a café to write down my impressions of Ostend. I like the fact that it has stopped calling itself the Queen of the Belgian Resorts. Ostend has decided instead to reinvent itself as a city of culture by opening a museum of contemporary art in an abandoned department store and a cultural centre in the former post office. It combines the quirky charm of a faded seaside resort with the edgy art of a big city. It is Brussels with seagulls.

Oostende station

I have mixed feelings about Ostend Station. It brings back memories of sea crossings on the Dover to Ostend ferry. After a couple of hours, you would see the coast of Belgium through the grubby windows. At first it looked like a long line of cliffs, but then you began to realise that this was a continuous barrier of grey concrete apartment buildings, a modern Atlantic Wall.

The ferry was never really glamorous, not even when you caught a whiff of French perfume coming from the duty-free shop. It always had the smell of fried food and engine oil. Now the ferries no longer run and the harbour looks desolate. I came across a Facebook campaign to bring back the Ostend to Dover ferries, but I'm not planning to click "Like".

Weg naar Vismijn

The tram follows a meandering route from the station around the old port, past vast piles of gravel and a handsome 19th century bridge with locomotives carved in the stonework. It stops on the far side of the port near the fish market. I get out to look at Fort Napoleon, a massive brick fortress built in the dunes in the early 19th century. It was recently restored by the Ostend architects Govaert & Vanhoutte to create a museum and an upmarket restaurant.

Bredene

It is not far to Bredene, so I decide to walk along the beach. I come to a large forbidding sign that reads NAAKTSTRAND 200m, translated into French, German and English. It reminds me of those stern Cold War signs you used to see in West Berlin that warned people: YOU ARE LEAVING THE AMERICAN SECTOR. Somehow Bredene manages to instil a similar sense of totalitarian terror.

Bredene used to be a quiet family resort until the municipality voted to create the first nudist beach on the Belgian coast in 2000. It is still the only nudist beach in the country, whereas The Netherlands has almost 70 along its coastline and inland lakes. I am not sure that Belgians are really relaxed about their one short stretch of nudist beach. Some complain that it has become a gay cruising area. Others murmur about voyeurs taking photographs. I do not risk going beyond the sign.

De Haan

The tram runs through the woods to De Haan. I get off at a pretty station with half-timbered walls and steep pitched roofs. De Haan is different from the other resorts. I walk along quiet lanes lined with romantic villas. Everything is neat and well-maintained. I come across a statue of Albert Einstein sitting on a bench in a small park. He was travelling back to Germany when he learned that Hitler had seized power. He could not go back to Germany so he stayed in a little villa in De Haan for six months.

De Haan was one of Leopold II's resorts. He brought in the German urban planner Hermann-Josef Stübben to draw up a plan. Stübben insisted on low buildings surrounded by large gardens. Unlike other resorts, De Haan has barely changed. The houses have quaint names like Little Red Riding Hood and look like drawings in a German fairy story.

Blankenberge

The tram arrives in Blankenberge. This is a totally different kind of resort. It takes time to adjust. I walk down a side street and come to a row of fin de siècle seaside houses decorated with pretty painted tiles. Three of the houses have been turned into a museum of the Belle Epoque. I go inside and wander through rooms filled with nostalgic relics from the time when Blankenberge was the most elegant resort on the North Sea. The biggest surprise is a roof terrace with a replica Gaudi bench made with fragments of ceramic tiles salvaged from demolished seaside houses.

I wander along the promenade, past an exceptionally ugly casino with two large babies climbing the façade. They were created, I find out later, for a sculpture festival held on the coast some years ago. The modern apartment buildings along the beach are uniformly hideous, but the concrete pier has a certain rugged Art Deco charm. I sit with a coffee at the end of the pier facing out to sea. It is the only way you can avoid looking at the ugly buildings.

Zeebrugge kerk

I see a huge container ship from the tram. The port of Zeebrugge has bitten off a huge chunk of the coastline. I am curious to see the old port so I get off at Zeebrugge church and walk down to the waterfront. The huge fish market has been turned into a maritime theme park where a sleek Russian submarine is the main attraction. The fish market has moved elsewhere, but giant photographs of fishermen taken by Stefan Vanfleteren hang on the building.

Knokke

The tram arrives at Knokke. I am hoping for a grand finale, but there is not even a shelter. Nothing. The tram turns in a little grassy area. Terminus, the driver announces. The doors open. And that is the end of the longest tram journey in the world.

I walk down the long main street of Knokke in the direction of the sea. Knokke is considered the most glamorous resort on the coast, but I have never really liked the town. It is full of rich people who don't seem to be having much fun as they cruise around in conspicuous sports cars or ridiculous golf buggies.

The local council is rather mean spirited. It has banned cool boxes and kite flying and beach bars that play music after 8pm. I feel more comfortable in Blankenberge where cool boxes are permitted, or in Ostend where there are plenty of bars that play music until the early hours.

It is in Knokke that I see a strange vision of the future. An exhibition called Shifting Lands had brought together five architects who had developed a new radical vision of the coast. They started from the idea that the coastline should be restored to its old state with mudflats and tidal inlets. The towns would become more varied and interesting once this happened. Eventually the Atlantic Wall would disappear.

I walk along the Zeedijk, past the last beach bar in Belgium, the last palm tree, the last pampered dog. Soon I reach Het Zwin, the wild area of mudflats and screaming birds that marks the end of Belgium. I stand on the edge of the emptiness thinking that it used to be like this all along the coast.

Most people say the coast has been ruined by property developers. It is 70 kilometres of unsurpassed monotony. I might have agreed when I first set eyes on the coast from the deck of a Cross-Channel ferry. Now I see it differently.

I love the wild places that have survived, the little museums filled with model boats and seaside trinkets, the views of the greyish-green sea. I also like the ferry that chugs across Ostend harbour, the romantic paradises like De Haan and Het Zoute, and the quaint little chapel in Mariakerke filled with model ships and seashells.

At the end of it all, the coast is not just a stretch of sand or a row of apartments. It is a place where Belgians come to realise their dreams and desires. It is a 70-kilometre strip of fantasies.   ▪

© All photos by Jonas Lampens

Sailing Along the Dutch Coast

[THIJS BROER]

The North Sea was unwrinkled satin, the estuary of the Westerschelde deserted in the early morning light. In the distance, on the beach at Cadzand, a couple walked, small and dark against the white of the dunes. Behind them rose the apartment buildings of Breskens, like a monkey rock above the coast of Zeeuws-Vlaanderen. On the other side of the estuary the glowing dune landscape of the island of Walcheren turned into the serrated silhouette of Vlissingen, the first port city on the Dutch coast. A languid swell rolled past under the ship, the motor rumbled beneath my feet.

In spring 2013, I had cast off for a months-long trip over the North Sea, from Zeeuws-Vlaanderen in the south to Delfzijl in Northeast Groningen. By sailing my own yacht along the coast, I thought, I could investigate the relationship of the Dutch with the sea. The perspective would be different from everything I had read so far about the Netherlands and the sea. I would approach it from the water; become a tourist in my own country.

From the island of Marken, my home at the former Zuiderzee, I had set off through the inland waterways to Zeeland. On my way along the canals I saw the rusting cranes of abandoned shipyards, the silent remains of a disappearing culture, and, right beside them on the waterfront, brand new homes and senior citizens' flats, invariably with a gleaming sloop edged with rope in front of the door. Older couples in nautical striped jumpers drank coffee in the pale spring sunshine, contented behind the sliding glass doors. The waterfront had been taken over by the affluent middle class, Holland as a maritime nation seemed to be no more than a cultivated memory.

Early one morning I sailed through the Hansweert lock into the Westerschelde, alone at sea for the first time. A colossal container ship glided by, belching brown clouds, steaming in the direction of Antwerp. From the west a slow swell rolled towards me, the salt water foamed under the bow. A couple of weeks later I was bobbing about on the North Sea, close to Vlissingen. The journey had begun.

Sailing is outsourced

In the Vlissingen lock the metres-high walls were covered with rugged, razor-sharp oysters, dripping with seawater. I secured the ropes to the rusty chains hanging down from the lock walls. Gratingly the gates opened and the inland harbour appeared. From the Schelde, Vlissingen was a lively sight: town houses and holiday flats along the boulevard, the white-plastered nautical school, pilot boats on their way to the cargo ships on the anchorage. But the inland harbour was a dilapidated void. In the inner harbour fishing boats and old coasters lay rusting in the stagnant water. Immediately opposite the lock, weeds grew on a barren wasteland. The bankruptcy of the De Schelde shipyard in the nineteen-eighties had left a gaping hole in the city.

The monumental building of the former nautical college on the boulevard was deserted. A poster beside the door announced that the Maritiem Instituut De Ruyter, as it is called these days, would evacuate the building completely at the end of the week. In the last four decades the number of students wanting to qualify as maritime officers at the college had dropped from 1400 to fewer than 250. For reasons of efficiency the management had recently decided to dispose of the old building. It was sold to an investment club wanting to set up a care hotel there, an annex to a rehabilitation clinic. How ironic, I thought, as I stepped inside: the place where, for over a century, young Dutch men were educated for Dutch glory is being turned into a convalescent home for the elderly.

Julien Berthier,
Love–love, 2007.
Photo on paper.
© Fries Museum Leeuwarden

In the fifties, my Uncle Han raised here as a seaman. He sailed over all the seas of the world and went to live in South Africa. In those days the sea was an enticing prospect for a whole generation. The merchant navy grew tempestuously. But by the seventies and eighties there was little left of the romance of sailing, said Uncle Han, home on leave in the Netherlands. The ships were getting bigger, the crews smaller, and Dutch seamen were being replaced by cheaper sailors from China or the Philippines. Countless shipping companies went to the wall. According to the Dutch shipowners' association, KVNR, in 2013 there were fewer than 7500 registered Dutch mariners, including those working in sea fishing and hydraulic engineering. In half a century the percentage of seamen in the Netherlands had dropped by 90 percent. Seamanship was steadily seeping out of the public's experience.

The Netherlands is still considered internationally to be a leading maritime nation. Rotterdam is one of the largest and most efficient transhipment ports in Europe, Boskalis and Van Oord are among the biggest dredging companies in the world and the Netherlands still has maritime expertise. Yet the Dutch have outsourced seamanship; they rarely go to sea themselves.

Uncle Han retired in 1991, after nearly forty years of maritime service. When I spoke to him on the phone, just before my trip along the coast, he said from South Africa: 'Thijs, my boy, have a good trip and take care.' It was as if his voice came from the nineteen-fifties, from a ship somewhere on the ocean.

The Netherlands in 1574:
a realm of islands
(from: Sebastian Münster,
Cosmographia)

The literary sea

In the meantime the sea has gradually seeped out of literature too. On board I had a book that whole generations of Dutchmen read before they went to sea and that was more influential in determining the Netherlands' image of itself as a seafaring nation than any other novel in the twentieth century, if only for its title, *Hollands Glorie* by Jan de Hartog. It was translated into English as *Captain Jan*, but a literal translation of the Dutch title would be 'Dutch Glory'. I opened it on one of those evenings in Vlissingen by the light of a petrol lamp. The novel, a thoroughly Dutch story about a stubborn seaman who manages to wrest himself from the yoke of a profit-hungry shipowner, was published in September 1940 but is still read today. Jan de Hartog's work was part of a long tradition of Dutch sea stories, like Herman Heijermans' *Op hoop van zegen (The Good Hope)*, Arthur van Schendel's *Het fregatschip Johanna Maria (The Frigate Johanna Maria)* and the work of Jan Jacob Slauerhoff, the seafaring poet from Harlingen.

Part of the Dutch's relationship with saltwater was a sacred awe of the sea. Perhaps that was at the core of Dutch glory, I thought that evening in Vlissingen: the sea is the symbol of freedom, but it is also the natural power that sweeps pride from the deck.

After the nineteen-fifties, though, seafaring in literature increasingly slipped into the background. In the seventies there was only one seafaring writer of any significance in the Netherlands, Maarten Biesheuvel. I had read his best-known tales of the sea as a schoolboy: *Opstapper* (Passage worker), for example, *In de bovenkooi* (In the top berth) and *Brommer op zee* (Motorcycle at sea), in which, with great imagination and self-mockery, he told the story of his saltwater adventures.

After Maarten Biesheuvel few Dutch writers chose the sea as their subject. Typical of those who did was Thomas Rosenboom. His *De nieuwe man* (The new man, 2003) tells the story of the taciturn Groninger Niesten who, early in the twentieth century, builds a ship in a water-logged meadow at the Damsterdiep but fails, despite his desperate toil, to succeed in launching the iron colossus on the sea. Rosenboom based his novel on a true story, but chose a different ending. The change is telling. In historical fact the ship went to sea, a hundred years later in literature it remained stuck in a water-logged meadow.

What to do if the water comes?

In the weeks following my visit to Vlissingen I sailed around the former island of Walcheren. Since the Delta works were built, after the great flood of 1953, Zeeland has become a mecca for water sports. Nearly all the gaps between the islands, which used to be filled with swirling sea currents, were closed with heavy dams and a storm surge barrier. Nowhere in the Netherlands could you sail on salt water as light-heartedly as between the islands of Zeeland. That is how it was on that afternoon on the Veerse Meer, too. With wind force 6 from the northwest it was bedlam on the North Sea, but on the inside of the dam scores of sailing boats and surfers skimmed over the smooth water. Festive flags flapped in the wind above the beaches, where in early June the summer seemed to have begun already.

It was difficult to imagine that almost the whole island was still under water in the first year after the war. In October 1944 the Allies had bombarded the dykes to cut off the German bunkers at the coast from the hinterland. The sea surged in twice a day, month in month out, over a disconsolate, sodden landscape full of the rotting corpses of drowned horses and cows. Walcheren was very nearly surrendered to the sea. Heavy storms and the strong currents wore deep channels in the breaches in the dyke, so that it became increasingly urgent to act. With courage born of despair the dyke workers heaved the steel torpedo nets left from the war into the breaches, hurled stones and sandbags on top of them, and then lumps of concrete, clay and mud. The holes were closed just in time for the winter storms of 1946.

When I sailed round the former island, Walcheren was peaceful and prosperous, like the rest of the Netherlands. After the construction of the Delta works the sea stayed put behind the dykes, apparently for good. Dyke monitoring was subsequently professionalised and ceased to be of interest to the public. The Department of Waterways and Public Works, which was still spoken of with awe in the nineteen-fifties, was gutted by cost-cutting. No one was concerned about it. In 2010 'Waterways' even disappeared from the name of the ministry, which was to become 'Infrastructure and Environment'. The danger posed by the water was gradually forgotten.

Now and then someone did pull the alarm bell. Like Minister Melanie Schultz van Haegen, who had discovered in recent years how badly prepared the Netherlands was for a new flood. 'The chances of something going wrong sometime are increasing,' said the Minister, when I spoke to her in her office. 'The sea level is rising, and so is the water in the rivers, while the Netherlands itself is receding. We only need one hole to develop in the dunes with a springtide and a northwesterly storm and a large part of the Netherlands will be under water. But the wider public is barely aware of the threat.'

That is why the Minister was busy with a programme to increase people's ability to help themselves and a campaign to raise awareness, including via the internet. Soon everyone should be able to click on the postcode of their home in a special app to find out what they should do if the water comes.

A thirteen-year-old girl sails solo round the world

On nice summer days at the beach I had often seen little white sails, slowly gliding along the horizon. They had evoked a great feeling of freedom and a vague longing for what lay beyond the horizon. Now I, too, was one of these sails and could see the coast of Holland pass by slowly in the distance. The low line of dunes was interrupted here and there by buildings. I could identify the coastal villages with map and binoculars: Katwijk with the Old Church on the seafront, the white flats of Zandvoort, the beach huts of Bloemendaal.

In front and behind me I could see white triangles in the infinite space: other sailing boats, on their way to the south or the north, like me. In the summer thousands of pleasure boats sail along the Dutch coast, often heading for destinations further afield, in Belgium, France or Scandinavia.

In recent decades water sport has grown explosively in the Netherlands.

Dozens of large marinas have been built along the coast, some of them outside the dykes in salt water, like the marina at IJmuiden, which I was heading for on this summer day.

In 1978 Eilco Kasemier sailed in here with his Bylgia, after a round-the-world sailing trip lasting two years. He was the first Dutch solo sailor to round Cape Horn from east to west, against the current and the storms. Fifteen thousand people stood along the banks of the North Sea Canal cheering him, the Queen congratulated him by telegram. After Kasemier there were countless other Dutch sailors who undertook similar dangerous journeys on the seas of the world. But something strange happened. As the number of marine yachtsmen defying death rose, so media interest in marine yachting fell.

When a thirteen-year-old girl, Laura Dekker, announced in 2009 that she wanted to sail solo around the world – with her father's consent – she hit the news all over the planet. Yet in the Netherlands people were interested not in the extraordinary adventure awaiting her at sea, but in the question of whether such a long, dangerous journey would be bad for her development. After months of legal tussles with the youth and family service the judge ruled that she could go after all. Two years later Laura arrived back safe and sound, and radiant with health. As the youngest round-the-world sailor ever she once again hit the news worldwide. But in the Dutch media the news about her journey and arrival were completely obliterated by all the fuss with the youth and family service that had preceded her departure. In the Netherlands we were much more interested in the anxious objections beforehand than in the adventure itself.

Protocol for stranded whales

The waves foamed around the Razende Bol, the sandbank in the sea between Den Helder and Texel. As it lay deserted under the clear sky, just a couple of seals splashed about in the surf at the tide line. But six months earlier the Razende Bol had been the scene of great consternation when a whale was stranded on the sandbar. The twelve-metre-long humpback was even given a name, Johannes. After four days of media commotion Johannes died of natural causes, to the fury of various nature organisations, who felt excluded. On the seafront in Den Helder a silent lamp-lit procession was held for the whale after dark. 'He was my friend,' said emotional participants. 'We are determined this should never happen again.' In the Lower House the animal rights party demanded that there should be a special whale protocol, to prevent there being any more such tragic cases in the future.

When I sailed past the Razende Bol a protocol on beached live great whales had just been made public: eighteen pages of instructions, from the appointment of a stranding coordinator to palliative care if the animal should prove impossible to save. A few days later in the port of Oudeschild on the island of Texel I spoke to Hans Eelman, former deep-water seaman, wreck diver and assistant wreck master on the Razende Bol. 'Sometimes I think we've all gone completely crazy,' he said. 'When I was ten, in the nineteen-fifties, and we found a young seal, we beat it to death and got five gilders for the skin. Now the secretary of state has made a protocol for beached whales.' He tapped his forehead.

A realm of islands

A rolling landscape with traditional Dutch farmhouses and fields full of sheep stretched out from the Hoge Berg, near Oudeschild. On the other side of the Marsdiep I could see the head of North Holland and to the east, in the hazy distance, lay Vlieland. Up on the Hoge Berg I suddenly realised that, from the point of view of the coastal inhabitants, the Netherlands was more a realm of islands than a unitary state. On old maps from the sixteenth and seventeenth centuries, not only the Wadden Islands and the Zeeland Delta but large parts of Holland, too, formed a rugged group of islands on the edge of the continent. As a result of the impoldering in subsequent centuries the Netherlands is now largely joined together. But the realm of islands can still be found in the deeper layers of our culture.

You do not need to dig very deep to find it. The inhabitants of the islands of Zeeland still take very little notice of the provincial government in Middelburg, on the other side of the water. And on Wieringen, which has not been an island since 1924, melancholic songs about island life are still being sung. On the mainland this island feeling is sometimes scorned as being conservative and out of date. But in recent years the number of initiatives that have been rolled out reflecting the singularity of the islands is striking. EVT, Terschelling's own ferry service, crossed swords with the Doeksen shipping company, which had had a monopoly of the ferry service as long as people could remember. And on all the Wadden Islands sustainable energy co-ops have been set up by the inhabitants themselves to allow them to be independent of the big energy companies. The island culture has acquired a new dimension, in the middle of the twenty-first century.

Insignificant at sea

For many Dutch people the sea has faded into the background, but during my trip along the coast I met several coastal inhabitants who were rediscovering it. In Den Helder I spoke to the young skippers of the Tres Hombres who, under the motto 'From A to B without CO2', have been transporting cargo over the North Sea and the Atlantic Ocean on their engine-less sailing ship since 2009. In Lauwersoog I went fishing for grey mullet with Jan Geertsema. With his wife Barbara he is breathing new life into small-scale, traditional fishing. They fish with gillnets, a centuries-old, sustainable fishing method in the channels on the Wadden Sea, and have opened a small restaurant in the fishing port where, at the weekend, they serve the fish they have caught. In the same harbour I met Nienke Dijkstra, a theatre maker, who sails over the Wadden Sea in her old fishing boat with overstrung managers and executive secretaries to let them feel how insignificant they are at sea and how chastening that realisation is. 'The sea has largely disappeared from our culture and our everyday experiences,' she said. 'We think we can have anything at any time, and can always control everything ourselves. The sea shows you that that is not so. The tides, the weather - they are all things over which you have no control and to which you have to adjust. Sometimes the sea forces you to carry on and sometimes to take it really easy. The sea is never still. In a storm whole dunes and entire sandbanks can be swept away. It is good to realise that growth and progress are not always certain.'

A flight of loudly cackling geese

In late summer I sailed through the mist over the Dollard, a bay in the Eems Estuary in Northeast Groningen, at the end of the Dutch coast. The sandbars on the two sides crept closer and seemed to float above the mirroring water. Slowly the ship glided through the channel. In front the green of the bank was suddenly visible. The fringe of reeds opened and there lay the Nieuwe Statenzijl lock, solitary between the green dykes. I moored the ship to a couple of large mooring posts with long ropes, because the water would drop three metres with the ebb tide. There was not a human being in sight. Cows grazed on the distant mud flats. A flock of hundreds of geese flew over, cackling loudly, high in the sky.

Late in the evening I heard a door slam in the silence and saw the bent figure of the lockmaster crossing the bridge on his way home. ▓

FURTHER READING

Thijs Broer, *Langs de kust. De Nederlanders en de zee,*
Uitgeverij Prometheus/Bert Bakker, Amsterdam, 2014

Thierry De Cordier, *Mer Du Nord, Étude n°1,* 2011
Oil paint and enamel on canvas, 120 x 150 cm
Courtesy the Artist and Xavier Hufkens, Brussels. Photography © Dirk Pauwels, Gent

Translated by Lindsay Edwards

One Port for the Delta?

[JAN BLOMME]

Europe has a long maritime tradition. The long coastline, the high population density, the dense river network in north-western Europe, industrialisation combined with the wave of colonisation in past centuries, and the emergence of the welfare state after the Second World War, have all led to intensive goods traffic between the European continent and the rest of the world. After 1990, the globalisation of the world economy added a new dimension, leading to a striking increase in maritime traffic – which was then rudely interrupted by the global crisis of 2008/9. Yet despite this latter slowdown, the growth in the amount of goods traffic passing through Europe's ports over the last 150 years has been phenomenal, especially since 1950. In 1913, 19 million tonnes of cargo were transhipped in the port of Antwerp, and 28 million tonnes in Rotterdam; compare that with the figures for 2013: 191 million tonnes in Antwerp and 440 million tonnes in Rotterdam – a tenfold and fifteen-fold increase, respectively, within the space of 100 years. Even more remarkable, virtually all of that increase has taken place since 1950.

According to the European Commission, 90% of the EU's external trade volume and 40% of internal trade is carried by sea. In 2011, a total of 3.7 billion tonnes of cargo were loaded and unloaded in the EU-27 member states (Belgium, Denmark, France, Germany, Greece, Ireland, Italy, Luxembourg, Netherlands, Portugal, Spain, United Kingdom, Austria, Finland, Sweden, Cyprus, Czech Republic, Estonia, Hungary, Latvia, Lithuania, Malta, Poland, Slovakia, Slovenia, Bulgaria and Romania), while 385 million passengers were carried on ferry services. Europe remains a very open economy today; the value of merchandise imports and exports amounted to 27% of GDP in 2012 in the EU-28 (EU-27 plus Croatia). The European Union remains the biggest trading region in the world: number 1 in the world when it comes to exports, just ahead of China, and number 2 for imports, after the USA. Until recently, ports were also key locations for investments in industry because of the space they offered, the synergy with other businesses and the logistical advantages (groupage and bimodal or trimodal transportation to the hinterland).

It is therefore clear that a well-functioning port system plays a crucial role in creating wealth and raising the efficiency of the economy for those countries and regions that are served by that system, and the Delta ports do indeed

provide a strong stimulus to prosperity in the Benelux. Not only are they crucial for maintaining the competitiveness of our industry but, as integrated logistical and industrial clusters, they generate a substantial proportion of Belgian and Dutch wealth from a small area. In 2012, for example, the direct and indirect value added contributed by ports amounted to 7.9% of Belgian GDP and 6% of Dutch GDP, while they were responsible for 7.9% of employment in Belgium (Flanders: 9.9%) and 3.3% in the Netherlands. Moreover, a substantial slice of the major industries remaining in these countries is located in the ports (fuel production and petrochemicals in Antwerp and Rotterdam, petrochemicals in Zeeland Seaports (Vlissingen and Terneuzen), steel in Ghent and Amsterdam and car assembly in Ghent). The Belgian and Dutch ports cannot be seen in isolation from the logistics sector in the two countries. Within the Flanders in Action programme, logistics has been designated as a core sector, and its success will in large part depend on a strong performance of the ports cluster. Similarly, ports in the Netherlands play a key role in the concept of the Holland International Distribution Council, whose aim is to make the Netherlands the most important European base for value-added logistics companies.

In relation to the size of the Netherlands and Belgium and their populations, the Benelux ports punch far above their demographic and economic weight. The Delta ports are far and away the most important gateway in north-western Europe for the import and export of commodities, industrial products and consumer goods. Within their range, the Delta ports have built a market share that over the last 20 years has remained consistently at around 70%.

© Port of Rotterdam   **Transhipment**

Ports have traditionally been compared principally on the basis of the results of their core tasks, the throughput of maritime cargo between ship and quayside. This comparison provides a good impression of the importance and maritime typology of ports.

Chart 1

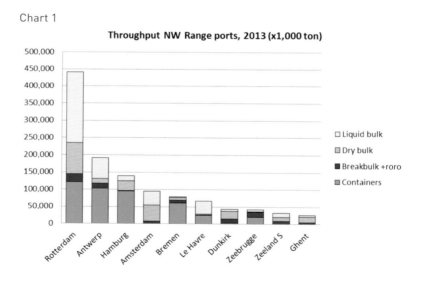

In volume terms, Rotterdam, with a total transhipped volume of 440 million tonnes per annum, is the biggest of the North-West European Range ports, i.e. ports partially serving the same hinterland region in north-western Europe. Antwerp, Hamburg and Amsterdam follow at some distance with just under 200 million, 150 million and 100 million tonnes, respectively. However, Rotterdam's strong position is largely explained by the impressive volume of transhipped

bulk products: liquid cargo such as oil and fuels accounts for almost 50% of the total transhipped volume in this port, while dry bulk such as coal and ore makes up 20%. If only general cargo is considered, i.e. containers and break bulk (goods that have to be loaded individually rather than in intermodal containers or in bulk), a quartet of ports emerges in which transhipment volumes are fairly similar: Rotterdam, Antwerp, Hamburg and Bremen.

Within the North-West European Range, Rotterdam and Antwerp are the only seaports where all categories of maritime traffic have a pronounced presence. The German ports are heavily focused on container transhipment. Amsterdam, Dunkirk, Zeeland Seaports and Ghent are predominantly bulk cargo ports, often specialising in a particular category (Roll-on/Roll-off (RoRo) ferry traffic for Dunkirk, break bulk for Zeeland Seaports and RoRo for Ghent). Le Havre and Zeebrugge focus mainly on two cargo segments: both ports specialise in handling containers, while Le Havre also focuses on liquid bulk cargo and Zeebrugge on RoRo traffic.

Ports are more than piers

However, modern ports are more than just piers for the transhipment of cargo; large, modern ports such as Antwerp are integrated maritime logistical and industrial clusters. Despite this, ports are still compared mainly on the basis of their total cargo transhipment volumes. In reality, a better way of measuring the true economic contribution of a port is the value added it creates, rather than the number of tonnes transhipped (from 'tonnage port to value port'). This value added has for many years been estimated for Belgium by the National Bank of Belgium (Economic Importance of the Belgian Ports: ... Report 2012) and for the Netherlands by Erasmus University Rotterdam in the 'Port Monitor' compiled on behalf of the Dutch Ministry of Infrastructure and the Environment (Havenmonitor 2012). Although there are a number of methodological differences (a bottom-up approach in Belgium via individual businesses and a more top-down approach in the Netherlands based on more general statistics), the estimates are more or less comparable and constitute a unique source for understanding the structure of the Delta ports better.

A comparison between the main Benelux ports shows that – if allowance is made for a number of differences in the methodology used – value-added indicators allow a much more detailed comparison of the importance and structure of the different ports than the obligatory 'tonnage approach'. For the Dutch ports, the Rotterdam-Rijnmond region was used for Rotterdam, the North Sea Canal region for Amsterdam and the Scheldt Basin region for Zeeland Seaports, because these areas correspond most closely with the geographical definition of the Flemish ports. Some of the results are shown in Chart 2.

Chart 2

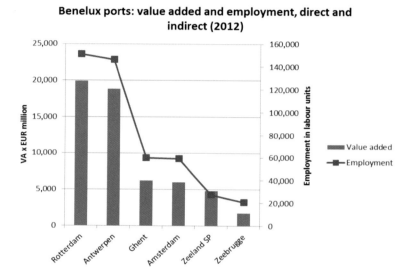

The analysis shows that the size of a port expressed in terms of value added and employment presents a totally different picture from the comparison of the transhipment volumes in the respective ports. The two main ports (Rotterdam and Antwerp) each contributed value added of almost EUR 20 billion in 2012. These two ports account for approximately two-thirds of the value added and employment provided by ports in both countries. Services and industry are more or less in balance. The two main ports are followed by three important industrial ports, Ghent, Amsterdam and Zeeland Seaports, where the share taken by industry in the total value added ranges from just over 50% to almost 80%. With an industry contribution of barely 25%, Zeebrugge is the port with the least distinct maritime profile in this group. These differences are magnified further in the employment figures.

The employment figures involved in goods transhipment and storage, the core activity of any port, are striking in this regard. Despite a global transhipment volume in 2012 that was almost two and a half times as great as that of Antwerp (440 million tonnes versus 191 million tonnes in Antwerp in 2013),

Rotterdam employed fewer people in this segment than Antwerp (9,016 FTE in Rotterdam versus 14,161 FTE in Antwerp). This is of course explained by the different cargo and activity mix in the two ports, with much more labour-extensive transhipment of bulk cargo in Rotterdam compared with the greater importance of labour-intensive break bulk cargo transhipment and more intensive seaport logistics in Antwerp.

What if...?

One question that has to be addressed in relation to greater cooperation is the degree to which Benelux ports are competitive or complementary. Although the ports sector is by definition characterised by competition, and especially between Rotterdam and Antwerp, there is nonetheless a degree of complementarity between Benelux ports as regards goods flows and industrial specialisation. On the other hand, when it comes to container traffic, there is unrelenting fierce competition between the ports of Antwerp, Rotterdam and Zeebrugge.

What if...? In some parts of the world, such as China and North America, regional ports have been created from which other ports, sometimes several kilometres distant, are jointly managed and promoted. The six largest ports in the Benelux are located a maximum of 250 kilometres (Zeebrugge – Amsterdam) from each other, less than three hours' drive. The combined traffic passing through the six biggest Benelux ports, a total of 827 million tonnes in 2013, makes this the largest contiguous port region in the world. Suppose that Antwerp and Rotterdam were one day to become a single port; they would then form the third largest port in the world, handling 626 million tonnes of cargo (2012) – smaller than Ningbo and Shanghai but larger than Singapore and Tianjin. If Antwerp and Zeebrugge were to merge, the new entity would be the largest general cargo port in Europe. And if Zeeland Seaports and Ghent were to integrate, they would form a medium-sized global port. And there are

plenty of other examples.

But this is just playing with figures. The reality is that, with the exception of Vlissingen and Terneuzen (Zeeland Seaports), there are no regional ports in the Benelux. Why not? Most ports in Belgium and the Netherlands have a long local tradition and are firmly rooted in their local communities (the 'Hanseatic' tradition). And most port authorities in the Delta region have developed from local municipal administrations. The situation in the rest of Europe is different: around 45% of ports are owned by higher-level public authorities (the state, region, province), with 'only' 35% of port authorities having a direct link to the municipality. Moreover, many European countries also have a strong centralistic tradition which imposes its stamp on port management and policy.

For many years, the majority of Benelux and North-West European Range ports have co-operated on non-commercial matters, mostly in relation to less controversial topics such as joint lobbying on European ports policy or the creation of a level playing field in areas such as environmental policy and mobility.

Believers and Non-believers

A move has also been under way for several decades in Flemish political circles to work towards a closely integrated port landscape. Some may still remember the proposals made by former Minister-President Luc Van den Brande who, in the mid-1990s, called for the creation of a single port authority, to be known as Flandria Port. As long ago as 1995, private port associations had already made the case for joint marketing of the main Flemish seaports. New proposals on far-reaching cooperation between the Flemish ports were submitted to each new minister with responsibility for the ports. Although some reasonable attempts have been made in recent years to raise the profile of Flanders and its logistics capabilities abroad through a collaborative model (Flanders Logistics, which includes a section devoted to ports, in the Flanders Port Area), the tangible results have been modest. In practice, these initiatives have not really gone beyond being largely declarations of intent, which in periods of more intense competition have

often proved to be more cosmetic than real, an attempt to mask the heightened oppositions from public opinion. This is of course also connected to the often political and commercial fragmentation of the port landscape. In the Netherlands, too, there is a debate about further cooperation, but unlike in Flanders, the mainport concept, with a leading role for Rotterdam, is fairly generally accepted. The Dutch ports policy has in recent years focused more on the role of the state in ports policy and its direct participation in port management.

To some extent, the debate about a single Delta port can be compared with the polemic surrounding the retention of the euro and closer European integration. The debate on further port unification also contains high-profile camps of visionaries and sceptics, or utopians and realists. Neither side is afraid to resort to phrases such as 'ivory tower mentality' or 'Soviet dirigisme', and more besides.

The central tenet of the Believers is a belief in the feasibility of a planned economy. Some go so far as to use a SWOT analysis of the Benelux ports as a basis for the steering of goods flows (and therefore of shipping traffic). Port cooperation and integration combined with more central control can avoid overinvestment and overcapacity, they argue. Not entirely without justification, Believers claim that the competition between individual ports and the related competition for government investment in infrastructure often leads to the development of large terminals at considerable public expense, which are later not used or underused (e.g. container terminals in Zeebrugge or Amsterdam). They also point to the risk of a price war in a bid to fill the (newly created) capacity. The end result is often value destruction in the ports concerned, partly because international port authorities are played off against each other by the shipping lines in tariff negotiations. Believers also argue that the differences between the Delta ports are largely lost on shippers and shipping lines on other continents. Cooperation and mergers would make it easier to develop a coordinated policy that prevents waste and avoids a scattergun approach to clients. Moreover, the lack of coordination can mean additional environmental costs.

For their part, the Non-believers point to the advantages of competition and market forces which stimulate credible initiatives and punish initiatives that are inappropriate. Goods flows and the choice of ports by shipping lines and shippers cannot be imposed from above, but often follow traditional patterns, sometimes going back centuries. Shippers and logistics service providers know better than anyone else the advantages and disadvantages of the different ports. Some ports show wide variation in costs, accessibility and additional services. Mergers will consequently inevitably lead to additional costs for clients, stifle customisation and (sometimes) lead to artificial and more expensive solutions. They also underline the importance of ports for the local economy and the potential costs of any relocation of traffic and investments for towns and communities that have links to the port.

To date, only one successful merger has taken place between larger port authorities in the Benelux, when the ports of Vlissingen and Terneuzen merged in the mid-1990s to create Zeeland Seaports (formalised on 1 January 1998). Set against this one success are a number of notable failures. Attempts to amalgamate Ghent with Zeeland Seaports ran aground in 2006 when Zeeland Seaports said 'no'. In late June 2014, during a visit by the Benelux Parliament to the port of Ghent, calls were once again raised for more cooperation, but not a merger. An interesting experiment was the creation of the Scheldt-Meuse Operating Company (Exploitatiemaatschappij Schelde Maas – ESM) in 1995, a joint-venture between Vlissingen Port Authority and the Port of Rotterdam Authority. The aim was to develop a joint port facility and river container terminal on the River Scheldt in Vlissingen. If the project could be realised quickly, it could bridge the lack of space in the Port of Rotterdam until the Maasvlakte 2 terminal came on stream, whilst at the same time launching a direct attack on the Antwerp cargo handling facility. Rotterdam would provide the funding for the project, offer technical know-how and a substantial part of the value added and employment would come to Zeeland. Procedural problems meant that the project dragged on much longer than expected and its raison d'être disappeared following the development of container capacity at other ports. A final decision to wrap up the initiative was taken in the wake of the crisis in 2009.

Realism

To some extent, the roots of this debate lie in the 'container fever' in the period from around 1995 to 2009 and the scarcity of handling capacity in north-western Europe. Many smaller ports saw their chance and dreamt of promotion to a higher league by building their own, new port capacity, often in segments with which they had previously had only limited experience. Some ports were partially successful in attracting niche cargo by playing to the full the competitive advantage card (e.g. container transhipment or handling specific break bulk commodities). However, the onset of the crisis in the maritime sector shuffled the deck once again from 2009; goods flows returned to their most cost-effective logistical routes and to their old established connections with the traditional main ports. This may well create opportunities for rethinking forms of cooperation that are more realistic and which take more account of the essence of what the different ports have to offer.

It would seem logical to base further cooperation on the concept of 'the best logistical route', with the cargo types and the most efficient supply chain being the central factors and each port focusing on its own strengths. It is key that these initiatives come from the port authorities themselves; initiatives imposed by higher agencies almost always conflict with the particularism and autonomy of the port authority. Combining goods flows by creating critical mass is essential here, and increasing the responsibility of port authorities in expansion projects could potentially reduce the risk of overinvestment.

The creation of one Delta port is not something that will happen tomorrow, and possibly not the day after. However, more tangible cooperation on things such as the connectivity of our ports with the hinterland is certainly a possibility in the shorter term. It is easier first to explore the opportunities within our own national borders, because this is less commercially sensitive and less legally complex. From the perspective of the Benelux, too, there is scope for joint action on this topic, for example in seeking to attract German and Central European cargo for which the Delta ports offer cost and logistical benefits. ■

Translated by Julian Ross

© Port of Zeebrugge

Life is a Beach

Hours of Idleness During the Summer of 2014
Somewhere at the Belgian and Dutch Coast

© All photos by Jonas Lampens

Seafood

Of Sprat, Herring, Cod and Mussel

[NICK TRACHET]

The Low Countries by the sea didn't acquire their name by accident. While for most people in the world a coast is one that has cliffs and inlets, mountains and rocks, the country between Calais and Helgoland is straight, flat and rock-less. The wind has swept the sand into dunes, but those are mostly no higher than ten meters.

The North Sea is even shallower here than elsewhere, the seabed either undulates slightly or is flat. Nowhere are there little caves or hollows for fish to hide in. Unless they dig them themselves!

People are attracted to the coast. It's the same everywhere. One can wax about it romantically but the crux of the matter is that a coast has always been a place where there's an abundance of food, just for the taking. Hunting bison or aurochs requires a lot of effort, speed and stamina, but on a beach one only has to bend down. Shells are washed up or stick on poles and stones; fish and shrimp stay behind in tidal pools. This is easy nutrition and people have always liked the taste of seafood.

Again, on rocky shores it's easy picking. But on the sandy expanse along the North Sea it took lots of searching, digging and hard work to feed oneself. Most people in those parts lived with their backs towards the sea. They farmed, right up to the dunes. The beach provided them with free fertilizer in the form of washed-up seaweed; and potatoes like sandy soil. For extra money farmers would fish from the shore with cast and fyke nets, and fishing lines too. They caught shrimp with a push net and then sold them to the well-off people in the towns inland.

But over time there would be technology. Boats, pulled in from the beach, put out nets and caught sprat (*Sprattus sprattus*) and herring (*Clupea harengus*). It turned into a whole industry, though it was only seasonal. The North Sea herring assembles at our coast in the fall. In Boulogne and Dunkirk the new herring season is celebrated at the end of October: '*hareng de toussaint, hareng plein*'. The Dutch herring season, however, is based on herring that arrive from afar, from the Norwegian coast or sometimes even from Canada. Here the herring season starts in June, when the 'new herring' is very fat and very tasty. In Belgium and Germany we use the Dutch term *maatjes* for these. At one point this fishing was so important for the Netherlands that even today one can hear it said that Amsterdam was built on herring bones. The herring catch and the

export of herring to the rest of Europe was the basis of the Dutch Golden Age. But that is a different story.

Shrimp fishermen on horseback in Oostduinkerke © Gemeentebestuur Koksijde

Sprat became a Belgian speciality. It was smoked and then canned, in huge quantities. But after the Second World War the schools of sprat disappeared from the coast and slowly the whole industry disappeared as well. The smoke stacks in Nieuwpoort and Bruges are reminders of that lost activity. The last canning factory in Belgium has now been moved from Ostend to Charleroi, a hundred kilometres from the sea and not near a harbour but on a highway intersection. The sprat comes from afar and the location of a factory depends on subsidies from the European Union.

Cod is a foreign species

Traditionally cod and haddock came from the north. Cod had been of vital importance to the Low Countries since the Middle Ages. But it wasn't caught here. Instead it came dried (stockfish) or salted (salt cod) from Bergen in Norway. Fresh cod was unknown here. In France this is actually still a problem. 'Morue', the French name for cod (*Gadus morhua* being its scientific name), is so synonymous with salted fish, that French cooks didn't know how to put the fresh version on the menu, once it became available. They timidly spoke of *morue fraiche* but that didn't sound too appetizing. Later they gratefully accepted *cabillaud*, borrowed from the Dutch, although *kabeljouw* was originally a Basque word that entered the Dutch language via Spanish. The Basque were the first Southerners to venture out to the Grand Banks off Newfoundland to harvest the fish themselves. On the way they discovered America too, but they forgot to mention this to the historians. Even today fishermen are cagey about where they go.

The inhabitants of Dunkirk later started harvesting cod off Iceland. Flemish farm boys came along. It was hard work. The cod was salted on board. Later, when cooling techniques became more common, the fish was also transported fresh. But before the Second World War no cod was caught in the North Sea. Were there none there? Were they not using the right technique? It is too late to answer these questions now, but it is rather ironic that all the talk these days is about the disappearance of the North Sea cod, while seventy years ago no cod was caught there at all. If we were referring to a different kind of creature, we would call it a foreign species.

The cod fishing around Iceland started to peter out in the second half of the twentieth century, when Iceland introduced the exclusive economic fishing zone and was willing to defend it with canons. The rest of the world was very angry at first, but over the years all countries that border on a sea have done the same thing. The last Belgian boat to fish off Iceland was the O. 129 Amandine and its runs came to an end in April 1995. It is now moored on the quay in Ostend and has become a museum.

Small scale has the future

What we do find off our coast are flatfish. In sandy seabeds there are certain to be flatfish hiding. Lemon sole (*Microstomus kitt*) and plaice (*Pleuronectes platessa*), common sole (*Solea solea*) and turbot (*Psetta maxima*) are today the bread and butter of the fishing industry in the Low Countries. The herring catch is important to the Netherlands, but it has only a few (big) ships fishing for herring. The rest are after sole and plaice. Common sole is perhaps the most prestigious fish in European cuisine, popular in chic restaurants from Milan to Moscow - unless it is turbot, a fish that was served at the table of Roman emperors. Special cutlery was even designed for flatfish, the so-called fish knife, with which the diner can personally detach the filet from the bones.

In order to bring this lucrative fish to the surface, people started investing in beam trawlers. An intricate system of chains chases the flatfish from their hiding places under the sand. The fish are then swallowed up by the dragnet that follows behind. This kind of fishing is now under attack because it greatly disturbs the seabed, while all the bycatch, worth a lot less than the flatfish, is thrown overboard again, often dead.

Meanwhile, the flatfish stocks themselves are very healthy. Plaice stocks have even reached record highs in the last couple of years. Still, the sector needs to become more sustainable. Not least because these bottom trawlers use a lot of power, and diesel is becoming too expensive for this kind of fishing. So research into new harvesting techniques is being conducted on all sides. The Netherlands has embraced electric fishing, the so-called electric beam trawl, whereby fish are startled by electric shocks rather than heavy chains and the seabed isn't disturbed as much. But there is also mounting criticism of this method, not in the least by the fishermen themselves who don't seem to have any trust in its sustainability. With other fishing methods, like trammel netting or gill netting, virtually no motor power is required, as curtains of netting hang motionless in the sea and the fish become entangled while swimming past. These techniques are more selective than trawling too, while the quality of the fish is higher, as they aren't flattened during harvesting. Add to this the fact that this kind of fishing can be done in smaller boats and therefore provides work for more fishermen, who will bring a better fish to market, and it's obvious that small-scale fishing in the North Sea is the future.

Mussel © VLAM

Big crabs and lobsters need rocky bottoms in order to exist and are therefore rarely found on the coasts of the Low Countries; we see them only in certain wrecks and on the dikes and harbour installations that humans have erected. But there is one kind of lobster that digs a hole for itself, the langoustine (*Nephrops norvegicus*). The feasibility of harvesting these is presently being studied. For one thing, we want to guarantee sustainability, which shouldn't be too hard in view of the biology of the creature. Females carrying eggs seldom allow themselves to be caught and live hidden in burrows far from the threat of nets and dragging. Only bachelors out for a walk are caught by fishermen. But the quality of the catch still leaves room for improvement. Better known is the harvesting of brown shrimp (Crangon crangon), a speciality of the Dutch fishing industry in particular. It is possibly the tastiest kind of shrimp on the planet. Taste and colour are relative of course, but the little shrimp is truly a taste bomb of concentrated shrimp perfume. The use of these tiny creatures in a shrimp bisque or tomato with shrimp is justifiably famous in Belgian cuisine.

Smoked young herring © VLAM

Eating (mussels) for a good cause

But the most extraordinary form of seafood in Belgium and the Netherlands is undoubtedly the common mussel (*Mytilus edulis*). One country (the Netherlands) produces them and the other one (Belgium) eats them, which is comparable to the situation with the above-mentioned brown shrimp. In a report by the World Food Organization (FAO) about the production of mussels in the 1980s this remarkable sentence stands out: 'The consumers of mussels can be divided into two groups, the Belgians and the rest of the world'. Nowhere in the world do people eat mussels in such quantities and with such delight. And this in a country that hardly produces any mussels itself! The reason for this strange phenomenon can be found in the industrial revolution and the (post-) Napoleonic state administration.

Present-day Belgium was the first country on the European continent to undergo the industrial revolution. Already in 1720 the first steam engine was installed near Liège. In 1792 France annexed Belgium and under Napoleon industrialization really took off. With this, labourers began to stream into the cities and they had to be fed, of course. As the Netherlands had also become a Napoleonic vassal state in 1801, attention fell on the Zeeland mussel industry, since mussels could be delivered quickly to Liège, Brussels or Ghent via the big rivers – say within a day or two. This way the Zeeland mussel became a daily staple for labourers. In their eyes the mussel was cheap and abundant, manna, a real feast. In a great many families mussels were eaten once a week during the season, from September to March.

After the fall of Napoleon, Belgium and the Netherlands were united under a single crown again. It is remarkable that the first organization and regulation of the mussel production was formalized in the Netherlands in 1825, during the short period that the countries were together. After independence the taste for mussels among the Belgian population remained. In the Netherlands itself, where mussel beds could in prime years produce 100,000 tonnes of the Zeeland black gold, people rarely ate mussels. Only in recent decades, after a lot of marketing efforts by the big Zeeland mussel companies, have the Dutch returned somewhat hesitantly to the mussel.

Not only have the Belgians eaten extraordinary amounts of mussels in recent history, they have also done it in a way that's unparalleled anywhere else, at mussel feasts. It is a custom, certainly among people who do not prepare mussels themselves at home, to attend a mussel feast once or twice a year, a big event in any village or town, where mussels are prepared collectively for sometimes very big groups. A mussel feast is usually organized in aid of a good cause, like the Red Cross, or to contribute to the finances of a football club, a scout group, a political party or development organisation. Eating for a good cause is a phenomenon that hardly exists outside of Belgium, certainly not on such a big scale. If it were possible, the Belgians would bring an end to hunger in the world, simply by eating.

Traditionally mussels were eaten with bread, but during the last fifty years mussels have more and more often been served with fries, which is actually a difficult combination, as fries and mussels can't be served in the same dish. And *Moules frites* is really a culinary contradiction. Still, the biggest mussel event takes place outside of Belgium, in Lille in France, during their annual fair

Sprats © VLAM

in September. According to the French Wikipedia, in 2009 more than 500 tonnes of mussels (and 30 tonnes of fries) were eaten during this 24-hour event.

The Zeeland way of cultivating mussels (more ranching than farming) is unique. Holland is far from being the biggest producer of mussels in the world. It is not even the biggest in Europe. Mussels were already being farmed in the early 13th century (1235) in France. According to legend the idea came from an Irish monk, Patrick Walton, who was shipwrecked there. He cultivated mussels on ropes between poles. In the 20th century this type of suspended or rope culture became common, and places like Galicia in Spain and the Adriatic coast of Italy now produce a lot more mussels than the Netherlands, albeit of a different kind. South of Brittany the Mediterranean mussel (*Mytilus galloprovincialis*) proliferates and is bigger than the blue mussel (*Mytilus edulis*) found in Zeeland, but also tastes different and has a different texture.

Meanwhile, in the Netherlands on-bottom culture of the blue mussel continues. Wild mussel seed, or spat, is fished from the Waddenzee and put out in beds where the little creatures can grow for another year or two. In suspended culture the mussel seed is directly set out on ropes. These mussels then grow faster and are obviously free of sand and have a lighter shell than those from traditional on-bottom culture. The future of mussel production undoubtedly lies with suspended culture. But the true mussel lover swears by the sturdy black shells of the Zeeland on-bottom mussel. The taste is more intense and the shells are rarely damaged during transport or cooking.

In the last fifty years mussel consumption has changed. The Zeeland mussels are becoming ever more expensive. The Dutch authorities have (deliberately?) created a scarcity of mussel seed by prohibiting the harvest of mussel seed in big parts of the Waddenzee. According to them, the Zeeland mussel sector needs to become more sustainable, which is odd seeing that the harvest of mussels has been ongoing in the Netherlands for the last 200 years. Sustainability can only be ascertained afterwards and in this case the continuity, even in times when no one gave a thought to conservation, seems more than proven.

The popular mussel feasts are also in decline. As they are organized to make a profit, the mussels can't be too expensive or there won't be any money made. With mussel prices as they are, many organizers are switching over to spaghetti feasts or – a sign of the times - paella or couscous evenings. Mussels, on the other hand, are now also served in the better (white cloth) restaurants. Before 1970 that would never have happened. The custom of serving mussels in individual pots, a tradition that arose in the eating establishments of the Rue des Bouchers in Brussels, has also been adopted by these better restaurants.

Because of his familiarity with mussels, the average Belgian is also less afraid of other shellfish and crustaceans on the menu. Would that be why Belgians are at the top of the list of consumers of oysters and lobsters? And of champagne, too – although you can hardly expect anything else in a country where people know how to enjoy life. ■

Translated by Pleuke Boyce

Herring in vinegar © VLAM

Dutch Pirates

Why Dutch pirates never swing from a rope onto a British ship, a knife between their teeth and a pistol in their belt, to kill the captain with a sabre and get the girl

When it comes to buccaneers and pirates the Netherlands is no match for the United Kingdom, not as far as the rest of the world is concerned at any rate. Dutch literature has no *Treasure Island*. Neither did it have Hollywood on its side to complete what Robert Louis Stevenson had begun, first with Errol Flynn and then with Johnny Depp. That is why Sir Harry Morgan and Edward 'Blackbeard' Teach are known around the world, while no one has heard of Cornelis Jol - otherwise known as Peg Leg (*Houtebeen*) - or Claes Compaen.

Neither did the Netherlands have a Queen Georgiana, who personally went on board the Golden Hind to knight Francis Drake after his journey round the world. Her Dutch counterparts are the lofty members of the States General, in their habitual black garb, who voted for a marble tomb for the privateer Piet Hein but only coughed up the money for it when his widow threatened to settle the bill herself. It can still be seen in the Oude Kerk church in Delft.

Yet the whole romanticization of the buccaneers started with a book that was published in Amsterdam in 1678, *De Americaensche Zeerovers*. Written originally in Dutch by Alexandre Olivier Exquemelin, a French ship's surgeon, it immediately became a bestseller and was translated into English, under the title *The History of the Bucaniers* [sic] *of America*, and many other languages. All the scenes in the Errol Flynn films can be traced back to descriptions in this book. The same is true for *Pirates of the Caribbean*. Legendary buccaneers like François l'Olonnais, who ate the hearts of captured Spaniards, and Harry Morgan, the great freebooter from Port Royal in Jamaica, were made famous by Flynn. The problem is that Exquemelin had hardly any followers in the Netherlands. Dutch authors have rarely been inspired by homegrown pirates. An exception to that rule was Dick Dreux, a social-democrat with a kind of historical social awareness who, in Free Trade (*De Vrije Nering*, 1956), described the rise of a poor outcast who manages, after a career on the island of Tortuga in the Caribbean, to make it to regent in the widely admired commercial city of Amsterdam. Along the way he learns that a conscience and love for his fellow human beings only get in the way of social success in the early capitalist society. Dreux enjoyed a certain renown amongst kindred spirits. His books were sold with great success by the socialist publishing house De Arbeiderspers in the fifties and sixties of the last century, but Dreux was never officially recognised as 'real' literature, a judgement that should perhaps be revised.

Inside image: AFBEELDINGE IN WAT MANIER DE PIETER PIETERSEN HEYN / SILUER VLOOT VANDEN GENERAEL VEROOUERT IS Anno 1628.

Watergeuzen

Then there is Rum Island (*Rumeiland*) by the then highly respected author Simon Vestdijk. However, it plays in the eighteenth century in Jamaica and there is not a single Dutchman in it. The only privateer that really comes to mind in the Netherlands is Piet Hein, whom we mentioned above, and that is only because of a nineteenth-century folk song, written for the founding of the young nation by the poet doctor Jan Pieter Heije and composed by Johannes Josephus Viotta:

> Piet Hein his name's quite short
> But what a feat, oh what a feat
> He's beaten and captured the silver fleet.

> *Piet Hein zijn naam is klein*
> *Zijn daden bennen groot,*
> *Hij heeft gewonnen de zilveren vloot.*

Michiel de Ruyter might get a mention too, but the Dutch know him only as an admiral and naval hero - despite the fact that his surname is derived from the long-forgotten Dutch verb ruiten, meaning to plunder and ravage. That though

Piet Hein captures the Spanish Silver Fleet in the Bay of Matanzas, Cuba (1628)

Piet Hein, Delfshaven, Rotterdam

is about it. Nonetheless, seizing other people's ships played just as important a role in Dutch history as in British history. Piet Hein and Cornelis Jol were by no means the only ones. Indeed pirates were at the root of Dutch independence. The English Queen Elisabeth I played an important role in this as well, by opening her ports to the Watergeuzen, Calvinists rebelling against the Spanish King Philip II, who also ruled over the Netherlands.

Initially the Geuzen, or beggars (so called for the silver begging bowl they took as their symbol), formed an aristocratic movement demanding religious tolerance and respect for the local rule of law. When they got literally no response to their petition the more radical elements began a revolt that was put down harshly by Philip II's commanders. Some of the survivors started a guerrilla war in the woods, but most fled out to sea, on fishing boots and other largely unimpressive vessels, where they made a living by piracy. They sold their booty in British ports – not golden treasures, but whatever they could grab from a little two-master or a couple of loads of grain from Baltic vessels.

In the name of Orange, open up!

The Watergeuzen referred to themselves not as pirates but as privateers. Indeed you might say they had permits to operate, the so-called letters of marque, that were granted to them by Prince William of Orange, the founder of the Dutch House of Orange and one of the main leaders of the rebellion. Unlike common piracy, privateering was a regular part of waging war. Enemy ships were captured, not sunk, as they were by German U-boats in the Second World War. Privateers were therefore also supposed to leave neutral ships alone, not to mention those on their own side. But all too often that rule was disregarded, not least by the Watergeuzen, who were known on the North Sea as unpredictable, cruel, merciless and all too often mad.

Nonetheless, embroiled in a sort of cold war with Philip II, Elisabeth allowed them into her ports. In the winter of 1572, however, a period of détente broke out and the Queen closed her ports to the Watergeuzen. A disastrous turn of events for any pirate. Catching merchant vessels and fishing boats offers no comfort if there is nowhere to dispose of the booty. Many a pirate has roamed the sea with a full hold but hungry and thirsty because there were gallows waiting in every port. The Watergeuzen had to choose between certain ruin on the North Sea and onward flight. In the Dutch town of Den Briel, which they attacked, they lived up completely to their reputation for cruelty (their practices and religious fanaticism being similar to those of Caliph Abu Bakr Al-Baghdadi's jihadists). However, the Watergeuzen did bring about a large-scale popular rebellion that paved the way for the first independent Dutch state, the Republic of the Seven United Provinces. Subsequently they were skilfully sidelined by more moderate forces, but the same generation that sang the song about Piet Hein lauded their deeds in an ode too:

In the name of Orange, open up!
The Watergeuzen are at the gates of Den Briel.

In naam van Oranje doe open de poort
De watergeus staat voor Den Briel.

Piet Hein, 1629.
Copy after a lost original by Jan Daemen Cool
from 1625

Ears nailed to the deck

The tradition of piracy covered by letters of marque continued to be just as profitable though. The inhabitants of the island province of Zeeland applied themselves to this, in particular, as their source of income. With the flag of the lofty gentlemen of the States General on the masthead – a yellow background with a red lion on it bearing seven arrows – they hunted down ships flying the Spanish flag. But their own merchant navy was not safe either, because the Spanish King had in turn given letters of marque to seafarers from the pious Catholic city of Dunkirk (Dunkerque), which is now in France. These privateers were interested not only in the cargoes but in the crews too, who were held captive in the most wretched conditions until a high ransom was paid or death ensued. Suffering this fate as a fifteen-year-old boy, Michiel de Ruyter was one of the few that managed to escape and make his way on foot through the hostile Flemish countryside back home to the privateers' port of Vlissingen, in Zeeland. The Dutch did not play the ransom game. Dunkirk seamen who fell into their hands were likely to be nailed by the ears to the deck of their own ship before it was sunk.

Darcana Entertainment
or Pirates today

The most coveted catch for one of these privateers was a Spanish galleon full of treasures from New Spain, or a Portuguese carrack laden with spices from the Far East. Stories abounded in every port of whole fleets of ships laden with silver, which gathered in the Bay of Matanzas in Cuba ready for the crossing to Cadiz in Spain. Sir Francis Drake had once captured a couple of silver ships, but since then they had sailed home unscathed. In the Far East, too, English and Dutch merchants knew of a legendary black ship that ventured the crossing between Manila in the Philippines and Acapulco in Mexico, once a year. But, though it was much sought after, none was ever found.

The short and wretched lives of privateers

In the seventeenth century the authorities mistrusted economic freedom, which was associated in their minds with anarchy. Production by the various trades was controlled by the guilds and they wanted to control seafaring as well. England and the Netherlands each formed an East India Company that was given the monopoly on trade with the Far East. By analogy with this model, the Republic of the Seven United Provinces also established a West India Company, with the exclusive right to develop commercial activities in the two Americas. The Board of Directors of the West India Company, the *Heren XIX* or Lords XIX, appear to have understood this to mean privateering against the Spanish enemy in particular. Piet Hein and Cornelis Jol both sailed in the service of this company. The result was that the largest portion of the booty disappeared into the shareholders' pockets, while the crews had to make do with a bonus that was barely any bigger than their annual pay. It was Piet Hein who, in 1629, after many attempts in the Caribbean - both successful and failed - got his hands on a silver fleet. Worth around twelve million guilders, it was enough to reward the shareholders richly and to finance the siege of 's-Hertogenbosch, a heavily fortified town considered to be impregnable due to its location in the middle of a marsh. Thanks to the millions from the silver fleet the marshes could be drained and empoldered in the tried and tested Dutch fashion, after which 'Den Bosch', as the town is known colloquially, fell. When it became clear how little of the booty was left for the privateers who had captured the silver fleet, they rioted in Amsterdam. No one who risked his life sailing for the West India Company ever became rich. Piet Hein barely outlived his greatest success, dying fighting privateers from Dunkirk, and Cornelis Jol died of malaria on the island of São Tomé before the coast of Africa. Privateers' lives were short and the end was often wretched.

In search of other work

Privateering came to an end when the lofty members of the States General and the Spanish crown finally made peace in 1648, after eighty years of war. The province of Zeeland investigated whether it could continue the war on its own, as the loss of privateering against Spanish ships would cost it so much of its income. It could not. The Dunkirk privateers had to look for other work too. Their business enjoyed a brief revival in the last quarter of the seventeenth century, when seamen from the city – under the French flag now – obtained letters of marque from Louis XIV to attack the Dutch navy. It was during this period that the most famous Dunkirk privateer, Jan Baert, lived. Admitted to the pantheon of great French heroes under the name of Jean Bart, he died - unlike most of his colleagues - in bed, succumbing to pneumonia in 1702.

Rock Braziliano (in fact born in Groningen ca. 1630) was one of the more successful Dutch pirates in the Caribbean.
He was a brave man, a fine sailor and a dangerous psychopath.

ROCK, de Brasiliaen Genaemt
Gebooren tot Groeningen
Cap.t van een Troep Engelse Rovers.

West-Indisch huis, headquarters
of the West-India Trading
Company, Amsterdam

Barbary

Those interested in real free trade did better to go to the Mediterranean where
Muslim pirates, referred to as Barbary pirates, besieged Christian shipping
from ports on the North African coast. The crews invariably ended up on the
slave market but could usually be redeemed by their families. There was another way out though. Those who converted to Islam were often able to join
the pirates. During the first few decades of the seventeenth century a number of Dutch seamen were happy to take this opportunity; others volunteered.
They were usually privateers who wanted to be able to flaunt the booty they
had fought for so bloodily themselves and were not prepared to hand it over
to greedy shareholders with mansions beside a canal in some Dutch city. The
most famous of these was Simon de Danser, from Dordrecht, who ended up
owning a whole pirate fleet based in the port of Algiers. He was known along
coasts everywhere as *Dali-capitan* or Devil Captain.

A certain Jan Janszoon, who took the name Murad Raïs after his conversion,
operated from the Moroccan city of Salé. His most famous exploit is a slave
raid on Iceland. But the most notorious of these Dutch privateers in Barbary
attire was Claes Compaen, who called himself the *Neptune and King of the Sea*.
He, likewise, operated out of Salé. After coming to an arrangement with the
authorities in the Netherlands, however, Compaen returned in his old age to
his native village of Oostzaan, northwest of Amsterdam. That is not as strange
as it may seem. In the seventeenth and eighteenth centuries European rulers
tried to buy off attacks on ships sailing under their flag more often than they
sent out an expensive war fleet to track down the pirates. The lofty members of
the States General, too, usually tried to placate the Barbary pirates with money
and fine words, even though they occasionally sent out a fleet to give them a
bit of a fright.

The Dutch naval hero Michiel de Ruyter led one such expedition. The British knew very well what he was capable of after he sailed up the Medway in 1667 and did immense damage in the dockyards where the British fleet was laid up. He sailed off with the flagship, the Royal Charles, as war booty, proving that he was still a privateer at heart. In classic Dutch history teaching the raid on the Medway was seen as the perfect opportunity for teachers to give full rein to their storytelling abilities. In the nineteenth century, too, a popular song was composed about Michiel de Ruyter - by Richard Hol, a contemporary of Viotta - commemorating his rise from humble origins as a rope-maker's apprentice to admiral of the formidable fleet of the lofty members of the States General:

Clad in a blue check smock
The great wheel he turned all day
But Michiel's boyish heart was anguished
Aye, aye, aye, aye!

As a matelot swift and trim
He went on board - as befitted him –and sailed
To East India and the West, ah that was the life
Hoho, hoho, hoho, hoho!

And now he's the Admiral of Holland
Made of fire and steel, the terror of the seas
A real trooper, glorious on his horse
Heave-ho, heave-ho, heave-ho, heave-ho!

In een blauwgeruiten kiel
Draaide hij aan 't groote wiel den ganschen dag
Maar Michieltjes jongenshart leed ondragelijke smart
Ach, ach, ach, ach!

Als matroosje vlug en net
Heeft hij voet aan boord gezet, dat hoorde zo
Naar Oostinje, naar de West, jongens dat gaat opperbest
Hojo, hojo, hojo, hojo!

Daar staat Hollands Admiraal
Nu een man van vuur en staal, de schrik der zee
't Is een Ruiter naar den aard, glorierijk zit hij te paard
Hoezee, hoezee, hoezee, hoezee!

Classic Dutch history teaching – now sacrificed to the urge for renewal – was intended to offer subsequent generations an example of the heroes of the seventeenth century, known in the Netherlands as the Golden Age. Freedom fighters and naval heroes like Horatio Nelson were better suited to that than

Juan Bautista Maino, *The Recapture of Bahia*, 1635 © Museo del Prado.
The Dutch captured Salvador de Bahia from the Portuguese in 1624.
It was recaptured by the Portuguese in 1625.

pirates, which is why Piet Hein has been put in the same category as Michiel de Ruyter. He has been elevated to the glory of the naval heroes and his piracy has been relegated to the background. Real pirates like Simon de Danser or Claes Compaen are known only to specialists. This may explain why the Netherlands has never developed pirate literature, and why no Dutch pirates have lodged in the collective memory and popular culture, like Blackbeard Teach and Harry Morgan have. Although Arne Zuidhoek, a respected expert in this field, has combed the archives and found thousands of names of Dutchmen who were actively involved in classic piracy – not privateers that is, but real pirates - not one of them ever became really famous or even notorious.

Anti-piracy

The Netherlands and the United Kingdom have been united in the global battle against piracy for two centuries now. In 1815 a Dutch-British fleet bombarded the city of Algiers to such an extent that the local rulers considered it would be wise to stop allowing piracy from their ports. These days Dutch and British naval ships patrol the coast of Somalia. Even France has taken part - with a frigate bearing the name *Jean Bart*, ironically enough. And there is no question now of backing down. In the ports along the coast, people must know that pirates may set sail but they do not come back.

However, none of this changes the painful awareness that Dutch literature has never produced a character that can match Long John Silver. On the big screen we shall never see a Dutchman with a knife between his teeth and a pistol in his belt, swinging with a rope onto a British ship to kill the captain with his sabre and get the girl.

Pity. A real pity. ▪

Translated by Lindsay Edwards

The Law(lessness) of the Sea

[JAN BERKOUWER]

The first important step towards a law of the seas was taken by Hugo Grotius (1583-1645), now regarded as the father of international law of the sea. If his proposals had been put into practice at the time, it is arguable that the law of the seas in the seventeenth century would have been more than adequate. However, time does not stand still. In Grotius's time the right to sail in international waters was threatened mainly by pirates, though in the course of time that particular danger was virtually eliminated. (In recent years, however, it has begun to reappear.) More serious have been the problems of pollution and overfishing and the discovery of important mineral resources such as oil, gas and so-called manganese or polymetallic nodules. This has raised the extremely topical question of the ownership of resources that in law belong to nobody or, rather, belong to the whole of humanity. Overfishing and pollution are issues that nobody wants but that nevertheless occur. Their causes were discussed in 1968 by G. Hardin in a now famous article in *Science* entitled 'The tragedy of the commons'. By the *commons* he meant all those resources which everyone may use, but no-one has a legal right or any claim of ownership to. International waters are a prime example. Hardin called the underlying principle of the over- or misuse of the *commons* the 'free riders principle'. The chief cause of problems at sea is that there is no owner who is responsible for the sea and liable for its responsible use. No country has any *a priori* administrative, controlling or sovereign rights over it. That has tempted some states to make use of the sea in ways that they know are irresponsible but for which others, and not they themselves, have to pay the price. Overfishing is an obvious example, as is pollution.

These abuses have led to the drawing up of a treaty, *The Law of the Sea*, under the auspices of the United Nations. This is an important step forward which cannot be praised highly enough. But even here the drawback can be seen of not having a treaty which is universal, worldwide, and automatically binding if it is to achieve its ends. Every sovereign state may decide whether to abide by it or not, and the sanctions are weak. Moreover, several useful institutions which the treaty envisages have not yet been set up.

Hugo Grotius
by Michiel Jansz. Van Mierevelt

What are international waters?

We shall confine ourselves to the sea beyond territorial waters. It falls outside the jurisdiction or sovereignty of any national state. National territory extends 12 nautical miles (1 nautical mile is 1852 meters) out from the coastline while its jurisdiction extends a further 12 nautical miles. Beyond that, up to 200 sea miles from the coast, the state only has rights to the fishing and the mineral resources. These distances are all *maxima*; a state can always agree to less.

This demarcation of the legal rights of national states does not cause problems so long as three conditions are satisfied:
1. all other states must agree
2. when a coastline runs through onto the territory of a neighbouring state it must be straight
3. the coastlines of states that face each other must be separated by at least 400 nautical miles to prevent overlapping

These conditions are often not met. It is a potential source of conflict which is usually resolved through bilateral treaties.

Beyond territorial waters the freedom of the sea obtains, limited only by treaties against piracy, the slave trade, and off-shore transmitters. It should be pointed out that the weakest aspect of this regulation of international affairs by treaty is that the treaty is only binding on a sovereign state if it ratifies it. This is not normally a problem though there are unfortunate exceptions, especially where mineral resources are concerned. The United States, for instance, has not ratified the Law of the Sea because it cannot agree to the terms covering this subject. This leads to the possibility of *free riders* behaviour, the moral mis-use of power mentioned above. Recently there has been conflict over mineral resources in the South China Sea between China on the one side and Japan, Vietnam, Taiwan and the Philippines on the other (*The Economist*, 16/8/2014).

Mare Liberum (The Freedom of the Seas)

Hugo Grotius was a many-sided man. He had a range of administrative respon-sibilities, even outside the Dutch Republic, and his interests extended beyond the law to literature and theological subjects on which he published a number of important books. His most famous work is *De iure belli ac pacis* (On the Law of War and Peace), published in 1625, which became the basis for modern in-ternational law. He is also known for his argument for the free use of the seas in *Mare Liberum*. In general, he is considered to be one of the greatest jurists and he has had an enormous influence on international public law. His ideas about the law of the sea still form an important basis for the law that applies nowadays. Grotius argued that the sea was free for all to use and that nobody owned it. If this were not so, it would be to everyone's disadvantage. In modern times that last statement might be challenged. It depends on who the owner is, what form the attached rights actually take, and also whether all other states can really be bound to accept and observe those rights. As we shall see, the treaty structure which has been used until now has been unable to achieve this.

A few treaties

In international waters there is unfortunately no law that applies automatically and is binding on all countries in the way that it is within national states. The most important treaty that regulates the law of the sea is the *United Nations Convention on the Law of the Sea*, abbreviated to UNCLOS (1982).

The treaty was necessary because of the weakness of Grotius's concept of *Mare Liberum*, dating from the 17th century, which limited national rights to an area around the shoreline, normally up to a distance of three nautical miles (5.5 km). That distance was based by Cornelis van Bijnkershoek in the early 18th century on the firing range of contemporary coastal defences.

In the course of the 20th century, many countries wanted to extend these limits because of the presence of natural resources such as minerals and fish-eries, and in order to impose measures to protect the environment. The prin-ciple of the Free Sea was broken by the United States in 1945 when President Truman unilaterally laid claim to all the natural resources of the continental shelf. Other countries quickly followed suit. Between 1946 and 1950, Argentina, Chile, Peru and Ecuador extended their sovereign rights to 200 nautical miles in order to protect their fisheries. Other states extended their territorial waters to 12 nautical miles. By 1967, only 25 states still accepted the original territorial limit of three sea miles, 66 states had a 12 mile limit and 8 extended for 200 sea miles. In spite of the weaknesses inherent in all treaties, UNCLOS represents an enormous step forward. 158 states are signatories to it while 12 countries including the United States have signed up but have not yet ratified it. This forc-es us to face the fact that national states are free to sign up to or simply ignore international treaties. If powerful states make use of that, then the intentions of the treaty will not be achieved and the efforts and sacrifices of those states that do take part will have been completely or at least partially in vain.

The London Convention of 1972 is administered under the aegis of the Inter-national Maritime Organisation (IMO). It consists of a large number of agreements on the dumping of waste at sea. In the autumn of 1996, 43 states agreed that the dumping of waste at sea should in principle be forbidden. Before that, in 1993, there had already been an agreement to ban the dumping and burning at sea of radioactive materials and industrial waste.

It is, of course, excellent that action should be taken against such abuses. But that such action should be necessary speaks volumes about the lack of adequate regulation of international waters. It is also worth noting that nothing is said about waste being dumped on land and making its way into international waters via rivers, lakes and off the beach.

The *International Convention for the Prevention of Pollution from Ships* (1973), as modified by the Protocol of 1978, in short MARPOL, also came about within the IMO. It is one of the most important treaties relating to the pollution of seawater. The treaty consists of six annexes. They were signed at different times and not every country is a signatory to all the annexes. They comprise regulations designed to prevent pollution of the sea by oil and other harmful substances that are transported in bulk across the seas, by sanitary discharge and by the dumping of rubbish by ships and, finally, to prevent pollution of the air by ships.

The Ocean Cleanup. This concept for cleaning up the plastic pollution in the seas was developed by a young Dutch student, Boyan Slat. The pilot phase began after a crowd funding campaign in 2014.

The Convention was signed on 17 February 1973 but only came into effect after the addition of the Protocol of 1978. Once a sufficient number of states had ratified it, it finally came into force on 2 October 1983. By 31 December 2005, 136 countries had signed the convention. These countries represent 98% of the world's shipping measured by tonnage.

The OSPAR Convention (1992) is the instrument regulating international cooperation in protecting the maritime environment in the north-east Atlantic (including the North Sea). The most important goals of the Convention are:

1. the prevention and ending of the pollution of the maritime environment;
2. the protection of the sea against the harmful effects of human activity to safeguard human health and maintain the maritime ecosystem, and where practicable restore maritime areas which have already been adversely affected.

Furthermore, the convention is aimed at sustainable management of the areas concerned. This involves managing human activities so that the marine ecosystem can sustain the present level of legitimate use and can continue to meet the needs of future generations. To achieve this the signatories have agreed, jointly and severally, to take appropriate measures and harmonise their policies. In this a number of principles must be applied:

1. the principle of precaution: take preventive measures if there is reasonable suspicion that harm to the environment is likely, even where there is no proof;
2. the principle that the polluter pays;
3. the principle of best practice: the best environmental practices and the cleanest technology will be employed.

Critique of current international law

So, for the resolution of international problems, there are treaties and international law courts which can make binding pronouncements on conflict situations so long as the parties have given their assent. It is an illogical and, in fact, idiotic situation that national states should decide whether or not to participate in the resolution of problems which affect all states. The law of the seas falls into that category. That freedom, which is used and indeed abused on a wide scale, leads us to conclude that at the international level there is a high degree of anarchy. Many international issues are inadequately or not at all resolved or even tackled. The governments responsible, and below them the inhabitants of their states, must realise that great damage is being done to the common interest that they are deemed to serve. Nevertheless, it is certainly not the case that every state will gain an exclusive or even a partial advantage in the resolution of every international or transnational problem.

Compliance

International treaties, except for the European Union, do not bind their signatories directly. Normally their content has to be laid down in national legislation to which all ships registered in the country are also subject. Every country is free to do this in its own way. It is highly doubtful whether this always takes place entirely according to the letter and spirit of the treaty and all too often there is no check on it. This can lead to the actual application of the treaty being neglected. Moreover, the tendency in international treaties to include phrases like 'so far as possible' further contributes to such non-compliance.

Sometimes treaties include clauses which are impossible to fulfil. In Europe, for instance, it is often possible to dump the leftovers from tankers in a type of

French marines
capture Somali pirates

giant skip. In Africa, however, harbours are not equipped to deal with that kind of waste. If such failures were to occur in national legislation, the legislature would soon end up in trouble with the judiciary. But when regulation is by treaty these weaknesses are easily overlooked.

In reality, global issues involve more states and lead to more problems. To resolve them a world authority is needed or, put more bluntly, a world government with everything that implies: a budget and a steady income, expert and adequate staffing, a strong arm for situations where coercion is needed, and naturally democratic composition and supervision. Only then will it be possible to solve the problem of inadequate international law, including the law of the sea.

In game theory, the preceding example simply illustrates the advantages of cooperation. One might wonder why everyone does not see this and wholeheartedly support the idea of a world government. There are three reasons. The first is that for the average individual world government is a very distant prospect and there are very few who are (at all) ready for it. The politicians who would need to bring it about would have to jump the gun, as it were, and take the initiative. And that is not something that politicians are, to put it mildly, usually very good at. Even if they were, it is not at all certain that effective world government would result because of two other relevant principles of game theory.

The first is the *free riders* problem. This takes effect when one can clearly see the advantages of global measures but hopes that others will pay for them; in other words, there is the prospect of a free ride. This is a worldwide phenomenon. At the national level, it was what caused the collapse of communism. There were many who felt it was a good idea, but hoped that everyone else would put in the extra effort to achieve the ideal community so that they could proceed a little more slowly. When others noticed this, they also thought it a good idea and hoped, or believed, that they would be the only ones. But it did not take long for them to become the majority. People also try to get a free ride on public transport and the solution is well-known: effective checks. Precisely the same applies at the global level.

The second factor is known as the *prisoner's dilemma*. Roughly speaking, this amounts to showing rather less willingness during negotiations (in this case about treaties) to contribute to the solution than one's actual desire to find a solution. One does that to avoid having to bear a disproportionate share of the cost when others do the same. The result is that too little ends up being regulated. In this, trust is an important factor, the trust that one's fellow negotiators are showing their true preferences. Trust will come about if it is clear that a party is not playing games in order to reduce his share of the costs. But that takes time.

Naturally, it is necessary to keep a check on whether treaties are actually carried out. At present, when this is done it is almost always carried out by the national states themselves, which carries the risk that it will not always happen objectively. After all, charity usually begins at home. We shall not dwell on the dangers of corruption but they are certainly present, as they are at the national level.

Monitoring

International waters form the largest part of the earth's surface. In every hundred square kilometres of sea there are few if any ships, which means that any external monitoring of dumping from the air is virtually impossible. Monitoring from the ship itself is a more obvious solution and, subject to a couple of conditions, it would be more effective. We shall return to those conditions shortly. Effective monitoring is no small matter. In general, the state where the ship was registered has legal authority over it and is therefore entitled and, indeed, obliged to check that the ship abides by the regulations. But there are a number of problems which all too often make this kind of monitoring illusory. Firstly, there is no guarantee that the state concerned will carry out the checks. There are innumerable examples of this. But even if checks are carried out, the problem is still not resolved. In the first place the checks may be made by an employee of the company that owns the ship. In which case, one has every reason to question his or her independence. But even if the checks are carried out by a government official there is still a danger of bribery and it is certainly not unthinkable that a ship of his own state would receive favourable treatment, the problem of the *free* rider. Further on, we shall sketch out how the task of monitoring should actually be performed.

The damage

It is difficult to describe briefly how much harm is done by these shortcomings in the law of the sea but we shall attempt to do so in the case of overfishing as an example. Worldwide, 350 million people make their living from the sea. If the overfishing ceases to be profitable, they will have no income and most fishermen live in poor countries. We may assume an average income of €10,000 per annum and the same figure again per fisherman for the investments which are lost when their ships lose their value, as also the fish processing factories, means of transport and other capital goods used in the fishing industry. In total the capital losses would amount to a one-off total of 3.5 trillion Euros. A similar sum, but then *annually*, would also be lost in income. We are not talking of a situation where not a single fish is left in the sea, for that would be biological nonsense. These gigantic losses occur as soon as the fish harvest is no longer profitable, which will be long before the stocks of fish are exhausted - something which in fact will never happen. The moment when losses occur is therefore much closer than we might imagine at first sight. There is already talk of serious overfishing of certain species and in certain areas. Sometimes it is possible to switch to a different species, but the threat of overfishing would simply be transferred to that species.

The remaining damage to the environment, apart from the overfishing itself, is more difficult to quantify since it consists of the reduction in the number of species which is not recorded by the market. There is no price paid in money. Nevertheless, the loss of species is occurring, and on a large scale.

We must hope that we can prevent a time arising when fish are no longer affordable or available to our children and grandchildren and when the last elements

of biodiversity at sea will only be found in a few reserves which they must pay to visit. If we allow that to happen, we shall be endangering our own descendants.

What must happen

The treatment and solution of these problems, which are now manifesting themselves on a global scale, require a worldwide system of law. Unfortunately this does not yet exist and the well-being of the world's inhabitants is paying for it. There are, of course, innumerable treaties between states and a useful institutional start has been made in the form of the United Nations. But except for a few security issues, the decisions which it takes are binding on nobody. And it is there of all places that a number of larger states have been given a right of veto, which is crippling. We need to make this point because the most important underlying reason for the lack of a worldwide system of law is the refusal of a number of largely powerful countries to give up any part of their sovereignty. We should be aware that this not only harms the well-being of their own citizens but also that of the rest of the world's inhabitants. Nobody wants it, but it happens nonetheless. The solution lies in what J. Tinbergen called 'thinking far and wide'. Unfortunately, there are too few leading politicians capable of it. It would be much better if the world's inhabitants were to exert pressure to bring about a world order. 'Charity begins at home' may be a familiar proverb but it is all too often short-sighted. Everybody can profit from cooperation.

The law of the sea, like all international legislation, should satisfy the following conditions:
1. all countries should be obliged to participate;
2. it should be based on democratic principles;
3. its management should have sufficient powers to resolve issues adequately;
4. there must be proper monitoring of its observance, which is only possible if there are powers of enforcement and, if necessary, powers of coercion;
5. its management must dispose of sufficient financial means to carry out its task.

The present management of international affairs, including the law of the sea, does not satisfy any of these conditions. They would be considered completely normal at a national, regional or local level, so why not at the international level? The problems are serious enough to deserve it. ∎

Translated by Chris Emery

Left: Somali pirates captured by Dutch commandos

There is no Such Thing as 'Dutchness' or 'Flemishness' in Seascape Painting

[GARY SCHWARTZ]

In his gripping monograph of 1989, *Tempest and Shipwreck in Dutch and Flemish Art: Convention, Rhetoric and Imagination*, Larry Goedde wrote:

> 'The study of seascape has been constrained by the nationalist and temporal boundaries that have tended to divide most landscape studies. In view of the interwoven relationship of Dutch, Flemish and Italian seascape production over two centuries, however, it is sensible to make this survey of the pictorial tradition as broad as possible.' [1]

This is indeed a sensible observation, and it would be nice to think that it carried universal conviction. That has however not happened. National distinctions, whether or not based on political nationalism, continue to be taken for granted or emphatically insisted on, at the cost of the broader understanding sought by Goedde. On 26 September 2002, Christopher Brown delivered in Amsterdam the first Golden Age lecture of the Center for Golden Age Studies of the University of Amsterdam. He gave his talk the programmatic title *The Dutchness of Dutch Art*. The title was adapted from a famous book from 1956 by Nikolaus Pevsner (1902-1983), *The Englishness of English Art*. Brown said,

> 'Pevsner argued that the historical circumstances, economic, religious and social of English society in the eighteenth century produced a different kind of art, which was significantly different from the art produced by contemporaries elsewhere in Europe. This, applied to the Dutch Republic in the seventeenth century, is essentially my argument today.... It ... seems to me ... that the great majority of paintings made [in the northern Netherlands] between about 1620 and 1670 ... had very little to do with what was happening elsewhere and that the very special circumstances of the north Netherlands led to the creation of an art which is strikingly different from the art of elsewhere in Western Europe.' [2]

The subject has therefore wider connotations than merely the distinction between Dutch and Flemish seascape painting. If Dutch seascape painting, one of the signature products of the Golden Age, turns out to be not at all 'strikingly different from the art of elsewhere in Western Europe', then the basis will be undermined for the assertion that different historical, economic, religious and social circumstances necessarily lead to art of a significantly different kind.

Consider as evidence four stormy seas painted between 1630 and 1690. The painter of only one of them was born in the northern Netherlands, but he did most of his work in England. One was born in Ghent and worked in Antwerp and London as well as four different Holland towns. The third was born in Antwerp and never left there, while the fourth was born in Emden in German Frisia and became Mr. Amsterdam himself in seascape. They were all formed under different circumstances of the kind adduced by Pevsner and Brown and they worked in different environments. Yet it takes specialist knowledge of seascape painting to recognize the differences between them. An observer equipped only with knowledge of the social, economic and political circumstances in the Free City of Emden, the Dutch Republic, the Spanish Netherlands and Restoration England would have no way of linking this knowledge to the work of the Dutch-Brit Willem van de Velde the Younger (p. 89), the Flemish Dutchman Jan Porcellis (p. 90), the stay-at-home Antwerper Bonaventura Peeters (p. 91) and the Frisian-German Ludolf Backhuysen (p. 92). If such links exist at all, they cannot be said to have led to 'strikingly different' artistic results.

More widely separated in time and background than these roughly contemporaneous painters of storms at sea were the authors of the ship portraits on p. 93. Pieter Bruegel the Elder was a Fleming who initiated more artistic modes than seems decent for any single person. J. van Beecq (his first name is uncertain) was born in Amsterdam more than 100 years later than Bruegel. He worked in the Netherlands and England at the beginning of his career, but for the last forty years of his life he worked in France, for Louis XIV and high officers of the French fleet. One of his masterpieces, *The Royal Prince before the wind* of 1679 in the National Maritime Museum in Greenwich is so indebted to Bruegel, as in his *Four-Mast Man o'War*, engraved by Frans Huys in the 1560s, that we can speak of a measure of sheer common identity.

Willem van de Velde the Younger (1633-1707), *Ships in a Stormy Sea*, ca. 1671-1672. Oil on canvas, 132.2 x 191.9 cm. Toledo Museum of Art.

Ideological parti pris

There is a deeper problem lying beneath these comparisons in motif and approach. What is it that makes an art historian look for fundamental differences

Jan Porcellis (1583/85-1632), *Vessels in a Moderate Breeze*, ca. 1629. Oil on panel, 41.3 x 61.6 cm. Los Angeles, Los Angeles County Museum of Art.

between works such as these? What stands in the way of acknowledging that in the mid-16th century Pieter Bruegel created and published works that served as models for the main types of maritime subjects for the next few hundred years? Some Bruegel followers were Dutch, others were Flemings or Englishmen or Frenchmen or Italians. That each master brings to the task his own local, period and individual stylistic peculiarities is only to be expected. That certain developments, such as the introduction of tonal painting, will give the genre a new twist is a necessary sign of vitality. But why, in art-historical discourse, should those features be elevated above the strikingly *similar* features of European maritime art? And why should they be conjoined with the notion of national schools?

The origins of the issue are younger than you might think. In the standard sources, from Carel van Mander's *Schilder-boeck* (1604) to Christiaan Kramm's lexicon of 1857-1864, no distinction is drawn between the Dutch and Flemish schools. For centuries, it did not occur to the compilers of compendia that the work of artists from the northern Netherlands was strikingly different from that made by Flemings. Nowhere in all those thousands of pages is the predicate Dutch or Flemish used in connection with typical stylistic features. The origins of the sharp Dutch-Flemish distinction lie in the realm of political philosophy rather than art connoisseurship. The notion was fed by the German philosopher Georg Hegel (1770-1831), who preceded Pevsner and Brown in writing that Dutch artists broke all pre-existing molds because they lived in the first 'national state that fought for its own freedom, a country that reformed the church by itself, that wrested itself from the sea on its own; a country without aristocrats, with few peasants, ... inhabited largely by burghers, [who nurture] the bourgeois spirit, entrepreneurial drive and pride in business, concern for [the] welfare [of their fellow burghers], cleanliness, pleasure in the small [things of life].'[3] He saw the Dutch Republic as a model for the emerging Protestant, liberal German state that would put an end to history. Dutch art of the Golden Age, distinguished from Flemish, born in an autocratic Catholic realm, was

an important part of his proof. Among Hegel's kindred spirits were the French art historian and political activist Théophile Thoré (1807-1869), who wrote that Dutch painting of the Golden Age was 'absolutely incomparable to the rest of Europe',[4] to which he added the significant remark 'quite like present-day young American society, Protestant and democratic.' This phrase echoes the convictions expressed two years earlier, in 1856, in J.F. Motley's bestseller *The Rise of the Dutch Republic*. The American historian claimed as the true mother-land of the United States the low-church, republican United *Provinces*, rather than the Anglican, aristocratic United *Kingdom*.[5] Thoré, in his quest for political salvation and his belief in the Hegelian lockstep of art and society, invested Dutch art with qualities that of necessity *had* to be lacking in Catholic, aristo-cratic, Habsburg Flanders. This ideological parti pris generated a mindset in which admiration for the heroic, free Republic and a measure of disdain for the Spanish Netherlands came to be tied up with admiration for Dutch art at the expense of Flemish. Connoisseurs and art historians embraced this message fervently. It added philosophical profundity and nationalistic resonance – and with it, political support – to their inborn habit of dividing art into schools and making fine distinctions between qualities that lay people could not see.

Too inlandish

The first survey of Flemish and Dutch seascape painting, the book that set the terms in which the subject has since been discussed, was deeply rooted in the ideas of Hegel. The author was a German art historian with the English name Frederick Charles Willis. In 1910 he took his degree at Halle University with *Die niederländische Marinemalerei* (Netherlandish maritime painting). In the trade edition of the dissertation, he writes 'As in all branches of art, here too the tribal oppositions – *Stammesgegensätze* – between Dutchmen and Flemings are pre-sent, often in particularly sharp form.'[6] The Dutch succeeded in creating a more profound and internalized art, he wrote, while the few Flemings [in this field]

Ludolf Backhuysen
(1630-1708), *Warships in a Heavy Storm*, ca. 1695.
Oil on canvas, 150 x 227 cm.
Amsterdam, Rijksmuseum.

hardly rose above the level of surface charm. Moreover, the Dutch were children of the sea, while Antwerp was 'zu binnenländisch', too inlandish, to produce great maritime art. Flanders lacked the indispensable foundation of national rapture – 'nationale Begeisterung' – of the Republic.[7] Nonetheless, Willis is liberal enough to include Flemish masters in his survey.

In his sections on individual artists, Willis demonstrates exactly how these divisions affected the appearance of Dutch versus Flemish art. A good example is his entry on Adam Willaerts.[8] The art of the entire Willaerts family, he wrote, even the sons of Adam Willaerts, who were born in Utrecht, is more Flemish than Dutch. This manifests itself in the staffage, which is given lots of space, with larger figures than in most Dutch paintings. The dunes and rocky shores are constructed like stage sets. The coloring adheres to a strict tripartite division: brown foreground, dark green middle ground and bluish horizon. The Willaerts are completely insensitive to the delicate effects of the Dutch atmosphere. The depiction of shipbuilding and tackle lacks the loving attention to detail of the Dutchman Hendrick Vroom (1562/63-1640). Living as he did in landlocked Utrecht, Willaerts seems to have painted his compositions not from direct observation but from second-hand reports by others, 'Erzählungen anderer.' That is apparent from the uniform depiction of the sea, with its stiff, schematic waves. The early works, down to the early 1630s, show at least, despite their angularity, a certain Robinson Crusoe-like naïve delight in the exotic. Later he lost this fresh touch and reverted to his inborn Flemish love of wildly animated fantasies. 'An unpleasant example of this late period is the oval storm in the Rijksmuseum of 1644.'

Frans Huys (ca. 1522-1562)
after Pieter Bruegel
(ca. 1520-1569),
A Four Master Leaving a Harbor
(reversed), ca. 1561-1565.
Engraving, 22.4 x 29 cm.
Amsterdam, Rijksmuseum.

J. van Beecq (1638-1722),
*H.M.S. Royal Prince Before the
Wind,* 1679. Oil on canvas,
56 x 90 cm. Greenwich,
National Maritime Museum.

Julius Porcellis,
Fishermen on Shore Haul-
ing in Their Nets, ca. 1630s.
Oil on panel, 39.3 x 54.6 cm.
Greenwich, National Maritime
Museum.

Unfortunately for Willis's reconstruction of Willaerts's chronology and his belief that the artist reverted to genetic type in later life, the dating of the Rijksmuseum painting was misread in his time, and not just by a year or two. Not until 1960 did the Rijksmuseum hesitantly add thirty years to the age of its painting, revising the reading of the date from 1644 to 1614.

There is another historical circumstance unknown to Willis that complicates his derogation of Willaerts as a Fleming. When he wrote, it was thought that the artist was born in Antwerp in 1577 and not recorded in Utrecht until 1602. In that case he would have had his training in Flanders. We now know that he was born in London to a family of Protestant refugees from Flanders. The artist's father was registered in the Walloon Church of Utrecht by 1589. 'Adam must have crossed the North Sea about the age of ten', writes the new authority on the artist, Otto Nelemans.[9] In other words, neither Adam nor any other of the Willaertses who are arch-Flemings to Willis, ever set foot in Flanders, let alone wielded a brush there. Their entire training and careers were spent in the proud, free Dutch Republic. To call the work of Adam Willaerts Flemish is inadmissible and, the way Willis does it, to my mind even reprehensible. Willis discredits an entire school by associating it with a set of qualities he finds distasteful.

Willis's book may be nearly 100 years old, but it has never been criticized, let alone discredited by the field. Wolfgang Stechow still cited it approvingly in his 1966 book *Dutch Landscape Painting.*[10] Its only successor in monographic form is Laurens J. Bol's *Die holländische Marinemalerei des 17. Jahrhunderts* (1973) which however, like Stechow's book, leaves out southern Netherlandish paint-ing altogether. The same is true of the two large exhibitions on Dutch marine painting in Minneapolis, Toledo and Los Angeles in 1990-1991 and in Rotterdam and Berlin in 1996-1997.[11] Concerning Flemish seascape painting, Bol deploys a range of adjectives that are politer than those of Willis but also disparag-ing: 'basically documentary, with admixtures of fantasy, violence, animation and threat.' 'Terrifying, animated and dramatic.' 'Water and clouds are nearly explo-sively loaded, the glaring light forespeaks calamity.' 'Northern Netherlandish marine painting, which for the sake of simplicity will be called Dutch, is not

Julius Porcellis,
A Fishing Boat in Rough Sea
off a Rocky Shore,
ca. 1635. Oil on panel,
44.5 x 68.6 cm. Greenwich,
National Maritime Museum.

lyrical in its origins but narrative, descriptive. In the early years it displays affinity with southern Netherlandish land and seascapes in coloring – three-tone perspective and bright local tones in the clothing of the staffage and the banners – and in the coquettish, storytelling mentality and panoramic quality.'[12] Pieter Bruegel, the Flemish father of it all, would have turned over in his grave.

The connoisseurship and scholarship of marine painting is full of polar opposites such as these. Whether the study of this material – or any other form of art, for that matter – benefits from that categorical style of discourse I question. My own inclination is to begin with the assumption that differences between contemporaneous or successive schools and masters are marginal rather than essential, gradual rather than fundamental. However, even if one employs polar opposition for heuristic purposes, in the case of Flemish and Dutch seascape painting things got out of hand from the start and have never been repaired.

Mutual relations

In conclusion, a pair of images that illustrates these issues. On the right is a painting full of qualities that we have encountered above as typically Flemish: we see imaginary rock formations, large staffage figures in theatrical poses, dressed in garb with strong local tones. The water is 'badly painted, fluffy, and insubstantial.'[13] The fictiveness of the composition is evinced by the sharp contrast between the wind-still shore and the over animated sea. The other painting is as Dutchly descriptive as they come: small figures in tonally coordinated clothing engaged in utterly authentic fishermen's activities. 'Human activity is secondary to the prevalence of the immense sky.' The naturalism of the scene is substantiated by the unity of the composition. As you may have guessed, this is a trick opposition. Both paintings are by the same hand, that of Julius Porcellis, and both were made in the same years, that on the right about 1635 and the one on the left about five years later.[14] Julius Porcellis was born in Rotterdam as the son of

Jan Porcellis. Although Jan was born in Flanders and after emigration to the north returned there as a full-fledged Antwerp master before moving for the second time to Holland, he is nonetheless considered to be the main creator of the national Dutch school in the full sense. (This in itself should have been enough to block the assumption of a north-south dichotomy before it even started.)

The above reconnaissance into Netherlandish marine painting provides all the evidence needed, I propose, to support a resolve that we jettison reductive statements about Flemishness and Dutchness and renew the discussion about the mutual relations of the northern and southern Netherlands with fresh eyes and open minds. ■

Adam Willaerts (1577-1664),
Shipwreck off a Rocky Coast, 1614.
Oil on panel, 64.5 x 85.2 cm.
Amsterdam, Rijksmuseum.

NOTES

1. Lawrence Otto Goedde, *Tempest and Shipwreck in Dutch and Flemish Art: Convention, Rhetoric and Imagination*, University Park and London (Pennsylvania State University Press) 1989, p. 18.

2. Christopher Brown, *The Dutchness of Dutch Art*, Amsterdam (Amsterdams Centrum voor de Studie van de Gouden Eeuw, Universiteit van Amsterdam) 2002.

3. Dedalo Carasso, 'Beeldmateriaal als bron voor de historicus,' unpublished lecture held in the Rijksmuseum on May 26, 1982. A reliable paraphrase of passages in Hegel, op. cit., pp. 194-95, 561-64, 800-05.

4. William Bürger [pseudonym of Théophile Thoré], *Musées de la Hollande,* 2 vols., Paris (Jules Renouard) 1858-60, vol. I, p. IX.

5. 'In the third quarter of the nineteenth century a curious movement came into being in the United States. Its adherents opposed the view that Great Britain had provided the basis for American society. Well-known and less well-known, rich and not so rich Americans maintained that the Dutch Republic, which they endearingly called Holland, was the 'mother of America.' This was a fundamental change in the history of the United States. The American historian J.L. Motley first expounded this view in 1856, in his book entitled *The Rise of the Dutch Republic.*' See the website The Memory of the Netherlands, under 'Holland Mania.'

6. Fred. C. Willis, *Die niederländische Marinemalerei,* Leipzig (Klinkhardt und Biermann) 1910, p. 4.

7. Ibid., p. 27.

8. Ibid., pp. 25-27.

9. L. Otto Nelemans, 'Adam Willaerts (1577-1664), zee- en kunstschilder te Utrecht,' *Jaarboek Oud-Utrecht* 2001, pp. 25-56, p. 27.

10. Wolfgang Stechow, *Dutch Landscape Painting of the Seventeenth Century,* London (Phaidon) 1966, p. 110: 'a scholarly book of considerable substance.' Laurens J. Bol, *Die holländische Marinemalerei des 17. Jahrhunderts,* Braunschweig (Klinkhardt & Biermann) 1973.

11. George S. Keyes, exhib. cat. *Mirror of Empire: Dutch Marine Art of the Seventeenth Century,* Minneapolis (Minneapolis Institute of Arts) in association with Maarssen and The Hague (Gary Schwartz/SDU Publishers) 1990. Jeroen Giltaij and Jan Kelch, *Herren der Meere: Meister der Kunst: das holländische Seebild im 17. Jahrhundert,* Rotterdam (Museum Boijmans Van Beuningen) and Berlin (Staatliche Museen zu Berlin, Gemäldegalerie im Bodemuseum) 1996. A more inclusive criterion is taken by Admiral Sir Lionel Preston, K.C.B., *Sea and River Painters of the Netherlands in the Seventeenth Century,* London, New York and Toronto (Oxford University Press) 1937 and Colonel Rupert Preston, C.B.E., *The Seventeenth-Century Marine Painters of the Netherlands,* Leigh-on-Sea (F. Lewis) [1974].

12. Bol, op. cit., pp. 6,7.

13. John Walsh, Jr., 'The Dutch Marine Painters Jan and Julius Porcellis – II: Jan's Maturity and "de Jonge Porcellis",' *The Burlington Magazine* 116 (December 1974), pp. 734-745, p. 742.

14. Walsh, art. cit., p. 35, for the attribution of *Ships in a Storm near a Rocky Shore*, and Gaschke, op. cit., p., nr. 37.

Pounding on in Endless Wild Commotion

Ten Poems about the Sea

The Sea, the Sea pounds on in endless wild commotion,
The Sea in which my Soul itself reflected sees.
The Sea is like my Soul, for, like my Soul, the Ocean,
A Thing of Living Beauty, to itself a stranger is.

It laves its waters clear in eternal, pure ablutions,
And never it fails to turn and flow back whence it flees;
Expressing itself in waves, whorls, eddies, convolutions,
Singing its ever-joyous, its ever-mournful lays.

O Sea, were I like Thee, of myself as unaware,
Then, and only then, would true happiness be mine.
Then, only then, were I free from longing and despair

From the hunger for joy and pain for which the heart doth pine.
Then my Soul were indeed a Sea, and its freedom from all care,
Since greater It is than Thee, would greater be than Thine.

De Zee, de Zee klotst voort in eindelooze deining,
    De Zee, waarin mijn Ziel zich-zelf weerspiegeld ziet;
De Zee is als mijn Ziel in wezen en verschijning,
    Zij is een levend Schoon en kent zich-zelve niet.

Zij wischt zich-zelven af in eeuwige verreining,
    En wendt zich altijd òm, en keert weer waar zij vliedt,
Zij drukt zich-zelven uit in duizenderlij lijning
    En zingt een eeuwig-blij en eeuwig-klagend lied.

O, Zee was Ik als Gij in àl uw onbewustheid,
    Dan zou ik eerst gehéél- en gróót gelukkig zijn;
Dan had ik eerst geen lust naar menschlijke belustheid

    Op menschelijke vreugd en menschelijke pijn;
Dan wás mijn Ziel een Zee, en hare zelfgerustheid
    Zou, wijl Zij grooter is dan Gij, nóg grooter zijn

Willem Kloos (1859-1938)
Translated by James Brockway

Verzen. Dl.1. Amsterdam, W. Versluys 1902, tweede druk

Call of the Sea

I began thinking I would now find rest
And stay the winter in the town's walled space.
Take a house, set lucid lines in place,
For once keep women longer in my nest,
Once brushed off with kisses, make each my guest
And lie at length with them in an embrace,
So gradually their willing bodies' trace
Resembled much-sailed coasts in east and west.

In my own room I pondered thus, and yet
Tonight the autumn's stormy winds I hear;
The roof beams moan and like ship's rigging fret.

Far from the sea, by the sea I'm beset.
The crash of the surf cannot reach me here.
Why is it then so desperately clear?
Before year's end a new ship I will get.

Zeeroep

Ik ging gelooven dat ik nu zou rusten,
De winter in 't ommuurde stadje blijven,
Een huis bewonen, klare zinnen schrijven
En voor het eerst wat langer voortgekuste
Vrouwen hier bij mij hebben en, ter ruste
Met hen gegaan, lang in omhelzing blijven.
En langzaam werden mij hun willige lijven
Vertrouwd als vroeger vaak bezeilde kusten.

Zoo dacht ik zittend in mijn kamer, maar
Vannacht hoor ik de najaarsstorm aanheffen;
Het dakhout maakt als kreunend want misbaar.

Ik woon zoo ver van zee, zoo dicht bij haar;
't Storten der branding kan mij hier niet treffen.
Hoe kan ik zoo wanhopig klaar beseffen
Dat ik weer scheep zal gaan, voor 't eind van 't jaar.

Jan Jacob Slauerhoff (1898-1936)
Translated by Paul Vincent

Verzamelde gedichten. Dl. 2. 's-Gravenhage / Rotterdam,
Uitgeverij Nijgh & Van Ditmar, 1963, zevende druk

Paradise regained

With a flash sun and sea break open the skies:
their fire and silk fans they cast;
by blue, blue morning hills
the wind, an antelope, flies
past.

roaming among fountains of light
and past the radiant squares of the water,
I have a blond woman at my side,
singing so carefree along the eternal water

a clear, compelling, rapturous lay:

'the ship of the wind will soon sail away,
the sun and the moon are roses, snow-white,
the day's a blue sailor, so is the night –
back to Paradise we're underway'.

'Paradise regained'

De zon en de zee springen bliksemend open:
waaiers van vuur en zij;
langs blauwe bergen van den morgen
scheert de wind als een antilope
voorbij.

zwervende tussen fonteinen van licht
en langs de stralende pleinen van 't water
voer ik een blonde vrouw aan mijn zij,
die zorgeloos zingt langs het eeuwige water

een held're, verruk'lijk-meeslepende wijs:

'het schip van den wind ligt gereed voor de reis,
de zon en de maan zijn sneeuwwitte rozen,
de morgen en nacht twee blauwe matrozen –
wij gaan terug naar 't Paradijs'.

Hendrik Marsman (1899-1940)
Translated by Paul Vincent

Verzameld werk. *Poëzie, proza en critisch proza.*
Amsterdam, Em. Querido's Uitgeverij N.V., 1972

Westward

High through late light the white birds heading west
flew over that had not a thing to gain
from knowledge of twigs or building a nest.
I was still young, but won't forget again
the spirit, the whoosh of the wings, the cries
of the exalted ones; no joy or pain
holds souls together, obsessed by the skies
full of sea birds and the joyous refrain
of solitude. The late light in the west
remembers no joy, remembers no pain.

Westwaarts

Hoog door laat licht vlogen toen naar het westen
de witte vogels over, die geen weet
ooit hadden van boomtakken en van nesten.
Ik was nog jong, maar nimmer meer vergeet
de geest het vleugelsuizen en de kreten
van de verhevenen, geen vreugde geen leed
houdt ooit de zielen saam, die eens bezeten
raakten van zeevogels en de juichkreet
der eenzaamheid. Het laat licht in het westen
weet van geen vreugde meer en van geen leed.

Adriaan Roland Holst (1888-1976)
Translated by Paul Vincent

Met losse teugel. Verspreide gedichten. Den Haag,
Bert Bakker / Daamen nv, 1970

Sea

What you imagine is my voice, that rustling and complaint
that's how you gainsay me, you
who long for my silence.

I saw, luxuriating, a sacred landscape,
blessed even without your words, turned into myself.
Your hunting adds nothing to me,
you are nothing but your questions.

No, it is quite different,
even without you I have to be, but now that you're here,
those brief moments, I am the music.
You are only the strings.

Now try to dissolve me,
make your tones of water and mist,
sway with me in this light,
in my last, obscured rhymes,

and sit down and write.

Cees Nooteboom (1933)
Translated by Leonard Nathan and Herlinde Spahr

Zee

Wat jij denkt dat mijn stem is, dat ruisen en klagen,
dat is hoe je mij tegenspreekt, jij
die naar mijn stilte verlangt.

Ik ben, zwelgend en deinend, een goddelijk landschap,
ook zonder jouw woorden gewijd, gewend in mijzelf.
Jouw jagen voegt niets aan mij toe,
jij bent niets dan je vragen.

Nee, het is eerder heel anders,
ook zonder jou moet ik bestaan, maar nu jij er bent,
die korte momenten, ben ik de muziek.
Jij bent niets dan de snaren.

Probeer nu in mij te verdwijnen,
maak je tonen van nevels en water,
wieg met me mee in dit licht,
in mijn laatste, verduisterde rijmen,

en schrijf je gedicht.

Vuurtijd, ijstijd. Gedichten 1955 – 1983.
Amsterdam, De Arbeiderspers, 1984

The Great Flood

two days on the roof, she said
lately, but yes, they left
the hospital much later still

I was eight, just, my brother four – I don't
know as many fairy stories now as then:
Mother Hulda was a godsend on the roof

was there much water in her well?
he loved questions like that, my brother,
also later at Uncle Jos's house in Tilburg

it had been pouring there, February
the ditches overflowing, we'd hardly settled
in: my brother had never seen duckweed before

I'd meant to show him later back in Goeree
or casually tell him about it,
in a fairytale maybe

Arie van den Berg (1948)
Translated by Donald Gardner

Watersnood

twee dagen in de dakgoot, zei ze
laat, maar ja, ze kwamen nog
veel later uit het ziekenhuis

acht was ik pas, mijn broertje vier – ik ken
niet zoveel sprookjes meer als toen:
Vrouw Holle was een uitkomst in de goot

stond er veel water in haar put?
mijn broertje was verzot op zulke vragen
ook later nog in Tilburg bij oom Jos

het had daar hard geregend, februari
dus de sloot stond vol, we waren
er maar kort: mijn broertje kende nog geen kroos

ik had het hem later terug op Goeree
willen wijzen of beter vertellen, terloops
in een sprookje misschien

Mijn broertje kende nog geen kroos
Amsterdam, De Bezige Bij, 1971

Holland, they say ...*

The soil was marshy. We sang about
the lush green grass. What did we know?
One island further on as proof of this

the Biesbosch lay. Mudflats and silt
were closer still. I never went there.
I sat in the class, sung of a land
that lay almost beneath the waves.

At ebb my brother explored the creeks.
I believed nothing of his story.
Wind in the reeds? It was just a song.

My gumboots only came of use,
when there was no land, no luscious fields,
water was all there was. Indoors.
The ooze still lay there weeks on end.

So beautiful, that land? Story's end.
The polder out of bounds, the school
stayed shut, me scared, the song struck dumb.

Ad Zuiderent (1944)
Translated by Donald Gardner

*Zuiderent's poem is an ironic commentary on a traditional Dutch song
(Holland ze zeggen: je grond is zoo dras/ Maar mals zijn je weiden en puik
is je gras/ En vet zijn je glanzende koeien (…)) in praise of the landscape
of Holland that every schoolchild used to know.

Holland, ze zeggen...

De grond was dras. Wij zongen van
het puike gras. Wisten wij veel.
Eén eiland verder lag de Biesbosch

als bewijs. Slikken en gorzen
waren dichterbij. Ik kwam er nooit.
'k Zat in de klas, bezong een land
dat bijna onder water lag.

Mijn broer ging wel bij eb door kreken.
'k geloofde niets van zijn verhaal.
Wind in het riet? Dat was een lied.

Mijn laarzen kwamen pas van pas,
toen er geen land, geen malse wei,
alleen maar water was. In huis.
weken daarna nog lag er slik.

Zo mooi, dat land? Het einde van het lied.
De polder was verboden, de school
bleef dicht, ik bang, gezang verstomd.

Op het droge.
Amsterdam, Uitgeverij De Arbeiderspers, 1988

Winter on the Coast

The sky blasts its greys away, the lot.
Can a flock of seagulls pass by here,
please, to lend wings to the wind
and renounce it now and then?

And may we too fly through these lives
of ours, taking off with a mighty flap
and flutter, to squall and fall like
gulls in flight, and be forgotten.

Night falls. Something large over something small.
Silence is your hand over mine,
and thirty years later, the hand of your daughter
over the hand of mine.

Winter aan zee

Lucht jaagt haar grijzen voorbij, alle.
Kan hier een vlucht meeuwen
doortrekken alstublieft om de wind
te bevliegen en er af en toe af te vallen?

En mogen ook wij ons zo eigen leven zijn door-
gevolgen, aan groot gefladder opgestegen
om hemelhoog te gaan lallen en te vallen
zoals meeuwen nu eenmaal vliegen, en te worden verzwegen?

Nacht valt. Het grote over het kleine.
Zwijgen is jouw hand over de mijne,
en dertig jaar later de hand van jouw dochter
over de hand van de mijne.

Herman de Coninck (1944-1997)
Translated by David Colmer

Schoolslag. Amsterdam / Antwerpen,
Uitgeverij De Arbeiderspers, 1994

At Sea

I looked at you
you looked at nothing
you'd something special with the sea
its hissing roar
stole you away from me

your eyes I said
they are so blue
you closed them then
I asked myself
what you were thinking
you lay so quiet
I couldn't hear you breathe

I said I'd write
a book about us
or else a poem
in which I'd tell the world
how in the cinema
you talked out loud
well, well! you laughed
and stroked my hair from off my face

Miriam Van hee (1952)
Translated by Donald Gardner

Aan zee

ik keek naar jou
en jij naar niets
je had iets met de zee
haar ruisen
nam je weg van mij

ik zei je ogen
zijn zo blauw
je deed ze dicht
ik vroeg mij af
waaraan je dacht
je lag zo stil ik kon
je ademen niet horen

ik zei dat ik
een boek zou schrijven
over ons of een gedicht
waarin ik zou verklappen
dat je hardop praatte
in de bioscoop
zo, zei je lachend en deed
het haar uit mijn gezicht

Het verband tussen de dagen. Gedichten 1978 – 1996.
Amsterdam, De Bezige Bij, 1998

Crab

The border of sand and water
is vague with no clear lines.
By a clump of seaweed a white gull
nabs a green crab. Impatiently it pecks,
pecks, pecks the belly open and gorges
on the soft and flaky innards.
Flat-footed it knocks
on the rest of the crab,
which has long since stopped moving:
guts gone, legs hanging loose,
pincers, oh lord, wide in desperation.
That shell was a joke, crab.

Life is an order
and we are never hard enough.

Krab

De rand van water en zand
is niet erg precies en nergens is een heldere lijn.
Bij een tros zwart wier pakt een witte meeuw
een groene krab. De meeuw pikt, pikt, pikt
vol ongeduld de buik open en vreet
schrokkerig het zachte, schilferige binnenste.
Hij geeft met zijn platte poot een klopje
op de rest van de krab,
maar er beweegt allang niets meer,
ingewanden weg, poten half los,
tengels, o heer, in wanhoop wijd uiteen.
Dat pantser was een lachertje, krab.

Het leven is een bevel
en we zijn nooit hard genoeg.

Wim Hofman (1941)
Translated by David Colmer

Laat ons drinken. Dordrecht,
Uitgeverij Liverse, 2013

© Stephan Vanfleteren, *Oostduinkerke*, 2006

Anecdotes Evoke Poetry

On the Work of Jan De Maesschalck

What is the difference between a drawing and a painting? There would appear to be a degree of consensus here. Drawing has to do with lines and tone, with paper as its medium. Painting is about paint, colour and form on canvas or panel. Drawing is fast, painting slow. Drawings usually cost a lot less than paintings. Drawings can also be studies in preparation for a 'larger' work, but there are countless exceptions in this regard.

Sometimes the distinction is unclear or close to irrelevant, and this is the case with respect to the work of Jan De Maesschalck (°1958). He is, for want of a better expression, a painting drawer. Most of his work takes place on paper, although he also uses canvas and panel.

It goes without saying that backgrounds are important – canvas 'absorbs' very differently from paper. But for De Maesschalck it's all about painting. Or alternatively, making images with the material that suits him best.

For several years, a considerable portion of said images were produced for newspapers and magazines such as *Humo, De Standaard, De Tijd* and *De Morgen*. And while they may, as a rule, have been 'instrumental', De Maesschalck has in the meantime created his own world, image by image.

I have written elsewhere about De Maesschalck's work and I am once again confronted with the same question: how do you describe it? De Maesschalck has been active in the public domain for 25 years, and his works run into the several hundreds. But if you pick one at random, you're obliged to say: De Maesschalck. Why?

A few years ago I wrote the following about De Maesschalck's work: 'The images are somewhere between the ordinary, the strange and the impossible. It's a game designed to slightly unsettle. A frown, a smile, an association, sometimes momentary bewilderment. They conceal an inclination to melancholy, not the unbearable abysmal sort; rather the incurable but not life-threatening sort. There's also sarcasm from time to time, and the occasional splash of mockery, but never maliciousness. And we also see silence, an intense self-evident silence that makes us uneasy. The world in these drawings turns in a placid sound of silence, as if behind glass. It turns inside a head – you can almost hear it whizz. The head, of course, is the head of the artist, but there is

clearly a measure of distance. The glass isn't blurred, as certain artists prefer it to be. It's clear, but it's still there, and it buffers, muffles.'

Untitled (The law of gravitation) (2013), acrylic on paper, 41 x 58 cm

Mild melancholy and irony

Since I wrote the above I've seen new work on a regular basis and have had the opportunity to talk to De Maesschalck about it on occasion. And while what I wrote still stands, good artists tend to become clearer and more complex as they acquire a fixed place in our thoughts as years pass.

Jan De Maesschalck is a melancholy character, so much is clear. Few if any of his images do not testify to this either explicitly or implicitly. But his melancholy is mild, and inalienably combined with a mild irony.

Equally undeniable are his love for material, fascination for light, shadow and reflection, his focus on the female figure, his preoccupation with space and architecture, his need for cultural history, his incessant search for our facial expressions, our shapes and movements, from which perhaps something of the order of a 'soul' might speak – ironically he offers no opinion

From the 'soul' to God is only a few illusions away. And God, like the devil, is in the details. This is where the sensual complexity of his work is to be located. It swarms with detail, details that initiate countless tiny movements and feigned movements.

Piles of books pictured one by one, the meticulous rendering of the blue mosaic tiles in a swimming pool, a long drawn out row of identical benches, apparently endless furrows in a field, countless pebbles on a beach, rows of shelves in a cupboard, a large house with several open windows, uniform bare branches in a winter landscape, a painstakingly perfect manuscript: all bear witness to the pleasure of painting, pleasure that has its roots in the sensual, repetitive concentration of the monk at his desk.

Sensuality is unmistakable in the work of De Maesschalck. It is present thematically in his interest in the female body, for example, in light-filled spaces and landscapes, in the proximity of the everyday, in the muted glow that often characterises his figures. But it is also evident in his technique, shapes, tonalities and use of colour. Time after time we hear the words of the painter, content to leave traces of his 'quest', no matter how the patient, line-perfect 'draftsman' in him would like to go about his business.

Anyone examining these detailed, carefully crafted works will find such traces everywhere. They testify to a nimble swiftness (De Maesschalck works for the most part with quick-drying acrylic paint), to an unexpected lawlessness, to a monk who likes to freewheel and insists on it – without ever denying his place as servant of the images he creates.

Untitled (Valencia 1937) (2013), acrylic on paper, 53.5 x 82 cm

Longing for a scar

The said images often have two faces, a genuine face and a counterfeit face. Observers can't avoid noticing how 'photographic' De Maesschalck's work appears. In line with many contemporary visual artists, he also works from existing photographs or photographs that he has taken himself and, as he himself insists, he wants to make his images *accessible*. But 'contention' is located in the anomalies – some small, some less so – the shifts, the dislocations, in which the apparent realism transitions into soft surrealism.

I imagine this comes about while the work is being created, that drawing and painting induce their own countermovement, that the expert hand craves a moment of clumsiness, deviation, error. A scar.

A scar is a sign of the time, and time as we know is light; and light marks everything with two meanings. Without light, no shapes, no colours etc. At the same time, light erodes colours and shapes. Light facilitates both creation and decay and in this paradox melancholy thrives. In like fashion to Edward Hopper, whose work he admires so much, light for De Maesschalck is a primary character, or better still, the primary presence. He has painted countless manifestations of light: the light of every season; light in the morning, at noon, in the evening, at night; artificial light, angled light, floodlight, frontal light; light on houses, in interiors, on landscapes, in windows, in water, on our bodies, and also on our faces.

Light is inescapable for every painter, of course, and the painting of light remains an inescapable and perpetual question, an ongoing struggle. Edward Hopper maintained that he had only one ambition: to paint light on a wall. At the end of his life he succeeded and magnificently so.

De Maesschalck and Hopper succeed amazingly in letting light – their light – shine over our elusive presence in the world. They don't do so in a wispy, woolly manner, but concretely and with precision. It is with this precision that they come close to our riddle. And by rendering impermanent light time and again as something inescapable, all sorts of things begin to happen in, around and outside the painting.

By immortalising momentary light, and through the use of framing, perspective, carefully chosen moments, attention to isolated figures, tranquil interiors, unpeopled landscapes, reflective windows and mirrors, alienating objects, De Maesschalck creates a sort of vacuum between motionlessness and motion, between what we see in the image and what we presume before and after it. The precision of his images gives the impression that he has cut through time and space with a scalpel, like cutting into an ice-cream cake with a sharp knife. And things happen in that moment of splitting that are 'impossible', that only the creator of the image could have conceived. De Maesschalck thus draws our attention to the artificiality of his apparently 'lifelike' images.

Painting is also gambling

Having stated clearly and sufficiently that Jan De Maesschalck paints/draws 'keenly', with 'precision', 'realistically' it's now time for me to contradict myself.

It's my good fortune to have a few of his pictures in front of me on the table as I write. It's a pleasure to be able to explore his techniques, his paint, his

Untitled (2011), acrylic on paper, 27.5 x 36.5 cm

Untitled (2010), acrylic on paper, 27.5 x 36.5 cm

articulations, his colours, his light and shadow at close quarters and for as long as I like. But this proximity also has something important to teach me.

The more I look at his better images, the more I realise that De Maesschalck does indeed want to *paint* all the time.

Let me use the German painter Gerhard Richter to illustrate what I mean. 'Painting', Richter wrote, 'has nothing to do with thinking, because in painting, thinking is painting.'

In other words, painting has its own logic. And its own optics, kinetics and memory. And no matter how much a visual artist like De Maesschalck might want to maintain control over his images – they have to be 'right' – the brush and the paint ultimately do their own thing. Painting is also gambling.

Just as painting has its own logic, it also has its own capriciousness. Paint isn't printer's ink and that becomes very clear at close quarters.

In one of De Maesschalck's favourite drawings, we see a woman in profile sitting on a table or cupboard and holding a book in her hands, which rest between her legs. She's half naked, her legs and her rear uncovered. She's sitting in a dark space in front of closed grey curtains. We don't see her face. A successful and typical De Maesschalck drawing, both recognisable and alienating at one and the same time.

When I explore the details, trace the path of the paint, drawing merges into painting, as understood in the modernist sense. Splashes, blunders, 'untidy' fragments, untamed brushstrokes, blurred areas where colours overflow, tiny unidentifiable marks, traces of erasure: all evidence of the actions, hesitations and speculations that are barely perceptible in what appears at first sight to be a 'sharp' image.

In the image I have before me, as in many others, De Maesschalck handsomely combines the two souls inside his heart: the painter and the drawer take pity on one another, like a man shaking hands with himself.

And what does such an *entente* have to tell us? Here also two souls are visible, one epic the other lyrical; a prose writer and a poet. I know of few images by De Maesschalck in which both are not in evidence. The anecdote or narrative is rarely absent, yet poetry is also often verbally present. It's hard to conceive of the one without the other in his work. Anecdotes inspire poetry and poetry has need of the anecdote as its ground of existence. In De Maesschalck's best work both are simultaneous, like a leaf and the wind: inseparable.

Then it doesn't matter what happens. De Maesschalck likes to reveal, let us see how everything is inspired by a sort of elementary silence. Landscape, human being or interior, they're all still-lifes in essence. Two girls working at a table in a library deep in concentration, a snow-covered landscape with dark branches like Arabic calligraphy, women reading books in countless shapes and positions, a boy asleep, an abandoned bus stop or hotel room, children playing in a courtyard under excessive light, a grand piano in the middle of a building site: distinct images, but just like the humour and the 'surrealism' in each, the undercurrent of this work is silence.

It's not an unbearable silence – in fact it's even appealing – although it has its roots in the essential desolation of all things. De Maesschalck isn't dramatic about it. His solution is both simple and thorny in equal measure; beauty.

Untitled (Loop) (2012), acrylic on paper, 36.5 x 46.5 cm

And in the middle of it all – the silence, the melancholy and the humour – a great deal of looking is going on, especially by women. Indeed, 'women looking' is a constant in his work. And as we know, the eyes together with the hands are the most difficult to paint. Moreover, the eyes, the way someone looks, is also difficult to express in words.

What do the many female eyes De Maesschalck has immortalised have to say to us? All sorts of things. Vulnerability, loftiness, indifference, wonder, introversion. But especially silent amazement.

It seems obvious to suggest that all those eyes, all those looks, reflect De Maesschalck's own gaze; its restless amazement that can change into surprise and, now and then, into bewilderment. And the ever drawing, painting hand is its accomplice.

In the final analysis, I'm inclined to think that the eyes and the hand are here in search of harmony, rhyme in incongruity, grace in the merciless common-or-garden. Or the other way round: the unreal in the drudgery of the real.

That too makes De Maesschalck's work attractive; it shuttles lucidly and restlessly between deed and dream and is only at home in itself; in the imagination of the paint. ▪

FURTHER READING

Jan De Maesschalck 2005-2014, Teksten/Texts: Bernard Dewulf & Eric Rinckhout, Uitgeverij Hannibal, 2014

Translated by Brian Doyle

Untitled (2011), oil on wooden panel, 40 x 48 cm

With a View of the Landscape

The Poetic World of Miriam Van hee

[ANNE MARIE MUSSCHOOT]

The Flemish poet Miriam Van hee, born in Ghent in 1952, read Slavonic studies at university and has translated poetry by Anna Akhmatova, Osip Mandelstam and Joseph Brodsky into Dutch. She debuted in 1978 with *Het karige maal* ('The scanty meal') and has since published ten collections, including the anthology *Het verband tussen de dagen. Gedichten 1978-1996* ('The link between the days. Poems 1978-1996', published in 1998). In Flanders and the Netherlands Van hee is a cherished, award-winning poet, and internationally she enjoys an ever-growing reputation thanks to the many translations of her work into German, French, Spanish, Russian, Polish, Swedish, Lithuanian and Afrikaans. She was first introduced in English as one of 'Seven Women Poets from the Low Countries', by Hugo Brems, in the first edition of this yearbook, *The Low Countries 1* (1993-1994). Judith Wilkinson later translated an extensive selection of her poems under the title *Instead of Silence* (Shoestring Press 2007).

The special features of Van hee's very consistent poetic world were already established in her first collection: she writes hushed, hesitant, melancholy poems, searching for depth with a whispering, subdued voice and an entirely unique rhythm. The borders of this world are continually being marked out: the observation is determined by the internal space (typified by the title of the second collection, *Binnenkamers*, 'Interiors', published in 1980) but the reader's view is also focused on the external space, the distance, that which is out of reach or absent. Attention for the simple, 'ordinary' things surrounding us at the same time reveals a pressing need for the 'other', the need to understand the underlying structures and the unknown. Poetic composition emerges as 'a hesitation between silence and speech', as the poet herself calls it, a form of thinking, a search for clarity and explanation, for existential depth. This poetry is defined by uncertainty, by qualifications such as 'sometimes', 'barely', 'but' and 'however', by questions and answers which remain unspoken, and by penetrating self-perception: 'for we're no gods / not even seemingly / in our dreams' (in 'The scanty meal'). 'Great' feelings are expressed simply and unassumingly, in a manner averse to pathos and reduced to everyday proportions, in language closely resembling natural speech. The longing for distance is suggested by a passing train, a bicycle entering the countryside, and conversely the restricted immediate environment is always linked back to the need to break away. The longing for security, warmth and contact is paired with a longing for change, escape, distance.

Miriam Van hee (1952)
©Klaas Koppe

We're not the ones they're waiting for

These opposing poles are conveyed by recurring motifs which give the poems, at first sight so simple and accessible, a great dynamism and liveliness. In her small, intimate world, the poet is involved with the house, garden, husband and children, but the longing for other worlds and landscapes is never far away, bringing restlessness and tension. Direct observation and reflection are always connected. In Van hee's two most gloomy collections, *Ingesneeuwd* ('Snowed In', 1984) and *Winterhard* ('Winter Hardy', 1988), the central motif of winter snow is used with great detachment and objectivity to express the isolation and hope-lessness in the 'landscape of desolation'. The poet reflects on herself and her observations. At the same time there is a shift in perspective: the lyrical subject is doubled, adding a third person, or a second person who is directly addressed. Failure, the concept of 'fatal imperfection', is the focal point of these 'wintery' collections. There has been a parting, an emotional failure; what remains is simply the absence of togetherness. The nostalgia for the absent loved one is counterbalanced by an equally strong, even more urgently growing longing for a new future, for light, for distance, for travel, as in the poem 'that's how she'll leave' (see below). In 'Winter Hardy' Van hee consciously seeks out loneliness, because clarity can only be achieved out of the reach of the noise of others: 'until everything is clearly defined / the sun the water / the possibilities'. Looking and asking questions remains a way of registering loss:

> we're not the ones
> they're waiting for
> we're waiting ourselves for the morning
> for our benefits for the first
> tram, we're not the ones
> who slot in we look
> slowly out of the window
> the voice fallen silent
> still in the hand

The lyrical subject attempts to shield itself, to protect itself by cultivating habits ('habits to stave off the emptiness'). The space that accommodates the watchful waiting, the silent listening, the remembrance of unfulfilled togetherness, remains as desolate as usual: the foliage is rusty, there is snow, bald roadsides, railways and stations, bicycles in the landscape, even freight ferries and now airports, but especially windows – windows through which the lyric subject looks 'slowly' and longingly.

In the collections of the 1990s, *Reisgeld* ('Travel Money', 1992) and *Achter de bergen* ('Behind the Mountains', 1996), however, the poetry turns a corner, as indicated in the titles, reflecting a turn of events in the poet's personal life. The desolation is interrupted, confinement and loneliness are replaced by new love and travel. The word 'happiness' even occurs, albeit in the context of 'sums' of 'happiness and unhappiness'. New landscapes open up, both literally and figuratively. The French landscape of the Cévennes, where the poet stays for extensive periods in summer and winter, becomes a particular source of inspiration. This landscape is not threatening to the poet because she grants herself space and is able to transform it to human proportions: the house, the garden, the trees and the wind, the terrace, the river, the stones, 'the scent of blooming broom flowers' which remind her of Moscow. The experiential world of the lyric subject is never free of tensions; her searching and questioning are expressed in poems which represent attempts to 'gather her being together'. The classic themes of melancholy and fear are resumed here: fear of losing happiness and love again, melancholy over the uncertainties, the transience of things, all those unanswered questions. As in the poem 'les gorges du tarn':

> it's melancholy because we're
> not there, because we were nowhere
> so alone and together
> as here under the blue sky
> and we ask ourselves questions
> which are not questions
> our lives in the solar system
> where to and where from

But melancholy and fear can go their way here together in peace, trust and acceptance. The final poem of the cycle 'Behind the mountains', which ends the collection of the same name, reads as follows:

> and I thought everything was in place
> the deep blue of the sky
> and our purple shadows
> over the snow

This final chord expresses a rare phase of serenity in Van hee's world view.

Light brings transparency

The title of Van hee's latest collection, *Ook daar valt het licht* ('There too falls the light', 2013), is a variation on two verses from one of the poems, 'in the suburb': 'but here too fell the light in which everything had / to be seen'. In this collection, as in Van hee's previous work, it is light which truly makes things clear, transparent, allowing us to understand what 'the I' (also referred to as 'she') sees and what she remembers. We read in *De bramenpluk* ('Blackberrying', 2002) that 'light does not comfort / the point is / that it changes, / disappears and returns // wherever sadness may come from'. There are things which remain, catching the sunlight, if only temporarily: the light will not be lost, 'even when we / are gone'. The light here is a way of giving meaning, forming an image for Van hee which expresses the transience, the fleetingness of things. Paradoxically, the changeable light represents a positive, stable value in a world of uncertainty: the light will always be there, even when we are gone.

However, it is not time itself that is most prominent in this collection, but rather space, the locations in which things are fleetingly observed or stored in memory. 'Time is abstract,' we are told in one of the two *Brieven uit het noorden* ('Letters from the North', written for the birthday of the Flemish poet Leonard Nolens): 'it helps if you provide something concrete / in exchange, wash glasses, write letters or go on / a journey'; and 'light makes the landscape transparent, and / ourselves'. There is a great deal of looking in Van hee's poetry, not only in the here and now, but also there, on a journey or in the remembered past. In her previous collection *Buitenland* ('Foreign Country', 2007) most of the poems were devoted to journeys or the now familiar landscape of the Cévennes. In the latest collection these 'distant' images are still present, but the emphasis is on the immediate surroundings in which the poet grew up, on the space of the past. These memories were present earlier in her poetry but are presented here for the first time in a separate series of poems.

Home is where one starts from

The collection begins with several 'separate' poems, not in series, with the familiar 'views' of the village and the mountains. The gaze here primarily registers the 'spots of light' moving on the road, or the road itself in the snowy landscape; the middle of the road itself is marked with 'shining dots' which provide a safe guideline between the snowy edges. The view from the plane registers the temporary nature of things and the great absence which pervades everything, the view from a rock in the landscape itself shows how deceptively quickly the light can disappear. As always with Van hee, there are quickly alternating moods which almost dance along with the flickering sunlight: the sense of duality skims over things that are briefly present but then give way or cease to be. The small, concrete detail also encapsulates the great and the abstract: the trembling ripples in the morning coffee summon up the 'awakening grief' of the coming autumn. But despite the continually melancholy keynote of Van hee's poetry there is a never-ending tendency towards movement, towards breaking free, a longing to escape and 'go outside'. As in the penetrating 'once so far', in which the poet makes a firm choice to seek out a familiar part of the world: 'let's take the uncertain path / to be certain,' with the particularly beautifully formulated concept, 'there will always / be something we recognise, the yielding // ground under the pines we so loved.' This poetry exhibits a virtuosity of language and imagery which only comes into its own with repeated reading.

Between the two groups of poems presented as series, 'Het nulpunt' ('Zero') and 'Station Gent Dampoort' the two 'Letters from the north' are placed as a hinge, reading as key poems in Van hee's work: the poet, who has become increasingly conscious of form, searches for words to interpret the light, to set concrete things in opposition to abstract, elusive time. A key to reading the first series is also presented in the form of the quote from Herta Müller: 'Zero is the indescribable,' in which a few dreams are summoned into a world that can barely be named. Here the light comes 'hesitantly', 'inconspicuously', there is a journey with an 'empty destination' and a lane reveals a 'translation' of the wind and the light. The autobiographical commemorative cycle 'Station Gent Dampoort' is striking in Van hee's work, with a motto by T.S. Eliot: 'Home is where one starts from.' For Van hee it all started in Sint-Amandsberg, the suburb of Ghent where she grew up. The titles of the poems refer very precisely to existing places, in the broad surroundings of the station. There are the streets and the houses where she lived and dreamed. This is an environment in which she deliberately learnt to observe, where she looked for connections and from where she is 'drawn into the world': here, by a bus stop, there was 'always something to see'. The longing to begin, to leave, to enter the countryside, originates here, and the memory is as concrete as the reality, always in search of 'what's missing'. The series on Van hee's home city also contains a little pearl with the title 'op de watersportbaan' ('the water sports course'), which summons up the image of her father rowing: cycling on the bank beside him, she sees him rowing backwards towards land.

Seeing what others do not

It is not easy to penetrate the essence of these apparently accessible poems. Van hee suggests more than she says, leaves many thoughts unfinished and only renders glimpses of her reality. Spatial elements are evoked by a handful of images, or sounds which reveal the silence, in sentences which reflect a fleeting experience with minimal words. Silence can be described 'by wind, rain, fluttering / and further away a lorry / climbing the slopes / and moving earth'. The experience of love is 'described' by a simple image of the loved one in the doorway. Sometimes the everyday also reveals the sublime, there is a momentum that flashes up in the consciousness of the lyrical 'I'. Composition, which for Van hee is 'thought' and with which she attempts to gain insight into her own existence, makes her see things others do not. The poem 'for Jacob and Menno' answers the hypothetical question of 'what a poet was': 'that I could not know – as usual – what I should reply'. After this hesitation, however, she adds that a poet sees in daily reality what 'others' do not see: as on the occasion when she stood waiting for the train and 'saw a feather / sticking straight up out of the stones [...] pushed through / to the light / to reveal itself'. Writing is also 'digging up what is buried', and that 'digging up' can also be achieved through simple concentration on details. It is about a kind of alienation which in literary theory was seen as the essence of literature or, by extension, of art in general: the 'ordinary' can be isolated and examined in such a way that it becomes extraordinary. The focus on details leads to alienation, divergence.

With Van hee all this is paired with a precise, sharply refined formulation and an entirely individual rhythm which is barely perceptible on the first reading. The verses have very little punctuation, hardly a full stop or a comma, here and there a question mark (sometimes the only punctuation is a question mark in the middle of a poem). They are structured by rhythm, by a few blank lines and lots of enjambment, running sentences across verse boundaries. The most recent collections are even free of capital letters. This austere, hushed, subtle poetry might appear simple; it is a carefully thought-through simplicity which penetrates to the essence of things. ▪

Translated by Anna Asbury

Five Poems

By Miriam Van hee

The scanty meal

Under the lamp across the table
we eat silently; our hands
like white flecks dart to and fro;
our ringed fingers heedlessly
playing with the familiar bread.

There is no joy nothing special
in the sound of our
knives and forks.

And of course we feel nothing
of the happiness of travellers
in an evening train.

Het karige maal

Onder de lamp aan tafel
zwijgend eten wij; onze handen
als witte vlekken komen en gaan;
onze beringde vingers achteloos
met het vertrouwde brood spelend.

Geen vreugde niets ongewoons
is er in de klank van onze
messen en vorken.

En natuurlijk weten wij niets
van het geluk van reizigers
in een avondtrein.

From: *Het karige maal* (The scanty meal),
Masereelfonds, Gent, 1978

that's how she will leave	zo zal ze weggaan
slow and unflinching,	traag en vastberaden,
as happens in dreams	zoals dat gaat in dromen
no gesture she will wonder	geen gebaar waarover ze zich
about no words about	verwonderen zal geen woorden waarover
which she'll feel shame	ze zich nog schamen zal
no hand that will restrain her	geen hand die haar tegenhoudt
no outburst of anger to disturb her gaze	geen opstuiven dat haar blik verstoort
that's how she will leave	zo zal ze weggaan
before crack of day,	voor dag en dauw,
soundlessly as in dreams	geluidloos als in dromen
and always something forgotten, a bunch of keys	en altijd iets vergeten, een sleutelbos
an address, warm clothes, the station where –	adresse, warme kleren, het station waarheen –
leaving and yet staying	weggaan en toch blijven
waiting snowed in	wachten ingesneeuwd

From: *Ingesneeuwd* (Snowed in),
De Bezige Bij, Amsterdam, 1984

May on the A75

the scent of blooming broom flowers
made me think of Moscow
that's what the airport smelled of, the underground
or was it the footpaths
after such a cloudburst as never
stopped anyone
from his quest for what
is bygone or unattainable

just for a moment though
you are caught up in
something else and you search
to bring together again
what was interrupted, warily
and haltingly to make a path
around the lakes.

I don't write this to say
I've done this or been there
I write to gather
my being together

Mei op de A75

de geur van bloeiende brem
deed mij aan moskou denken
zo rook de luchthaven, de metro
of waren het de voetpaden
na zo'n stortbui die niemand
ooit heeft afgehouden
van zijn zoektocht naar wat
voorbij of niet bereikbaar is

alleen heel even wordt men
in beslag genomen door
iets anders en zoekt
wat onderbroken was opnieuw
bijeen te brengen, behoedzaam
en vertraagd rond de waterplassen
heen een pad te maken.

zo schrijf ik niet om te zeggen
dat ik dit heb gedaan of daar
ben geweest maar mijn bestaan
bijeen te brengen

From: *Achter de bergen* (Behind the mountains),
De Bezige Bij, Amsterdam, 1996

Light

light from another season,
creamy and white, has entered
the room gliding
slowly over the cupboard,
the Russian teapot, and falling
on the photo of a family
sitting round the table, one
day in the summer: cake, lemonade
in long slow draughts

light does not comfort
the point is
that it changes,
disappears and returns

wherever sadness may come from

Licht

licht uit een ander seizoen,
romig en wit, is de kamer
binnengekomen en schuift
langzaam verder over de kast,
de Russische theepot, het valt
op de foto van een gezin
rond de tafel, een dag
in de zomer: gebak, limonade
met langzame teugen

troost komt niet van het licht
waar het om gaat is
dat het verandert,
verdwijnt en terugkomt

vanwaar ook verdriet

From: *De bramenpluk* (Blackberrying),
De Bezige Bij, Amsterdam, 2002

the water sports course

there goes my father down to the water in a little boat
he rows with slow strokes in between each pull

it is still, he stirs his oar in the water
he makes ripples that reach the banks later

at a spot I'm no longer at, I'm cycling along the shore
I shout that he's doing seven and a half per hour

he sits with his back to my view, he sees
the spot where we were, I see what's coming, he's wearing

a Kirghiz hat, not a real one but one
of shot cotton because there is too much wind

for a cap, he says, and on his feet he's wearing
galoshes that belonged to his father-in-law

and which don't come off, he says, should he fall
into the depths, he loved the water,

as he did my mother because, as he used to let
slip, out there in the ocean she was all he missed,

and what about us then, I thought and waved him
goodbye, he couldn't wave back, I called

but he couldn't hear me, he was rowing, it looked
as though it was effortless, slowly he performed

his earthly task, looking at me now and then
on the bank, maybe he was moved but you

couldn't see from here, it could just as easily
have been a game I didn't know the rules of

and I thought I could leave him there, the water
understood him and carried him backwards

back to the land

op de watersportbaan

daar gaat in een bootje mijn vader te water
hij roeit met langzame halen waartussen

het stil is, hij roert met een spaan in het water
hij maakt golven die later de oever bereiken

waar ik niet meer ben, ik fiets op het land
ik roep dat hij zeven en half gaat per uur

hij zit met zijn rug naar mijn uitzicht, hij ziet
waar we waren, ik zie wat er komt, hij draagt

een kirgizische hoed, geen echte maar een
van verschoten katoen want er is te veel wind

zegt hij, voor een pet en hij heeft aan zijn voeten
galochen die nog van zijn schoonvader waren

en goed blijven zitten, zegt hij, mocht hij dan
toch in het diepe belanden, hij hield van het

water, zoals van mijn moeder want midden
op zee ontbrak alleen zij, zo liet hij zich vroeger

ontvallen en wij dan, zo dacht ik en wuifde
ten afscheid, hij kon niet terugwuiven, ik riep

maar hij kon mij niet horen, hij roeide, het leek
hem geen moeite te kosten, langzaam vervulde

hij zijn aardse plicht af en toe kijkend naar mij
op de oever, bewogen misschien maar dat was

van hier niet te zien, het kon evengoed nog
een spelletje zijn waarvan ik de regels niet kende

en ik dacht dat ik hem daar kon laten, het water
verstond hem en droeg hem achterstevoren

terug naar het land

From: *Ook daar valt het licht* (There too falls the light),
De Bezige Bij, Amsterdam, 2013

All poems translated by Donald Gardner

On Sheep and Plants

The 'Felt' Oeuvre of Claudy Jongstra

[DAVID STROBAND]

One day in 1994, Claudy Jongstra (°1963) visited the Textile Museum in Tilburg. There she saw a Mongolian yurt (nomad's tent) made of felt inlaid with all manner of patterns. Since that moment, now some twenty years ago, felt has been her material.

Jongstra trained as a fashion designer at the HKU, or University of the Arts Utrecht. Initially she designed ready-to-wear clothing, but the encounter with the felt nomad's tent set her career on a new course. It was the warm look and feel of felt, and its intense tactility, that attracted her most.

Since the mid-1990s, Claudy Jongstra has been on a quest to discover processes for using felt in imaginative ways. It could even be said that she has technically advanced and refined the centuries-old technique of felt-making. She has also stripped this unique material of its somewhat stuffy, frumpy image. The raw material for felting is wool, from sheep, goats, camels and even yaks. Felt is made by washing the wool fibres in warm soapy water, then 'agitating' them. Jongstra has developed more than a hundred felt recipes for a wide range of uses. All the recipes have been documented, and the possible uses recorded in photographs. But the processes must remain a secret. We are not allowed a behind-the-scenes glimpse at Claudy Jongstra's studio. And that is perfectly understandable, since her name has become a brand in itself. Initially she designed under the witty name *Not Tom, Dick & Harry*. She now operates under the name Studio Claudy Jongstra. The beating heart of the studio is located in rural Friesland where, in the village of Spannum, Jongstra finds the peace and concentration to research and think about new uses and designs. She has a permanent supply of the raw material, the wool, close at hand: she keeps a flock of some 200 sheep. The flock consists of a variety of European breeds, such as the Scottish Gotland ('a comical sheep with big Rasta curls', according to those in the know), the Schoonebeek and the Drenthe Heath sheep, a rare breed known for its long hair that numbers only 1,200 worldwide. The flock is also used to keep down the weeds on the dikes. Jongstra's sustainable approach means that the wool is dyed in vats on her own premises.

Capes for the Jedi

Claudy Jongstra engages in a wide range of activities. She has upholstered pieces of furniture by designers including Hella Jongerius (the Kasese Chair), Maarten Baas, the Italian designer Ettore Sottsass and Giulio Cappellini, another Italian designer. She has also created concepts expressed in felt for garments by fashion designers including Christian Lacroix, Donna Karan and John Galliano. In around 1997, indirectly and by coincidence, she came into contact with the costume designer for *The Phantom Menace*, the first of a three-part prequel to the original *Star Wars* trilogy, directed by George Lucas. She was asked to produce fifty metres of felt in just two weeks. The material was for the capes of the Jedi warriors. Jongstra had to call in the help of her brother, sister and father to meet the tight deadline.

This commission certainly helped to establish her international reputation. So that she no longer needs to call in the back-up troops, Jongstra has worked

with engineers to develop a 'felt robot'. The production process now requires slightly less manual labour but, in the final creative phase, human input is essential. Jongstra works on her labour-intensive production processes with a team of assistants, including locals. In the surrounding area there are still people to be found who can spin and card wool, two traditional skills. Jongstra is frequently visited by international fashion and art students who are keen to learn precisely these craft skills.

Robust, but elegant

Since 2003, Jongstra has worked closely with architects including Rem Koolhaas, Jo Coenen, the architects' firms MVRDV and Claus & Kaan, and the U.S.-based firm Tod Williams Billie Tsien Architects. In her work with the architects, she aims to create a specific ambience for each of the spaces. Jongstra strives for what she describes as 'creative equality'. She no longer works with fashion designers. In her view, they simply put a few stitches in her felt, then claim all the credit. An exception to this is Alexander van Slobbe, with whom she has created haute couture pieces in which felt plays a leading role.

The paradox in the look and feel of Jongstra's materials manifests itself in her interior designs. The felt can appear rough as well as smooth. The addition of metallic organza or delicate silk fibres makes it appear transparent. Many of the designs – large wall hangings or coverings – are to be found in modern buildings with designs characterised by clean lines. She has brought spaces to life, as it were, in Amsterdam's new public library, the Bank of Luxemburg and the Netherlands Embassy in Berlin. Some of her designs have been described as rough, warm, cool and vivid in the same breath. Or dense and insulating, but at the same time translucent. 'Robust, but elegant' is a much-used description. Colours play an important role in her interior designs. In the past, Jongstra had the dyes produced elsewhere, but she now produces them in her own dye-works, using plant extracts such as madder and woad. Her palette has changed over the years, from vivid colours such as indigo to more earthy colours such as yellow, brown and red.

A tapestry of twenty-one by six metres hangs in the entrance hall of the new Fries Museum in Leeuwarden. Colour plays an essential role in the tapestry, and it took Jongstra and her team four years to complete it. The work is a visualisation of the Frisian landscape, in which sky, water and earth are the main elements. The tapestry is made from wool and silk, dyed naturally with cochineal (purple), indigo (blue) and woad (yellow). The Frisian horizon is visualised using guipure, a richly embellished 18th-century lace technique.

Jongstra seeks to transmit the significance of nature as well as cultural heritage. She likes to make us aware of the rich cultural traditions we carry with us. She refers to the famous 17th-century painting *Girl with the Red Hat* (1655) by Johannes Vermeer, in which the colour red has a remarkable warm glow. This colour can only be made using natural extracts, such as madder, and cannot be synthetically produced.

For some time now, Jongstra has owned a piece of land in the Wadden area where, in cooperation with scientists from Wageningen University, she grows her plants. St. John's Wort, red clover and larkspur, among others, can be found there and form the basis for a whole range of dyes.

International and local

Jongstra is now entirely self-supporting. Her work can be found all over the world, but the production process takes place strictly in her own region. Since globalisation has taken hold, the local has become more important in Western society. And certainly, since the onset of the latest economic crisis, there has been a renewed emphasis on self-sufficiency. In principle, we have access to the whole world through all manner of media, but there is a growing awareness that we should look to our immediate environment to support ourselves.

Jongstra's approach is characterised by the drive for sustainability, and a strongly evident awareness when it comes to heritage (from the perspective of culture as well as nature). Her oeuvre has been exhibited in locations including the United Nations building in New York and at the World Economic Forum in Davos, places where political and economic vistas are defined. These venues gave Jongstra's work an added dimension of social and political engagement.

In a vast hall of the new Barnes Foundation building in Philadelphia, she created fifteen felt-wrapped panels, each with a different structure. The softness of the felt integrates beautifully with the architecture of the U.S.-based firm Tod Williams Billie Tsien Architects. The building – limestone, steel and glass – houses a valuable collection of modern art, including works by Paul Cezanne, Vincent van Gogh and Pablo Picasso. The felt panels clearly have an acoustic function too. Wool absorbs sound and also conducts it.

Two large walls of a room at the Lincoln Center for the Performing Arts in New York are clad with two large hangings in a palette of natural colours, gold and grey.

Jongstra's designs are known for their lifelike character. They radiate intimacy, warmth and lightness. Jongstra herself says people often tell her that they experience her material as life-enhancing. She designed wall reliefs for waiting rooms in the Radiotherapy department at the University Medical Center Utrecht. Many of the patients who use these rooms are seriously ill. The rooms were originally designed with fairly cold materials such as glass, steel, copper and ceramic tiles. Jongstra suggested alternating the ceramic tiles with rectangular panels of felt (Merino wool, metallic organza and raw silk). Vertical and horizontal panels, varying in height from fifty centimetres to six metres, were placed in modules forty-five centimetres deep. Some of the panels display a wide range of grey tints, others a varied palette of warm yellows and reds. Within the room as a whole, the felts show all the colour gradations of the sky and earth.

Claudy Jongstra has proved that she is able to blend her designs with architecture so that they interact meaningfully. They inspire, in a stimulating, community-oriented way. In essence, they embody statements about today's screen-obsessed society. Their intense tactility, their intimacy and their traditional production method have the potential to form a welcome alternative to our fast-paced, functionality-oriented network society and, in fact, offer a vision of a reality beyond that society. ■

Translated by Yvette Mead

Above left
© Studio Claudy Jongstra.
The Lincoln Center for the
Performing Arts, New York, 2010.

Below left
© Studio Claudy Jongstra.
University Medical Center, Utrecht.

Right
© Studio Claudy Jongstra.
Entrance Hall Fries Museum,
Leeuwarden, 2013.

Community Arts: the Theatre of the Future?

[WOUTER HILLAERT]

Community arts in Flanders are unique in the world for at least one reason: they are known as 'social arts' (*sociaal-artistiek*) rather than 'community arts'. This immediately tells us a great deal about how they evolved and how they are perceived. For ten years now, they have been an integral part of arts policy. They may one day be the model for all artists – although the rest of the arts field has yet to realise it.

In 2014, the social-arts field in Flanders had two anniversaries to celebrate, but they went unnoticed. The first of these was the twentieth anniversary of the General Report on Poverty, published by the King Baudouin Foundation in 1994. The report is generally held to be the cradle of what would later become 'social arts'. The Report was based on the accounts given by people living in poverty, and it emerged that they felt cultural exclusion at least as deeply as material deprivation. For the poor, not taking part in the culture production of Flanders was just as much a problem as not having enough money to buy new clothes or pay the electricity bill. This was news to welfare workers and policymakers alike. Cultural participation became an additional key aspect in tackling poverty. Budgets were made available for artistic initiatives actively aimed at people experiencing poverty. Theatre proved to be a unique way to encourage them to tell their story, by literally making themselves heard and daring to make themselves visible to others.

This wondrous chemistry still takes place in community theatre: learning to act increases your self-esteem and greater self-esteem makes you a better actor. And even: the greater the artistic value of a project, the greater its social quality. Hence the term 'social arts'. In theory, at least. In practice, social-arts work evolved out of welfare work, and projects were led by culturally engaged welfare workers rather than established directors. In those days, the aim was not primarily to make art but to tackle poverty in a non-material way.

This is how the origin of social-arts practice in Flanders differs fundamentally from the often much older traditions of community arts in many other countries. It was not so much about political emancipation, as under the apartheid regime in South Africa, or attempts at peacekeeping, as in Northern Ireland, or keeping youngsters with no future prospects off the streets, as in occupied Palestine. In Flanders, community arts did not evolve as a bottom-up emancipation movement among cultural minorities, as has usually been the case in Britain, or as an effect of the political theatre of the 1970s, as in the community-based Rotterdams Wijktheater in the Netherlands. The birth of Flemish social arts was a top-down policy decision.

And it was at least a decision that fell on fertile ground. In 1994, Flanders was dealing with the aftermath of Black Sunday, the first major electoral success of the far-right racist party Vlaams Blok on 24 November 1991. The victory was a shock for civil society and the cultural field alike. Surely, when excluded citizens in the working-class neighbourhoods voted for a party that turned their exclusion into its trademark, it was time to put more energy into winning these citizens over to democracy again? Social-arts practice was not only a way of combating poverty, but also an emancipating cultural-participation project. When Antwerp was cultural capital of Europe in 1993, one of its official slogans was 'Can Art Save the World?' It was in this context that social-arts work was born. It was not only about the cultural emancipation of the poor, but at least as clearly about the social awakening of the cultural elite from postmodernism – out of the 'black box' of the so successful 'Vlaamse Golf' (Flemish Wave) and into the community!

Tartuffe, Platform K & NT-Gent, Photo by Arnold Van Herreweghe.

The art of the social arts

The second anniversary that went unnoticed in 2014 was the tenth anniversary of the Arts Decree (*Kunstendecreet*), a subsidy system introduced in 2004, with which the Minister for Culture, Bert Anciaux, brought together, in a single policy approach, all arts disciplines that did not have a fund. His strong commitment to 'culture for all' prompted his decision to integrate the nascent social arts in the new decree, alongside performing arts, visual arts, music and architecture. It is difficult to overestimate the impact of this voluntaristic decision. Suddenly, the five pioneering social-arts organisations – Victoria Deluxe and Bij' De Vieze Gasten (both in Ghent), De Unie der Zorgelozen (Kortrijk), De Figuranten (Menen) and Sering (Antwerp) – no longer had to scratch together project subsidies from all manner of sources year after year, but could now apply for structural funding for four years, and therefore finally establish a professional operation.

Buffalo Forever, Victoria Deluxe.

More importantly, after 2004 the artistic aspect gained ground. Social-arts productions had now extended their reach to local residents, senior citizens, prisoners, people without documents, young people from migrant backgrounds, psychiatric patients, et al. And, according to the Arts Decree, these performances didn't necessarily have to be of the same standard as professional theatre. Nevertheless, organisations took as much pride in creating an artistically convincing product as in the social process. They wanted to make worthwhile art. It was just as much about 'developing a new artistic language' as providing a platform for stories that receive too little attention in the cultural space. Today, in fact, hardly anyone refers to combating poverty, except as an integral part of the 'empowerment' of voices in society that are not so easily heard. Over a period of hardly twenty years, 'social arts' has transformed from disparate welfare practices to a fully-fledged sector of the arts landscape.

The inclusion of community arts in arts policy is something else that makes the Flemish situation unique. In Flanders, it is first and foremost the capacities that art encompasses – creativity, critical sense, sensitivity, alternative thinking, awareness of form – that shape the social aspect of community arts. Naturally, there has been intense debate during the ten years on the relative emphasis on the social and the artistic. For example, does the artistic emphasis provide sufficient scope for more accessible and above all process-oriented projects involving truly vulnerable people? Nevertheless, there is a broad consensus among those involved in the social arts: the Arts Decree was a blessing.

It extended the initial focus on theatre to other disciplines – from film and choral song to circus and visual arts – to the extent that many organisations today have a multidisciplinary approach. It has led to a situation in which the first, fairly documentary human-interest productions – actually real-life accounts thinly disguised as theatre pieces – have now made way for more abstracted general stories about the state of society in which there is also scope for humour and self-criticism. Call it an artistic 'coming of age'. It is thanks to the Arts Decree, after all, that professional directors and artists have been persuaded to approach social-arts organisations, that a prestigious civic theatre like NTGent makes co-productions with Platform K (for artists with a disability), and a major arts centre like Vooruit sets up projects with Victoria Deluxe.

Whereas community arts in other countries sometimes tend to operate in a somewhat insular fashion, in Flanders there is increasing interaction and branching. It is no coincidence that theatres such as the KVS (Royal Flemish Theatre, Brussels) and Antigone (Kortrijk) engage in social-arts projects, or that cultural centres such as De Warande in Turnhout or De Spil in Roeselare set up broad community projects based on similar methods. Social-arts practice is becoming much more a specific artistic approach than a separate, securely fenced-off field of the arts.

A broad patchwork

Yet it still cannot be said that there is one single approach. There are as many approaches as there are companies, and even projects; the approaches are as diverse as the casts. For a long time, Victoria Deluxe followed a target-group approach whereby almost every new project involved new players, ranging from detainees in Ghent prison (De Nieuwe Wandeling) in music-theatre performances behind closed doors, to intergenerational projects involving young people and senior citizens from a retirement home. Today it is just as interested in working on film documentaries (e.g. about AA Gent supporters and their love of the club) as on theatre productions with a returning and socially very diverse group of Ghent residents, based for example on Walter Benjamin's 'difficult' cultural criticisms. Victoria Deluxe is by far the most political social-arts organisation in Flanders, consistently opposing all manner of antisocial tendencies in society, for example by engaging players and audiences against the migration policy of the City of Ghent, new regulations of the Public Centre for Social Welfare, or the Israeli occupation of Palestine. In this context, community arts contributes to a global re-politicisation of the cultural field. Culture broadens the civic consciousness.

By contrast, Tutti Fratelli, a younger Antwerp theatre company led by the renowned actress Reinhilde Decleir, focuses on the classic theatre repertoire, from Shakespeare to Bertolt Brecht. While most organisations produce new works that are the result of dialogue with their participants, Tutti Fratelli enables its players to 'become someone else' by offering them the safety of existing fictive characters. In order to do justice to the characters, a high artistic standard is set through a purely artisanal approach, with professional training in voice, stage movement and self-presentation on stage. The director Ivan Vrambout, in his work with companies including De Figuranten and Cie Tartaren (Leuven), also chose to adapt well-known works such as *Antigone* and *Uncle Vanya*, which regained a certain originality thanks to the stark authenticity of their small companies of players. The value of such an approach lies not so much in its contribution to social emancipation, but in the unique interpretations of the classics that depend purely on who performs them. When his characters are played by people recovering from depression, Chekhov's work is suddenly *more* – not less – Chekhovian.

At the Unie der Zorgelozen, the emphasis is on the sense of family within a neighbourhood, expressed in works written by the Unie's own artistic director Geert Six. Phenomena such as cycle racing or the local bar frequently serve as metaphors for what small communities do to each other, or for what higher authorities do to them. The Unie also offers 'development tracks': experienced participants work on their own creations or act as mentors for newer participants. In this context, social arts are about the resilience of an entire community. Productions can also relate to a context of urban renewal, as in Ghent's Rabot district, where theatre-maker Simon Allemeersch spent more than two years living in a controversial social housing block that was due for demolition. On the basis of his impressions, he worked with the residents to create a film and a one-man production. Other companies work on an international level, one example being Sering, which has worked for many years developing local productions from an international virtual network with other community-arts organisations in South Africa, Peru and Canada.

But there is no standard approach. Some organisations build on the work of a single theatre-maker, while others continually invite new directors to work with them. Participants form single, highly diverse groups that develop over the years, or share the same vulnerable profile and become involved in the arts just once. There are initiatives that operate on project subsidies or resources from a local OCMW, and others that employ several permanent staff and are involved in many projects simultaneously. Some organisations have their own premises,

Lysistrata, Tutti Fratelli. Photo by Cuauhtémoc Garmendia.

where participants can be received on a daily basis, and others are based in cultural centres. Social-arts practice in Flanders is thus evolving into an ever-larger patchwork that one day engages in a heated debate about the appropriate ideological approach, and the next day unites to lobby the Minister for Culture to increase the overall budget for community arts. And to think that the social-arts sector didn't even exist twenty years ago - a great deal has happened in that time.

Peripheral or central?

But a great deal still needs to happen. Community arts in Flanders are still not taken entirely seriously by the arts world as a whole. At best there is collaboration – for example between NTGent and Platform K – but this seems to be a PR strategy on the part of the civic theatre rather than a genuine artistic choice. Community arts still have low symbolic capital, particularly in a theatrical field in which artistic autonomy is so important, and in which 'engaging with society' is still regarded to a certain extent as an artistic addendum, a peripheral requirement to justify funding. The real level of interest is evident at events such as Enter, the biennial festival at which the social-arts field gathers to show its best work. At the most recent Enter, in 2012 in Ghent – the capital of the community arts in Flanders – in the whole ten-day period, there were hardly any arts programmers or arts-centre representatives to be seen. Do they not believe that anything happening in the social-arts world is relevant in terms of art itself?

One artistic benefit of community arts in Flanders (and probably worldwide) is the renewed appreciation of historic forms of popular culture. Without the existence of a definite plan, social-arts theatre is increasingly drawing on the traditions of the circus, fair, masquerade, carnival, variety, musicals, mediaeval fables, and even 'catch' (professional wrestling) and Kermesse cycle races. In capitalist societies these have become commercial events, but social-arts practice is restoring their original meaning: colourful protests by society's underdogs against the powers that be. Beneath the sensuous adornments, and with the necessary humour and irony, they present sharp political stories about the state of society. This makes for critical theatre *and* theatre with which many people can identify. It is proving to be an ingenious alternative to the traditional documentary mosaic, which mainly presented stories of the individual as a victim. The community arts have discovered their ideal metaphoric dramaturgy in the historically popular forms. They are also a useful solution in terms of staging productions involving large groups – often with as many as twenty or thirty players. While conventional theatre has fewer and fewer resources for staging large-cast productions, Tutti Fratelli & Co. are reinventing the subversive mass spectacle.

And there are other senses in which conventional theatre companies can learn from social-arts practice. At a time when support for subsidised arts is shrinking – to the accompaniment of populist cries of protest about 'subsidy-guzzling' and the arts being 'a leftist hobby' – arts organisations will have to demonstrate a stronger commitment to their social anchoring. Although Flemish politicians are considerably more convinced of the importance of the arts than their counterparts in Britain and the Netherlands, Flanders is also facing a new round of cutbacks. In terms of the future of the arts, the ability to forge connections with the rest of civil society will likely prove more important than establishing a unique artistic profile. Let that ability to connect be the speciality of community arts. For twenty years they have been building expertise in establishing a dialogue with new audiences, tapping into and maintaining broad networks, and persuading the non-involved to support culture. Soon these competencies will have to be part of every artist's basic skills package.

Nonkel Wanj, Cie Tartaren.
Photo by Sander de Wilde.

This shift is already taking place in the Netherlands, where, in 2011, one-third of the arts budget was cut. Young artists are now breaking away from the theatres and basing themselves in 'art factories in the cities. Half of their work involves communicating with the public. Their creativity is no longer purely in the artistic, it is also in the social aspect of their oeuvre. In Flanders too, a new generation of art-makers has emerged over the past ten years who no longer distinguish between working with professional actors in the theatre and being involved in participatory projects with illegal immigrants or prisoners. They do both, within a single artistic line. By nature, artists such as Thomas Bellinck, Simon Allemeersch, Michiel Soete, Lucas De Man, Jozef Wouters, Tom Dupont and many others want to be at the centre of things, and are much freer in their relations with the institutes that the generations before them established as autonomous beacons. They are aware that, in the 21st century, the most exciting work is not being done at the centre but on the periphery, in the desolate borderlands around the community. Although they do not refer to their work explicitly in terms of the social arts, they often work with similar approaches and from similar convictions: dialogue, open processes, co-creation.

Perhaps that is why social-arts anniversaries in Flanders shouldn't be celebrated. In the long term, community arts could well become the standard rather than the exception. Is that unique role ahead of us, rather than behind us? A great deal will depend on the critical sense with which artists continue to explore the objectives of arts policy. In today's neoliberal participation society, community arts are all too easily used as an underfinanced cultural fig leaf to conceal the harsh reality of the social dismantling of the welfare state – a process that is taking place throughout Europe. Should social-arts organisations allow themselves to be used to that end, or offer every possible resistance? ■

Translated by Yvette Mead

Maustrofobie, CC De Spil.
Photo by Fabian Parent

Quatre-Bras and Waterloo Revisited.

A Belgian and Dutch History without Glory

[JEROEN VAN ZANTEN]

Napoleon had no doubt; the defeat at Waterloo was all Marshall Ney's fault, not his. After his second exile the fallen French Emperor did not like to talk much about the fatal campaign of 1815. But the days on St Helena were long and every so often he couldn't resist saying something about Waterloo. The four loyal officers who voluntarily followed him into exile then eagerly noted down his words for later inclusion in their official memoirs of the Emperor. To one of them, Baron Gaspard Gourgaud, Napoleon commented at the end of February 1817 that it would have been better if he 'had placed Soult instead of Ney on the left flank'. He then added immediately that he had never expected that Ney, who after all had pressed upon him the importance of Quatre-Bras, would neglect to take control of the crossroads. [1] However there was no point in speculating about what might have been. In his opinion Waterloo was a closed chapter. There was no such thing as *the* historical truth, he remarked: 'You will not find two accounts agreeing together in relating the same fact'. [2]

After the battle, Napoleon's adversary Wellington agreed. The truth about Waterloo would never be fully known, let alone the battle array and the orders that had led to victory. In a letter to the Irish politician and historian, John Croker, Wellington wrote:

> 'The history of a battle is not unlike the history of a ball. Some individuals may recollect all the little events of which the great result is the battle won or lost, but no individual can recollect the order in which, or the exact moment at which, they occurred, which makes all the difference as to their value or importance.' [3]

The lack of trust shown by both Napoleon and Wellington in historical writing is, to say the least, striking since neither of them missed any opportunity after 1815 to claim possession of the true account of Waterloo. In contrast to his defeat at Leipzig in October 1813, Napoleon succeeded in turning his defeat at Waterloo into victory. Through his defeat and exile on distant St Helena, the myths surrounding him grew ever greater. After his death in May 1821, in France and even Belgium and parts of Germany, he would become a martyr. By mid-19th century, the French no longer regarded Waterloo as a painful defeat but as a glorious and heroic highpoint in their national history: Napoleon and his army had put up a wonderful fight and indeed had almost won. [4] 'Waterloo!

Hat and Coat of Napoleon
© Musée de l'Armée, Paris

'Waterloo! morne plaine!' [*Waterloo, dismal plain*], wrote Victor Hugo. Wellington used Waterloo primarily to enhance his political influence. Through his victory, he and the British troops had brought about peace. 'Waterloo did more than any other battle I know of towards the true object of all battles – the peace of the world'.[5] In 1828 he became Prime Minister. Although he always denied it, and on occasion even demanded satisfaction when he was accused of it, the Duke made full use of Waterloo for political and personal advantage until his death.

By their denial of historical truth almost immediately after the battle, Napoleon and Wellington fired the starting pistol for a fresh struggle, a battle for the memory of Waterloo and even more importantly for the direction of European history. The Belgian historian Johan Op de Beeck rightly concludes in his recently published book on Waterloo that the Emperor and the Duke 'each in their own way' have made a satisfactory final assessment of Waterloo permanently impossible.[6] After 19 June 1815, Waterloo would have losers other than those who lost the battle itself: the Prussians and especially the Dutch and the Belgians, 35,000 of whom had fought alongside the English.

The contribution of these countries to Waterloo was and still is mainly played down in British historical writing. Important Belgian-Dutch officers such as Jean Baptiste Baron van Merlen, the Prince of Orange, Jean Victor de Constant Rebecque and Chrétien Henri Scheltens are often missing from English works. But the appropriation of Waterloo by the British is most obvious in the way 19th and 20th century English historians described the battle of Quatre-Bras.

In the early morning of 16 June 1815, two days before Waterloo, there was a fierce encounter at these crossroads between German, Belgian and Dutch troops under the command of the Prince of Orange and a superior French force led by Marshall Ney. Through a courageous tactical intervention by Belgian and Dutch troops, the Prince of Orange's officers were able to prevent Ney from taking the strategically important crossroads and so delayed the advance of the French towards Brussels. Initially, Wellington had overlooked the importance of Quatre-Bras and on the evening of 15 June had unsuspectingly attended a gala ball in Brussels given by the Duke and Duchess of Richmond. During the gala dinner preceding the ball he was informed of the French troop movements and only then did he realise that the loss of the crossroads would prevent the Anglo-Belgian-Dutch army from linking up with the Prussians, thereby enabling Napoleon to reach Brussels practically unhindered. Luckily for the Duke, the Dutch Chief of Staff Jean Victor Baron de Constant Rebecque and General Hendrik George de Perponcher-Sedlnitsky, acting against Wellington's orders, had sent extra troops to Quatre-Bras and instructed the 2nd Battalion Light Infantry under Major Von Normann and the regiment of Colonel Bernhard van Saksen-Weimar[7] to guard the crossroads.

Had this not happened Wellington would never have been victorious. In 1817, Napoleon stated that the Battle of Waterloo was lost not on the 18th of June but on the 16th at Quatre-Bras:

'To sum up, I had banked on a victory. Defeating the enemy was the key to my whole campaign. Everything depended on a great victory that would throw the enemy back behind the Rhine, and without the heroic decision of the Prince of Orange, who with a handful of men dared to take up a position at Quatre-Bras, I would have caught the British army by surprise. On that day, the Prince showed that he had a sharp insight into and a clear understanding of warfare. He deserves all the credit for this campaign. Without him the British army would have been destroyed before it could have struck a blow.'[8]

Napoleon recalled that on that very day he had successfully started off by defeating the Prussians at Ligny[9], but because of Ney's failure, the entire campaign failed. If the Dutch, Belgian and British troops had been overrun at Quatre-Bras, Wellington would have been unable to take up a position at Waterloo and the Prussians would never have arrived in time to give him support.

Wellington's casual attitude and his decision to leave Quatre-Bras unguarded while he attended the Richmond ball have taken on a mythical status in English historiography.[10] To go dancing on the eve of battle! A more stirring symbol of chivalry and manliness can hardly be imagined. Wellington's charm, his calm and imperturbable manner, made him the embodiment of 'Britishness' and, like Nelson, an 'essential English hero'. Thomas Hardy referred to the ball in his three part drama *The Dynasts* as a 'memorable gathering'.[11] William Thackeray described the festivities at the Richmond residence as historic:

'There never was, since the days of Darius, such a brilliant train of camp-followers as hung round the train of the Duke of Wellington's army in the Low Countries, in 1815; and led it dancing and feasting, as it were, up to the very brink of battle. A certain ball which a noble duchess gave at Brussels on the 15th of June in the above-named year is historical.'[12]

Wellington's biographer, Elizabeth Longford, concluded that the ball was the highpoint of the Duke's 'psychological warfare'.[13] According to her, it was a conscious decision to grace the ball with his and his officers' presence, despite the French threat, to give everyone the impression that they had everything under control. However, whether Wellington deliberately employed this somewhat roundabout style of psychological warfare is doubtful. After all, the French could not have known that the Duke had been invited to the ball and the general public was only vaguely aware of Napoleon's rapid advance. Many other explanations have been given in the British histories, but it does appear that on 15th June Wellington miscalculated the speed of the French advance and had every reason to be grateful for Constant's and Perponcher's military insight.[14]

However, matters went beyond simply glossing over Wellington's actions on 15 and 16 June 1815. In the mid-1840s the English historian William Siborne, in his *History of the War in France and Belgium,* claimed that many Belgian-Dutch troops deserted at Quatre-Bras and that the Prince of Orange on several

occasions had been slow to give the order to form squares in response to the attacks of French cuirassiers on the Bossu Woods, leading to an unnecessarily high death toll among the allied troops.[15] William's inexperience was apparently also a factor at Waterloo. According to Siborne the Prince sent Colonel Christian Friedrich Wilhelm von Ompteda to his death by ordering him to storm the farmstead of La Haie Sainte after the French had captured it. But judging by the evidence that can be found, these accusations do not hold water. At Quatre-Bras it was not William but Major Lindsay of the 69th Infantry Regiment who failed to give the command to form squares.[16] And in the case of the unfortunate Von Ompteda the order to storm La Haie Sainte was given by Von Alten. It was when Von Ompteda raised objections to the order that William reminded him of his duty to obey orders.[17]

The discrediting of the Belgian-Dutch troops and the Prince of Orange as a commander by Siborne and British historians up to the present day has been inspired by British chauvinism.[18] 'Slender Billy' was portrayed as a 'meagre', 'weak' and 'inexperienced' commander, who was incapable of commanding troops without Wellington's support. Siborne, and British historians after him, seem to have forgotten that a large number of the Belgian-Dutch troops were experienced and decorated soldiers who had served under Napoleon or had fought on the side of the allied powers during the first Coalition wars. The number of Belgian and Dutch casualties at Quatre-Bras and Waterloo says enough about their share of the fighting. At Waterloo the Belgian-Dutch army lost 3,000 officers and men out of a total of 17,000, i.e. one in six. At Quatre-Bras the losses were even higher. Here the Belgian-Dutch contingent lost more than a quarter of its men.[19]

The Lion's Mound, Waterloo, indicating the spot where the Prince of Orange was wounded.
© Michiel Hendryckx

Like the input of the Belgian and Dutch troops, the actions of the Prince of Orange in the 1815 campaign need no apology. However, some differentiation would not be out of place. William was certainly rather impetuous and, in the words of the military historian François de Bas, as a commanding officer showed evidence of a certain recklessness, 'une certaine témérité' in his ideas.[20] However, he was no fool in military matters. Soldiers and officers respected him as an officer and not just because of his title. In Portugal and Spain, where he fought with Wellington between 1811 and 1813 in an extremely dirty guerrilla war, he had, in spite of his youth, proved himself able to take independent command of troops and earn respect by example, something which few European princes could have done at that time.[21] The claim of Siborne and many English historians after him that William only held out at Quatre-Bras and Waterloo because of Wellington's guidance is disproved by the sources. The Duke himself stated on 19 June 1815 that the Prince was directing the troop movements so well that it was unnecessary to send him any orders.[22]

English criticism of the performance of the Belgian-Dutch troops at Quatre-Bras and later on at Waterloo is closely connected with the development of Great Britain after 1815. The victory over Napoleon marked the beginning of a period of British ascendancy which was to last until the death of Queen Victoria, in 1901. In addition to Trafalgar Square, London got a Waterloo Bridge in 1817, a Waterloo Road in 1823 and Waterloo Station in 1848. Britain's newly acquired status as a Great Power was attributed to national heroes such as Nelson, Wellington, Uxbridge, Picton and others. Wellington, as the personification of *Britishness,* had saved Europe from tyranny.[23] The Prince of Orange, Blücher, Bülow and Gneisenau had no place in this picture. Their role was downgraded or even suppressed, as in the case of the Dutch General Chassé, whose courageous move against the French guards at the end of the battle is often not mentioned at all by British historians.[24]

The Belgian-Dutch Waterloo myth

Until about 1830 the Dutch and the Belgians shared the same history of Waterloo, and national historians, writers, poets and painters made huge efforts to make the battle their own. Catholic, South-Netherlandish poets, such as the Antwerp-born Jan Antoon Pauwels, presented the victory as a deliverance, as an end to French domination. Belgian officers who had fought courageously at Quatre-Bras and Waterloo were lauded as heroes. General Jean Baptiste Baron van Merlen, for instance, who died at Waterloo, received from the poet Adriaan Jozef Stips a stirring epitaph: 'Citizens of Antwerp! Sprinkle your tears upon this holy ground where now lie the heroic deeds of your fellow townsman'. ['Antwerpenaer! Besproey deez' heylig' aerd met traenen. Waer 't heldenryk in rust, van uwen stadgenoot'].[25] In particular, Dutch poets sang the praises of the Prince of Orange and emphasised in their rhymes the close historical ties between the house of Orange and the protestant Northern Netherlands.

Incidentally, William I used Waterloo shamelessly to enhance his own legitimacy, just as his forebears had done during the Dutch Revolt. He saw the battle as the moment when the United Kingdom of the Netherlands came into being and declared June 18 to be a national holiday. 'Promises have been backed

Jan Willem Pieneman, *The Battle of Waterloo*, 1824, oil on canvas, 567 x 823 x 1822.7 cm.
The Duke of Wellington hears that the Prussians are on the way. The Prince of Orange,
later King William II, lies wounded on a stretcher. © Rijksmuseum, Amsterdam

up by deeds', he declared in his address from the throne in September 1815. He ordered innumerable prints which celebrated the heroic deeds of his son and the Dutch-Belgian troops during the campaign against Napoleon.[26] Medallions were struck and painting and poetry competitions were held, all to the greater glory of the nation. The wife of the writer Willem Bilderdijk, Katharina Wilhelmina Schweickhardt, summarised the feelings of the nation poetically:[27]

How William battled for his people as did William's forebears
How Batavians and Belgians brought down tyranny
And how their illustrious swords caused the French to fall.

[Hoe WILLEM voor zijn volk als WILLEMS afkomst streedt.
Hoe *Batavier en Belg* den dwingland nedervelden.
En hoe hun roemrijk staal zijn Gaulers vallen deed!]

A pyramid with a bronze lion was placed on the spot where the prince was wounded.[28] The battlefield became a tourist attraction drawing visitors from all over Europe. In the summer of 1816, a year after the battle, a panorama of the battlefield was built on the Leidseplein in Amsterdam for Dutchmen unable to make the journey to Waterloo. Its initiator, the publisher and bookseller Evert Maaskamp, proudly announced that the panorama had been assembled from genuine sources and that the noble Prince had inspected it in person before it was opened to the public.[29] A reviewer from the literary journal *Vaderlandsche Letteroefeningen* who visited the opening in 1816 compared it with the London panorama of Burnet and Barker that had opened shortly before in Leicester Square. The English, according to his commentary in the *Letteroefeningen*, had appropriated Waterloo for themselves and the London panorama reeked of historical falsehood:

To me it is incomprehensible how anyone could dare to present such a thing to the English people, how one could so disgrace the uprightness of the English character. [...] Waterloo has become the pinnacle of English inspiration; everything that is a reminder of that victory is dear to the heart of the nation.[30]

Frederika Louisa Wilhelmina of Prussia, first Queen of the Netherlands, '…ran immediately to her suffering son'.
© Atlas Van Stolk, Rotterdam

Except for 'the person of the Prince of Orange' not a single Dutch commander was represented on the London panorama, according to the reviewer. The Amsterdam panorama was much more faithful to nature and to the truth. 'In it one can see what the Dutch paintbrush is capable of; in it one can see that the Dutch school has remained true to its traditional character.' In accuracy and charm, the Dutch artists stood head and shoulders above the English.

In 1846, two years after the appearance of Siborne's work, the Dutch Lieutenant-General Willem Jan Knoop published a 'rebuttal' of 'the imputations against the Dutch army'. Knoop took great care to refute all of Siborne's charges.[31] His view of Siborne was unflattering. In his opinion, all the British accounts of Waterloo compromised themselves by 'a spirit of jealousy and national envy'. Historians like Siborne, he emphasised, 'attempted to enhance England's fame' at the expense of 'the honour of other nations'.[32] This was a serious accusation. It was not long before the 'Siborne affair' was being discussed in newspapers and journals, not least because Prince William, now King, had given his approval to Knoops 'Rebuttal'.[33] Like Siborne, Knoop had allowed national sentiment to sway him. In the summer of 1846 there were even rumours that he and Siborne intended to fight a duel. But in the end the affair was no more than a storm in a teacup.

A Belgian and Dutch nuance?

Nowadays outbursts of pique like those of Knoop and Siborne are rare. Which is just as well since that kind of chauvinism is not very productive. Although ... nowadays anyone visiting the battlefield at Waterloo will hear and see nothing else but Napoleon and Wellington. A battle involving around 140,000 men has been reduced to a struggle between two historical figures. Waterloo has degenerated into an account of Wellington's victory over a brilliant Napoleon, a cockfight between two military geniuses.

Is it right that Belgian and Dutch heroes such as Baron Jean Baptiste van Merlen, the Prince of Orange, Jean Victor de Constant Rebecque and Chrétien Henri Scheltens are forgotten? Surely the historiography of Waterloo is in need of a Belgian-Dutch revision? The Germans had a good advocate in the person of the 19th century publicist Julius von Pflugk-Harttung, especially because the historian Peter Hofschröer made his work accessible to British historians in the 20th century. At the start of the 20th century a joint attempt was made in the Netherlands and Belgium to rescue Waterloo from the hands of British historians: between 1908 and 1909 the Belgian Major General Jacques de T'Serclaes de Wommersom and the Dutch Colonel François de Bas published the four volume *La campagne de 1815 aux Pays-Bas d'apres les rapports officiels Néerlandais*. However, the work made little impact on British historians because it was written in French. This still remains a problem. The most recent Belgian and Dutch studies of Waterloo, by Luc de Vos, Nicolaas Vels Heijn and Johan Op de Beeck, are all written in Dutch.[34]

At Waterloo-commemorations the opposite seems to happen. In 1965, the celebrations were strikingly international in Belgium and the Netherlands. In that year, while the English held an extravagant dinner in Whitehall at which the Queen, the Duke of Edinburgh, Prime Minister Harold Wilson and members of the English elite drank toasts to the British victory at Waterloo, in the Netherlands frantic efforts were being made to make the commemoration of the battle as European as possible. Members of the Commemoration Committee, who included Princess Beatrix, wanted to eliminate all martial nationalism and more or less forbade a re-enactment of the battle in the Goffert Stadium in Nijmegen.[35] In Belgium, Waterloo was an even more sensitive issue because the Flemish nationalists claimed ownership of the Waterloo Lion. The Royal Library of Belgium made every effort to stay neutral in this national conflict and organised an exhibition of stamps and prints of the battle.[36] The Belgian government went a step further. The politicians placed the battle in the context of European history and represented Waterloo as one in a long list of hostilities to have taken place on Belgian soil. Between 1914 and 1918 and 1940 and 1945 other states fought their wars here at the expense of the small, neutral state of Belgium. Perhaps that holds the answer to the question of how the British have got away with expropriating Waterloo unpunished for 200 years: small neutral countries like Belgium and the Netherlands simply do not have great and glorious histories.

1 Gaspard Gourgaud, *Journal inédit de Ste-Hélène*, vol. I (Paris 1899), pp. 500-504. This contribution is largely based on: Jeroen van Zanten, *Willem II*, (Amsterdam 2013).

2 *Memoirs of the life, exile and conversations of the Emperor Napoleon by the Count de Las Cases*, volume IV (London 1836), pp. 179-180.

3 Wellington to John Croker, 8 August 1815. Quotation taken from: John Keegan, *The Face Of Battle: A Study of Agincourt, Waterloo and the Somme* (London 1976), p. 117.

4 *Jeremy Black, The Battle of Waterloo. A new history* (London 2010), pp. 199-200.

5 *Croker Papers, volume II* (London 1884), p. 235.

6 Johan Op de Beeck, *Waterloo. De laatste 100 dagen van Napoleon* (Antwerp 2013), pp.377. See also: Jean-Marc Largeaud, *Napeleon et Waterloo. La défaite glorieuse de 1815 à nos jours* (Paris 2006), passim.

7 H.M.F. Landolt. 'Z.K.H. Hertog Karel Bernhard van Saksen-Weimar-Eisenach', in: *Militaire Spectator* (1862), pp. 507-511.

8 Charles Tristan de Montholon, *Récits de la captivité de l'empereur Napoléonà Sainte-Hélène II* (Paris 1847),pp. 182-184.

9 Gaspard Gourgaud, *Journal inédit de Ste-Hélène,* tome I (Paris 1899), pp. 500-504.

10 P.W. Sinnema, *The Wake of Wellington: Englishness in 1852* (Athens 2006), passim.

11 Thomas Hardy, *The complete poetical works of Thomas Hardy, vol 5: The Dynasts. Part Three.* (Oxford 1995).

12 William Makepeace Thackeray, *Vanity Fair: a novel without a hero* (New York 1848), p. 136.

13 E. Longford, *Wellington. The Years of the Sword*, pp. 416-417. See also: Jeroen van Zanten, *Willem II*, (Amsterdam 2013), pp. 189-236.

14 For a good analysis of Wellington's position on 15 June 1815 see: Richard Holmes, *Wellington. The Iron Duke*, pp. 222-224. The leading military historian Jeremy Black sets Wellington's reaction in June 1815 against the background of his 'defensive tactics'. Cf. Jeremy Black, *The Battle of Waterloo. A new history* (London 2010).

15 For a negative judgement of William see William Siborne, *The Waterloo Campaign 1815* (Westminster 1900, originally published in 1844), pp 177-179. See too a work based on Siborne: George Hooper, *Waterloo, the downfall of the first Napoleon: a history of the campaign of 1815* (London 1862), pp.130-131. See further for criticism of William, P.J. de Bruine Ploos van Amstel, 'De Prins van Oranje bij Quatre-Bras', in: *Tijdschrift voor Geschiedenis, Land en Volkenkunde* 23 (1908), pp. 25-38. And also the novel by Georgette Heyer, *An Infamous Army* (London 1937), passim. See too Jac Weller, *Wellington at Waterloo* (Barnsley 2010), pp. 31-33 and 212. Weller wrongly makes William out to be a military nitwit who failed as a commander on several occasions at Quatre-Bras and Waterloo. Weller attributes success entirely to Wellington and the English. For criticism of Siborne see Malcolm Balen, *A Model Victory. Waterloo and the Battle for History* (London 2006).

16 Longford, Wellington. *The Years of the Sword*, p. 431 and Herbert Siborne (the son of William Siborne), *Waterloo Letters* (London 1983), pp. 336-338.

17 Barbero, *Waterloo. Het verhaal van de veldslag*, pp. 270-271.

18 For the background to Siborne's work and his influence on historical writing about Waterloo see David Hamilton-Williams, *Waterloo. New Perspectives*, pp. 11-30.

19 The number of casualties cannot be established exactly because no lists were drawn up immediately after 16 and 18 June. The figures and percentages cited here are therefore approximations and based on the figures given in F. de Bas and J. de T'Serclaes de Wommersom, *La Campagne de 1815 aux Pays-Bas III*, pp. 202-204; Wüppermann, *De vorming van het Nederlandsche leger na de omwenteling van 1813 en het aandeel van dat leger aan den veldtocht van 1815*, pp. 141-142 and W.G. de Bas, *Quatre-Bras en Waterloo*, p. 162.

20 F. de Bas en J. de T'Serclaes de Wommersom, *La Campagne de 1815 aux Pays-Bas I*, p. 183.

21 For the Prince's Spanish and Portuguese experiences see Jeroen van Zanten, *Willem II*, pp. 97-150. Elizabeth Longford writes that English historians have been too hard on William. She argues in her biography of Wellington that it was 'a fault in the system' that William at twenty-two was given command of a regiment, but that the Prince himself was not to blame. In spite of this concession, Longford is consistently too negative about William's military achievements and experiences. Longford, *Wellington. The Years of the Sword*, p. 474.

22 Jeroen van Zanten, *Willem II*, pp. 189-236 and Bosscha, *Leven van Willem den Tweede*, p.344. See also E. Maaskamp, *De veldslag van het schoon verbond*, p. 36.

23 P.W. Sinnema, *The Wake of Wellington: Englishness in 1852 (Athens 2006), passim*. See also L. Colley, *Britons. Forging the Nation 1707-1837* (London 1994), pp.327-328; R. Colls en Ph. Dodd, (ed), *Englishness: politics and culture 1880-1920* (London 1987) and Paul Langford, *Englishness identified: manners and character, 1650-1850* (Oxford 2001). For Waterloo en *Britishness* see Peter Kellner, 'What Britishness means to the British', in Andrew Gamble and Tony Wright (ed), *Britishness: perspectives on the Britishness question* (Oxford 2009), pp. 62-71, esp.p. 63.

24 Chassé to William, 4 July 1815, F. de Bas and J. de T'Serclaes de Wommersom, *La Campagne de 1815 aux Pays-Bas III*, pp. 354-357.

25 Janneke Weijermars, *Stiefbroeders. Zuid-Nederlandse letteren en de natievorming onder Willem I, 1814-1834* (Hilversum 2012), pp. 49-57.

26 Bergvelt, 'Koning Willem I als verzamelaar, opdrachtgever en weldoener van de Noordnederlandse Musea', in: Tamse en Witte, *Staats- en Natievorming in Willem I's Koninkrijk*, pp. 261-285, esp. pp. 263-268.

27 *Vaderlandsche uitboezemingen* (Leiden 1815), pp. 121-137, esp. 136-137 and *De dichtwerken van vrouwe Katharina Wilhelmina Bilderdijk. Deel 3*. (Haarlem 1860), p.132.

28 Guido Fonteyn, 'Waterloo: de Leeuw. Over de slag bij Waterloo die nog altijd aan de gang is', in Jan Bank, Marita Matthijsen (ed.), *Plaatsen van herinnering*, pp. 72-81; Philippe Raxhon, 'De Leeuw van Waterloo. Een trefpunt van verleden, heden en toekomst', in Jo Tollebeek (ed.), België. *Een parcours van herinnering. Plaatsen van geschiedenis en expansie* (Amsterdam 2008), pp. 179-189.

29 Cf. Eveline Koolhaas-Grosfeld, *De ontdekking van de Nederlander. In boeken en prenten rond 1800* (Zutphen 2010), pp. 299-301.

30 'Comparison between the London and the Amsterdam panorama of the Battle of Waterloo; in a letter to a friend. Amsterdam, 22 October 1816', in 'Mengelwerk', *Vaderlandsche Letteroefeningen* (Amsterdam 1816), pp. 671-682.

31 See for Knoop's 'nation-rousing historical writing': Remieg Aerts, *De letterheren. Liberale cultuur in de negentiende eeuw: het tijdschrift De Gids*. (Amsterdam 1997), pp. 257-258.

32 W.J. Knoop, *Beschouwingen over Siborne's Geschiedenis van den oorlog van 1815 in Frankrijk en de Nederlanden en wederlegging van de in dat werk voorkomende beschuldigingen tegen het Nederlandse leger* (Breda 1846), pp. 1-8.

33 See for example: *Vaderlandsche Letteroefeningen* (Amsterdam 1847), pp. 128-129 and E. Maaskamp, *De veldslag van het schoon verbond* (Amsterdam 1815), pp. 10-11.

34 Luc de Vos, *Het einde van Napoleon: Waterloo 1815* (Leuven 1999), Nicolaas Vels Heijn, *Waterloo. Glorie zonder helden* (Amsterdam 1990) and Johan Op de Beeck, *Waterloo. De laatste 100 dagen van Napoleon* (Antwerp 2013).

35 Jasper Heinzen, 'A Negotiated Truce: The Battle of Waterloo in European Memory since the Second World War', *History & Memory,* 26, Number 1, (2014), pp. 39-74 and Martin Steegmans, 'Vergetenglorie? De slag bij Waterloo in het collectievegeheugen van Nederland, 1815-1965' (Unpublished Master's thesis, Erasmus University Rotterdam, 2011).

36 Bibliothèque Albert I, *Waterloo 1815: Estampes, documents, dessins* (Brussels 1965).

Translated by Chris Emery

It's the Journey, Not the Destination

On the Work of Frank Westerman

[TOMAS VANHESTE]

It's not uncommon that a band's first album is its most exciting. The debut has a raw power. The first light of all the stars that will twinkle in this musical universe can be discerned. Later work may gain in technical control, compositional sophistication and musical depth, but it loses energy and originality. After the explosive first fruits – OK, if you're asking me for examples: The Piper at the Gates of Dawn (1967) by Pink Floyd, Three Imaginary Boys (1979) by The Cure and Beautiful Freak (1996) by Eels – there may be lots more good music to come, but nevertheless the work gradually becomes shrouded in an air of predictability. As if you already know the formula.

Something similar can be said about some literary oeuvres. To some extent, fortunately not entirely, this applies to the work of Frank Westerman (Meppel, 1964). Over the past twenty years, the Dutch grandmaster of literary non-fiction has produced a rich and varied oeuvre. His most recent full-length book, *Stikvallei* (Choke Valley, 2013), is without question a highlight. Yet the thought of his debut, *De brug over de Tara* (The Bridge over the Tara, 1994), makes me nostalgic. It's the only one of Westerman's works that's out of print and can only be found in second-hand bookshops. Perhaps this is because it's slightly dated, having been written during the war in the former Yugoslavia, before the drama of Srebrenica came to an end and the signing of the Dayton Peace Agreement. A less generous critic could also say that it's not really a wonderfully composed book, rather a collection of journalistic reports.

This might well be true, but The Bridge over the Tara was and is a pearl. Right from the opening sentences of his debut, Westerman shows he's a master of atmospheric description. 'That evening, we smoked Arabic Hollywoods and drank coffee from a fildžan, a Turkish coffee cup the size of a thimble. Eighty kilometres away raged the battle for the fildžan state, as the Muslims came to call the lost war.' In his debut, he demonstrates his great talent for finding just the right words to penetrate to the heart of a situation. Although The Bridge over the Tara sparkles with fine sentences, his prose is at the service of the story and occasionally, in his urgency to record what happened, also clunky and rough. His later work sometimes gives the impression of endless polishing. The sentences are often too perfect, which sometimes makes his prose sound a little affected.

Frank Westerman (1964)
© Klaas Koppe

The mystery of war

In his first book, Westerman practises the methods that he refines later on. In *Ingenieurs van de ziel* (*Engineers of the Soul*, 2002), he picks up the trail of the Soviet writer Konstantin Paustovksy. Just as in The Bridge over the Tara he follows in the footsteps of the Dutch novelist A. den Doolaard, who considered Yugoslavia as a second home. Westerman's books often have a puzzling question as their point of departure. In *De moord op de boekverkoopster* (The Murder of a Bookseller, 2014), a journalistic long read which was published as an e-book, the mystery is how an intelligent bookshop owner from Wageningen could fall for an illiterate charmer who would go on to murder her. In *El Negro en ik* (El Negro and Me, 2004), it's the identity of the stuffed black man who was on display in a glass case in Bayoles, Spain, until 1997. In *Engineers of the Soul* (2002), it's how the Gulf of Kara-Bogaz-Gol, the subject of Konstantin Paustovsky's 1932 book of the same name, seems to have disappeared off the face of the earth. In The Bridge over the Tara, it's 'the riddle of war: the towering, blazing difference between groups of people who were completely identical.'

Just such a conundrum is the point of departure for a journalistic quest. When it comes to journalists, Westerman is the real deal. He was one of only a few reporters to meet the Serbian war criminal Arkan and reach the Muslim enclave at Srebrenica. 'Death to journalists, we're going to put you lot against the wall,' one Serbian soldier told him at a checkpoint. As well as courage, he also possesses a huge amount of perseverance. After innumerable attempts, he eventually gets to speak to Mirjana Markovic, the wife of President Milosovic. 'The result is a fascinating interview, in which Markovic passionately attacks the nationalists who destroyed the multi-ethnic state of Yugoslavia, as if her husband were not among them.'

However, it never remains a journalistic quest in search of facts to solve a mystery. Westerman's investigations are always to do with social, sometimes almost philosophical issues. In *De graanrepubliek* (The Republic Of Grain, 1999), he uses the histories of three different gentleman farmers from Groningen to explore how the region and the farming industry fell prey to the ideology of progress, expansion and industrialisation, and how this ideology reached its limits. In *Engineers of the Soul*, he tries to understand how it was that in the Soviet Union *fiziki* and *liriki*, engineers and writers, forged a mass alliance in order to establish physical and intellectual realities on a Socialist footing. In El Negro and me, he investigates the once flagrant, now more hidden tradition of European racism and the always problematic relationship to the Other. Ararat (2007) is an attempt to shine light on the love-hate relationship between science and religion, a subject he revisits in Choke Valley, in which he juxtaposes mythical and scientific explanations for the disaster that struck the African valley.

Goodbye to journalistic distance

In attempting to answer these questions, Westerman also throws his own experiences and personality into the fray. Even in his debut, he's already begun to abandon the journalistic credo of objectivity. 'I became involved, when I really should have kept my distance,' he writes. 'Involvement would cloud my perception. I'd braced myself, but once it was there I began to give in'. Until 2002 he worked as a journalist, first as a correspondent for *de Volkskrant* in Belgrade, then as a correspondent for *NRC Handelsblad* in Moscow, and his books were characterised by a journalistic approach. Later he decided to become a full-time writer, and his work became increasingly literary and personal.

The prominence of his relationship with the world is evident from the programmatic title of El Negro and me alone. His investigations into the origins of El Negro and into how it was that white men came to desecrate the grave of a black man, skin the body, and stuff and mount it like an animal is also a confrontation with his own experiences of racism. Westerman studied tropical land development in Wageningen. Later he formed the opinion that 'development originated from motives that were basically racist. The urge to teach others 'our' techniques or lifestyle or articles of belief presupposed that 'we' knew better than 'them', that white civilisation was superior to non-white civilisation.'

Even closer to his personal obsessions is the subject of *Ararat*. In this book, Westerman climbs the mountain on which, according to Genesis, Noah's ark ran aground. The writer has heard this story umpteen times as a child. He comes from a strict Dutch Reformend Church background. His mother froze one time when he showed her a piece of work that began with the sentence, 'Although humans descended from apes...' He may have shaken off his parents' faith, but not his fascination with mythical stories. In fact, his ascent of the holy mountain is a sort of test: does he really want to break free of his parents' heritage, can he really resist the lure of higher things? But the mountain doesn't yield any mystical experiences, only physical hardship and fear, and he doesn't reach the top. As he suffers, he thinks about his young daughter, and about how she uses the term 'counting letters' for numbers. He comes to the conclusion that her creativity and his imagination come closer to the miracle of reality than the set forms in which religion tries to capture things that are beyond comprehension.

The main theme of Ararat is the strained relationship between science and religion. It was the sciences that first shook Westerman's faith, but not because reason overcame imagination and broke the spell. He tells how imaginary numbers bewitched him as a schoolboy. With a number which, when squared, gives a negative result – impossible in the world of common sense – you can create a world of countless practical applications. 'For me, this touched on the divine.'

Food, drink and fairy tales

His most recent full-length work, Choke Valley, is yet another exploration of the relationship between science and myth. When, on 25 August 1986, 1746 people and thousands of animals drop down dead in a remote valley in north-west Cameroon, a desperate search begins to find out the cause of this terrible event. What in God's name happened? The situation leant itself, writes Westerman, 'to an almost creepily perfect way of investigating the way stories sprout and produce shoots'. And people live by stories, argues the writer. 'Everyone in the world raises their children on food, drink and fairy tales.'

To start with, two different and conflicting scientific explanations are put forward. According to the French éminence grise on volcanology Haroun Tazieff, a volcano erupted beneath Lake Nyos. Volcanic gases shot straight through the water and a cloud of carbon dioxide and sulphur vapour took the lives of man and beast. CO_2 is definitely the culprit, agrees rival Icelandic scientist Haraldur Sigurdsson. However, he contests that this was a case of active volcanism, arguing instead that a huge bubble of carbon dioxide that had accumulated in the lake was released when the balance of the top layer of water, which had acted as a cork, was disrupted by an unknown trigger.

In the first part of Choke Valley, Westerman achieves a masterful depiction of the conflict between these two figures and their adherents. In so doing, he proves he has what it takes to produce a literary form of scientific journalism: the ability to demystify complex issues combined with a feel for the social and psychological sides of science. He is the ideal combination of artist and scientist.

It would be implausible in a novel, Westerman writes, but it's true none the less: the first people to enter the valley of death were three white missionaries, two of whom were Dutch. They came from different directions, but met each other on a deserted road. In the part entitled 'Myth bearers', Westerman tells the story of the Dutchmen, who each tried in their own way to grasp the horrors they were confronted with and help the survivors. One chose to explain the disaster using the Bible story of the Tower of Siloam, which collapsed killing eighteen people as a warning to sinners. The other reached the conclusion that his spiritual care was irrelevant, and lost his faith.

And then there's the version of the 'myth makers'. One of these is the Cameroonian lecturer in drama Bole Butake, who wrote the play Lake God. According to Westerman, Bole 'is not satisfied with the answers offered by Western religion or science. Looking closer to home, he examines each scene one by one to find out what went wrong among the people themselves. Bole describes the feuds that took place in the run-up to the catastrophe'.

Such a story is certainly no less persuasive than the scientific version of what happened, suggests the writer. Just as a scientific theory is hung on facts but is never completely convincing, myths contain a skeleton of historical facts. Westerman does not side with any of the stories, even in the scientific debate. 'I can't get away from the impression', he writes, 'that the volcano theory shrivelled and died partly because Sigurdsson's story is stronger (and more unusual) than Tazieff's story, and therefore more likely to spread.'

The final part is a mishmash of stories from survivors of the disaster, passages from *Lake God*, conspiracy theories about neutron bomb testing, explanations put forward by Cameroonian tribal leaders, and speculation regarding the myth-makers. It is as if the book becomes increasingly fragmented. And perhaps this fits with the idea that searching does not necessarily lead us to the truth and that the world is a cacophony of stories.

Choke Valley is vintage Westerman. The continuing quest, the ever changing routes towards the puzzle. The part-journalistic, part-philosophical search. The searching and not finding. A critic might say that, over the years, the skeleton of his method is at times a bit too visible through the flesh of his story. The enthusiast would counter: of course there is a certain familiarity, because the author has found his own distinctive voice and developed a unique form of literary non-fiction that combines literature and journalism, science and art, Westerman and the world. ▪

More information about Frank Westerman's books is available at www.frankwesterman.nl.

Translated by Rebekah Wilson

Frank Westerman hosted a TV Documentary
'Nederland in 7 overstromingen' (The Netherlands in 7 Floods)

An Extract from *Choke Valley*

By Frank Westerman

I love stories, be they true, plausible or pure fantasy. As a writer, I occasionally plant a new story in the forest of existing tales. The idea for this book came to me in 2009, the Year of Darwin, when Teylers Museum in Haarlem invited me to participate in an exhibition about two legendary ships: Noah's Ark and Darwin's Beagle. The former represented the myths of the Scriptures, the latter scientific truth.

'In the final room we'll have a theatrical finish,' the curator promised. 'We'll have the Beagle ram the Ark amidships and sink her. What do you think?'

I could already picture the breach in the hull. Later, however, it occurred to me that Noah's Ark has not sustained the slightest damage from Darwin's discoveries on the Beagle expedition. The impossible survival story of man and animal on that heaving sea, lapping against the earth, simply makes a stronger impression on the imagination than the young Darwin's research voyage. Before children have had the theory of evolution explained to them, they have already seen a procession of Noah's Arks go by – in books and films, Lego or Playmobil sets. Figments of the imagination can nestle so comfortably into reality that they become part of it. The missing room 13 in a hotel. The closure of the AEX index on Ascension Day. Newspaper horoscopes. Everyone in the world raises their children on food, drink and fairytales.

As a small child I was told time and again, wrapped up in the creation myth of Genesis, that the serpent in paradise brought injustice into the world. How? By tempting Eve to eat from the tree of knowledge of good and evil. Later, as an adult, I came to see all religions as mythical stories interfering in the lives of billions with 'thou shalts' and 'thou shalt nots' – to the point of cutting off one's nose to spite one's face.

What species of animal would do such a thing? When it comes to questions of life and death, the majority of the world's population prefer to put their faith in fiction rather than in fact. People are animals who tell one another stories; we are continually telling each other made-up tales to which we attribute significance at the very least, if not literal belief, as if voluntarily imprisoning ourselves in a cage of self-invented stories.

I wondered about the origin of myths which hold such formidable strength that they become mixed up with reality. Did they start small? And how?

Then I had a flash of inspiration. I thought back to the valley of death in Cameroon and saw in it the ideal test for what I wanted to know. The whole setting lent itself to an almost spine-chillingly perfect method of investigating how stories bud and bloom. Just imagine it. The Nyos valley is an orderly, clearly delineated area. On 21 August 1986, on the new moon, between nine and ten in the evening there is an explosion. This is my zero hour, the big bang with which everything begins. Sunrise is as quiet as quiet can be – even the crickets have stopped chirping. Not a word or a sign from the valley floor. Only afterwards does the sound of human voices swell again; in the days, months and years they speak, lament, dispute, speculate and make up fables regarding the valley of death.

I would like to tease apart all, or at least most, of what has been said and written about it. By disentangling the material thread by thread, I hope to discover the words that have attached themselves to the facts, and how they became woven into sentences, metaphors and stories.

A quarter of a century may be short. I don't expect to find a full-blown, perfected 'death valley legend'. It must be possible, however, to observe the germination of new mythical narrative strands.

From *Choke Valley* (Stikvallei),
De Bezige Bij, Amsterdam, 2013

Translated by Anna Asbury

Representing the Netherlands

The Rijksmuseum and the History of the Fatherland

[JO TOLLEBEEK]

The contrast could not be greater: on the one hand, the debacle of the Netherlands National History Museum, on the other, the triumphant reopening – in April 2013 – of the Rijksmuseum in Amsterdam. Yet initially the National History Museum had a lot of support too. Politicians from very diverse persuasions had come to the conclusion, in 2006, that the Dutch did not know their history and had therefore become 'rootless'. A 'house of history' would reverse the crisis – that was the idea in the dark years after the murder of the Dutch politician Pim Fortuyn in 2002, just as the compilation of a canon of the history of the fatherland was expected to provide solidity. But five years of quarrelling ensued concerning the location of the museum and what was considered to be the directors' overly postmodern concept of history. Then in 2011 the Government cut off the subsidies - an ignominious end.

In the meantime the Rijksmuseum's major renovation campaign was underway. In 1885 Pierre Cuypers had erected a building on the Stadhouderskade which was both city gate and museum, a richly decorated *Gesamtkunstwerk* – not an 'ossuary' full of dead art, he wrote, but a living institution showing society the heritage of their fathers. One renovation after the other subsequently turned the colossal building into an impenetrable labyrinth. The great clean-up began in 2003. The Spanish architect-duo Cruz y Ortiz restored the transparent structure of the museum and opened up the inner courtyards, which had been completely built over, to create a proper entrance. A specialised architect restored – at least partly – Cuypers's original decorations. The interior architect painted the museum halls grey (*noir de vigne*) and made the decision to present the artworks in an extremely discreet manner. It was an absolute success.

Moreover the mood of anxiety and turmoil that had accompanied the plans for the National History Museum subsided. In the reborn Netherlands, the renovated Rijksmuseum was presented unabashedly as an institution with ambition. Indeed, it was a national museum, without the universal reach of the Louvre, for example, but it was nonetheless the 'Museum of the Netherlands'. What that meant could be seen from the motto it proudly bore: 'The Rijksmuseum gives visitors a sense of beauty and a realisation of time.' In other words, the eight thousand objects exhibited not only allow visitors – a million in the

Left
Pieter de Hooch,
A company in the courtyard behind a house
(ca. 1663-1665)

Right
Jan Asselijn,
The threatened swan
(ca. 1650)

first four months after the reopening – to enjoy Dutch art, they also reveal the history of the nation, its life in time.

The remarkable dispute that developed in 2010 around the pistol with which Fortuyn was murdered illustrates the historical ambitions of the Rijksmuseum. Director Wim Pijbes was clear: he wanted the *corpus delicti* in his museum. Critics were astonished – that banal object between the Rembrandts and the Vermeers? – and accused the director of poaching on the preserve of the National History Museum, which was under construction at the time. Pijbes was not impressed. Was a new 'house of history' really necessary? After all, the Rijksmuseum was already the museum of Dutch history, the place where the historic evolution of the Netherlands was presented? That was in the statutes too, was it not?

Well then, let us visit the museum and examine whether and how the Rijksmuseum has realised its ambition. To what extent is it, as a 'Museum of the Netherlands' a history museum as well as a place of art? What is the relationship between art and history there? And how is the nation represented? The answer is anyone's guess, the balance between art and history varies considerably.

Enhanced enjoyment of art

Those who decide to take the shortcut from the new entrance hall to the heart of the museum, with the groups of international tourists, will pass the majestic Front Hall first. Cuypers' creation has been restored in all its glory here, from the terrazzo floor with its mosaics to the wall hangings made by the Austrian historical artist Georg Sturm. Next the visitor enters the Gallery of Honour where, in successive rooms, the great painters of the seventeenth century are exhibited: Saenredam and Frans Hals, Vermeer and Jan Steen, Ruisdael and Pieter de Hooch, with bare churches and Dutch interiors, portraits of merchants and apparently simple still lifes, landscapes with cattle and seascapes. Finally, at the end of the gallery, a room opens up to reveal the greatest masterpiece of all: the *Night Watch*, by Rembrandt. The draft there feels almost sacred because of it.

History is there in Cuypers's decor. The wall hangings in the Front Hall, on which great episodes from the Netherlands' past are depicted, and the pantheons of legators of the fatherland's (art) history in both the Front Hall and the Gallery of Honour make it clear how much the Rijksmuseum is also a monument to nineteenth-century cultural nationalism. Apart from that, though, history is absent. In the heart of the museum, art dominates completely. Here it is about pure enjoyment of art, an aesthetic experience that is not disrupted by any reference to turbulent history. Pijbes knows that many visitors to the Rijksmuseum would not want it otherwise, he is happy to give them what they ask for: 'You should do what you're good at.'

It is different in the rooms devoted to the Middle Ages, the seventeenth century – apart from the Gallery of Honour and the room with the *Night Watch* – and the eighteenth century. This is where history makes its entrance, not only – or not so much – in the didactic, guidebook-type room texts, but particularly in the often magnificent groups of exhibits that form the core of these rooms. Pictures are combined with all sorts of historic objects. In the basement room in

17th century gallery
© Iwan Baan

which medieval Christian art is displayed, for example, *The Adoration of the Magi* (ca. 1480-1485) by Geertgen tot Sint-Jans is accompanied by ivory reliquaries. In the room devoted to the birth of the Republic, paintings like Dirck van Delen's *Iconoclasm in a Church* (1630) are displayed together with items such as monumental cupboards, bronze figures and salt cellars.

The Netherlands that emerges from these rooms is one of power and independence. The Middle Ages (which begin only in the twelfth century) are not dark here, they are the precursor to the wonder of the Republic. The freedom, the economic vitality and the artistic blossoming of the Republic are unashamedly synthesised with the term that the early - nineteenth-century poets gave it, the 'Golden Age'. And with that the old realisation dawns again, seventeenth-century Dutch society owed its elevated state to the simplicity and sobriety of its bourgeois leaders, whom we can admire in Karel Dujardin's group portrait of the governors of the Amsterdam Spinhuis (1669). Fearlessness was a major factor too; Dutch power at sea was defended against its jealous neighbours with great military courage.

These traditional Dutch virtues and a high level of prosperity are also linked at the Rijksmuseum. The mercantile spirit and wealth are shown: in one room the luxury of the mansion houses, in another the large dolls' houses so beloved by the public, and in a third extravagant objects (a mechanical table decoration in the form of Diana on a stag for example). This image is reinforced in the eighteenth-century rooms: the importance of trade and industry, the great prosperity and its equal distribution. The global nature of these economic activities is emphasised in the room devoted to 'the Netherlands overseas'. It points ahead to the spirit of enterprise in the modern Netherlands later on. It is an historical image that inspires pride and contains a joyful message.

In other words, the presentation of the fatherland in this renovated museum has remained traditional. The history it contains is a recognisable story (the greatness of the herring fishing industry, for example), with equally well-known protagonists (Tromp and De Ruyter and so on). It is not without a moral either. Entering the eighteenth century one is warned against a life of 'outward show'. But visitors will forget that lesson fast, impressed as they are by the virtuoso art that is on display here too. The magnificent display case with animals in Meissen porcelain is so attractive. Likewise, further on, in the nineteenth-century rooms, criticism of colonial violence and slavery subsides among the dazzling, exotic art: the 'Lombok treasure' from 1894 does not fail to affect visitors.

It is telling, the halls devoted to the Middle Ages, the seventeenth-century halls – with the exception of the Gallery of Honour and the *Night Watch* room – and the eighteenth-century rooms are also primarily about art. History does not appear here for its own sake. It is there to explain the blossoming of art: the exceptional culture of the Republic resulted in the timeless beauty of Rembrandt and all those other artists. History adds lustre to artistic enjoyment. Its omnipresence in these rooms does not prevent it being, as a critic in *De Groene Amsterdammer* remarked, 'verse two'.

The Mauthausen concentration camp jacket of Isabel Wachenheimer

Tangible past

The history is instrumental then, at least in general, because sometimes it does break through and even take the foreground. That happens even in the Gallery of Honour. In one of the rooms visitors can admire *The Threatened Swan* (ca. 1650) by Jan Asselijn. This is an unusual painting, but not only as an animal picture. It is also noteworthy for the three inscriptions added in the eighteenth century: 'the Grand Pensionary', 'Holland' and 'the enemy of the state'. They turned the painting into a political pamphlet. In the context of the struggle between patriots and Orangists, the white swan portrayed Johan de Witt, who was murdered in 1672 having defended the country against its enemies. Suddenly visitors realise that this magnificent seventeenth century art, this sovereign beauty, could also be used historically as political propaganda.

And then history takes the upper hand, most explicitly in the nineteenth-century rooms. In the last of these rooms hang artists of the Hague School, who gave the Netherlands its 'national landscapes'. In the first of these rooms, though, the focus is on historical art. Once again the history of the fatherland forces itself on visitors as a recognisable entity – in and through the art itself – in a spectacular way. For who can fail to be impressed by the three great royal portraits with which the room opens? Who can fail to see the splendour of our contemporary monarchy, of Beatrix, Willem Alexander and Maxima, in Napoleon, Louis Napoleon and William I? And who has not heard of the Battle of Waterloo, which Jan Willem Pieneman painted on such a large scale in 1824? History reigns here like a picture book full of drama and heroism.

But even more than in and through this nineteenth-century historical art, history takes the upper hand sometimes in the Republic rooms. It is not the paintings, but the objects that are history's instruments there: objects that bring the past suddenly and unexpectedly close, making history so tangible that it doesn't feel as if it is past. It was Johan Huizinga who was the first to label this feeling with the term 'historic sensation', appropriately enough in an article published in *De Gids*, in 1920, about the major changes in the air in the museum

world. Historic details in a print or in a notarial act, he wrote, can 'suddenly give me the feeling of being in immediate contact with the past, a sensation as deep as the purest enjoyment of art, an almost (don't laugh) ecstatic sensation of no longer being myself'.

So let us retrace our steps. Which objects in the Republic rooms might evoke this historical sensation? First of all, there are objects that have acquired almost mythical status because of their origin. They come one after the other in the room devoted to the power struggle in the young Republic: the executioner's sword with which Oldenbarnevelt was beheaded in 1619 (Fortuyn's pistol ...), two sticks, one of which he (perhaps) used to climb onto the scaffold, the chest in which Hugo de Groot (possibly) escaped from prison. They are relics of the history of the fatherland, objects that represent and make the drama of this history tangible for both old and new Dutch citizens. A few rooms further on, the cup that Michiel de Ruyter got from the States of Holland, in 1667, plays a similar role. It gives the Admiral and the grand history that he embodies a powerful immediacy.

But even more than these mythical objects associated with the heroes of the fatherland, simple, often anonymous objects can also conjure up the historical sensation. In a showcase in the room dedicated to the overseas history of the Republic, four separate shoes are shown that were found on Nova Zembla. A little further on, a series of woolly hats is displayed; they were discovered by archaeologists in the graves of Dutch whalers on or near Spitsbergen. These shoes and hats show the fearlessness of the Dutch seamen, their expeditions and the winter hardships in an exceptionally direct way.

Like this, then, the Rijksmuseum offers visitors the chance to practically touch the 'great men' of their fatherland's past. They can see the bullet hole and traces of blood in the hat of Ernst Casimir, the loyal companion of stadholder Frederik Hendrik, who died in 1632. These anonymous objects show the workings of time itself too: the fabric, the grooves, the disintegration. All of these objects bear witness to the same, pride-inspiring history as the groups of exhibits, but they add something more. They turn the museum into a place of historic enjoyment, an almost sensual enjoyment that can sometimes be more powerful than the aesthetic sensation evoked by the Rembrandts and the Vermeers.

President Barack Obama and Prime Minister
Mark Rutte at a Press Conference in the
Rijksmuseum (24/3/2014)

20th century gallery
© Iwan Baan

Meagre representation

Does this make the Rijksmuseum a history museum too (like the National History Museum should have been in the opinion of those who conceived it)? The poverty of the representation of the fatherland's past is too obvious for that. Those who return to the eighteenth century rooms, for example, will be entranced by the magnificent portrait that Pierre Proud'hon painted of Rutger Jan Schimmelpenninck and his family (1801-1802). But it will tell him very little of the genesis of the modern Dutch state, in the decades round 1800, in which this patriotic citizen played such a prominent role. And the revolution, the Batavian Republic, the discussions on the new constitution, the reforms in education and finance? You can see a twig from a freedom tree and a member of parliament's ribbon, but that is about it.

The sparsity of the historical representation is most obvious in the twentieth century rooms, on the top floor of the museum. Attempts have been made in recent projects to synthesize the past century. On *The Dutch Floor*, the collective presentation of top pieces from the collections of the National Library of the Netherlands and the National Archives in The Hague, some thank-you letters written to Prime Minister Drees in 1947, the document with which Wilhelmina abdicated in 1948, and a treaty dating from 1949, in which the transfer of sovereignty to Indonesia is set out, illustrate the birth of the welfare state, the continuity of the monarchy and the difficult decolonisation. In the collection that the programme *The Memory of the Netherlands* published, in 2006, there are photos of a Limburg mine from 1909, the upper floor of the Albert Heijn in the Kalverstraat from 1934 and a poster from the Farmers' Party dating from 1968; they represent the process of industrialisation, the changing consumption culture and the success of populism. There is none of that in the Rijksmuseum; the twentieth century is nothing more than 'modernisation' and 'freedom'.

All the more painful is the presentation of what is shown: the Second World War and the Holocaust. In one of the small rooms dedicated to the first half of the twentieth century three objects are assembled. In the centre, the visitor can admire the chess set that the German SS leader Heinrich Himmler gave to Anton Mussert, the leader of the National Socialist Movement in the Netherlands, in 1941. In a showcase against the rear wall there is a photo album of the Wachenheimer family, German Jews who fled to the Netherlands. Above it hangs the concentration camp jacket of Isabel Wachenheimer. She wore it in Mauthausen, after having first been deported to Auschwitz, where her parents were murdered right after their arrival.

The camp jacket does not evoke the feeling of having immediate contact with this gruesome history, it merely evokes embarrassment. Amidst delftware from the Rozenburg factory in The Hague and the Mondriaans, the nostalgia of furniture from the Amsterdam School and the equally nostalgia-evoking documentary by Bert Haanstra about the damming of the Veerse Gat (1962), the peculiar double-decker built by Frans Koolhoven in 1918 and Rietveld chairs, the jacket is at risk of itself becoming an object of aesthetics and amusement. This shabby bit of cloth from Mauthausen, presented in isolation and without context, cannot convey the history of the war and the persecution of the Jews. Its presentation shows how the integration of art and history can fail completely.

For a foreign public the 'Museum of the Netherlands' shows the best of Dutch art: Rembrandt and Vermeer in a magnificent, contemporary museum – and Van Gogh too, at the end of the nineteenth century rooms, pointing the way to the next attraction on the programme. For the Dutch themselves the Rijksmuseum is certainly not a history museum either. Rather, it is a place where whiffs of memories of the (former) greatness of the fatherland waft towards them. A national community can be formed around these memories or be strengthened by them. The 'Museum of the Netherlands' disseminates consensus round a joyful representation of the Republic and the modern Netherlands. Who but a handful of conscientious historians will deplore the fact that this representation is a fiction? ▦

Translated by Lindsay Edwards

FURTHER READING

The album *Honderd jaar Rijksmuseum 1885-1985* (Weesp: Van Holkema & Warendorf, 1985) commemorates the history of 'the old Rijksmuseum' in photos and illustrations. For the formation of the nineteenth century collection see ELLINOOR BERGVELT's *Pantheon der Gouden Eeuw. Van Nationale Konst-Gallerij tot Rijksmuseum van Schilderijen* (1798-1896) (Zwolle: Waanders, 1998); for a biographical study of the architect see: A.J.C. VAN LEEUWEN, *Pierre Cuypers, architect (1827-1921)* (Zwolle / Amersfoort / Zeist: Waanders Uitgevers / Rijksdienst voor Archeologie, Cultuurlandschap en Monumenten, 2007).

The conversion to 'the new Rijksmuseum' is well documented and discussed in JENNY REYNAERTS's *Rijksmuseum. The Building as Work of Art* (Amsterdam: Rijksmuseum, 2013); JAAP HUISMAN, *The New Rijksmuseum. Cruz y Ortiz Architects* (Rotterdam: nai010 uitgevers, 2013) and CEES W. DE JONG and PATRICK SPIJKERMAN (ed.), *The New Rijksmuseum. Pierre Cuypers and Georg Sturm Exonerated* (Amsterdam: Pallas Publications, 2013).

For Huizinga: W.E. KRUL, 'Huizinga versus Schmidt-Degener. Twee meningen over het Historisch Museum', in: *Bulletin van het Rijksmuseum*, 43 (1995), 308-316.

There is extensive international literature about museal representation of the nation; see amongst others DAVID BOSWELL and JESSICA EVANS (ed.), *Representing the Nation: a Reader. Histories, Heritage and Museums* (London / New York: Routledge, 1999).

The 'Laugh-or-I'll-Shoot' Architecture of Zaandam

[JAAP HUISMAN]

It was a striking article in the paper: Dubai is going to build a replica of the Taj Mahal, but bigger, and not as a sacred place but as a shopping mall. In this instance, the Taj Mahal would be part of a park also containing copies of the Eiffel Tower and the leaning Tower of Pisa. This is a sample of the reinterpretation of classic icons that actually no longer surprises anyone.

Making copies is obviously one of man's primal necessities, since it happens not only in Dubai, but also in Japan, Las Vegas and many other places in the United States. And the copyists go for the greatest hits of Western architecture every time. We come across buildings reminiscent of Palladio's villas, Greek temples and French chateaux all over the world. And it's quite understandable – if you don't have the money to come to Europe, let Europe come to you. For Americans it's also part of their upbringing. Europe! Paris! London! You have to have seen them.

In Washington State I visited a small place called Lynden, whose population is made up largely of Dutch émigrés. They profess a strict version of Protestantism and at the same time keep up several Dutch traditions, such as the clog dance and a procession with floats. In the shopping area you will find a baker that makes fresh bread and there are old-fashioned Dutch delicacies on sale too. But the most striking thing is these emigrants' need for a Dutch backdrop. So we find a windmill (housing a restaurant serving 'poffertjes', or tiny pancakes), a small canal covered in duckweed, and imitation canal-side houses. As is frequently the case in the United States, these are cardboard facades on standard houses. And Lynden is not the only example. Ten kilometres down the road we find a replica of a Swiss mountain village and on the ocean Norwegians have settled down in a fishing community that makes them feel at home too. Seeing the Dutch archetypes in Lynden one becomes very much aware of what the icons of low-country architecture are, as they are imitated over and over again. One finds them in the form of a gin miniature on KLM planes and also as an amusement park in China. Mills, liftbridges, canals and stepped gables.

Call in the 'city surgeon'

It is notable that this sort of archetype only appears in distant foreign countries, never in one's own land. No one would ever consider building copies of the quaysides of Ghent or the palaces of Brussels in Belgium. For a long time it was a taboo in the Netherlands too: the ring of canals in Amsterdam was a one-off urban planning exercise. It was time, in the 20th century, for Modernism. The motto was: just act normally, that's crazy enough. But times change. Now the Modernist *diktat* has gone, space has been made for canals and imitation canal-side houses at several places in the Netherlands (specifically in the '*Vinex*' districts, sites for new building on a massive scale, often on the outskirts of cities). This too is understandable. Because there is a lack of points of recognition in newly built areas in the peat bogs. Since their residents work elsewhere, there is a need for a recognisable home, a glimpse of the past. The imitation canal-side houses and farmsteads satisfy the needs of nostalgia.

Inntell Hotel. Zaandam

The Zaan house is another icon. This is a wooden house, painted blue or green, in the Zaan region (in the province of North Holland, a stone's throw from Amsterdam), where the soil is so boggy that heavy building is impossible. Driving piles into the marshes around the River Zaan is out of the question: most of the houses stand on a concrete slab (and in the past on cow hides). The area round the town of Zaandam is the oldest industrial region in the Netherlands, with rice-husking plants, cacao factories and sawmills. When he stayed in the Zaan region in the 18th century, Tsar Peter the Great was so taken with this centre of industry and the architecture that went with it that it inspired him to build St Petersburg, which was in fact one of the first replicas of the ring of canals.

Zaandam has lost a lot of its charm as a result of the uncaring treatment of its town centre in the 1960s and 1970s. Canals were filled in, factories closed down and newly opened traffic routes disrupted the layout of the streets. The few remaining wooden houses looked like a silly reminder of past glories, but paled into insignificance alongside the colossal concrete office blocks of the *Albert Heijn* supermarket chain and *Rabobank*. In this respect, Zaandam is like other post-industrial towns such as Tilburg (in the south of the Netherlands) and Enschede (in the east), which are uncertain what to do with the legacy of abandoned industries. Empty spaces around the inner city create an inhospitable atmosphere.

It is therefore understandable that Zaandam town council has called on the Netherlands' prime 'city surgeon' for help: Sjoerd Soeters of the bureau Soeters and Van Eldonk Architects. This firm has made a name for itself by mending ruined inner cities and city centres with growing pains. This firm won several prizes for breaking open *Mariënburg* in Nijmegen and thereby creating an intelligent and agreeable connection between a forgotten square on the east side of the centre and a busy shopping street. The town of Nootdorp near The Hague asked Soeters to transform the former racecourse and trotting track into a shopping centre with homes on a raised indoor street above it. In both cases the architecture is given a historical look and is striking for its fine details. Embroidery patterns in the masonry, carefully designed facades and other elements are intended to give the residents the feeling they had lost in the formation of the city.

An XL transformation

Since Zaandam seemed to have lost its identity, Soeters came up with a brilliant plan. He suggested lining the walls of the pedestrian area between the station and the *Dam* (the central square) with Zaan-style houses. Not the tiny houses as in Peter the Great's day, but ten times bigger. Zaandam town council needed no persuading.

A Zaan House

Urban planning and architecture were to merge into one another and make for cohesion in the transformed *Gedempte Gracht* ('filled-in canal'). This canal has been opened up again so that the buildings are reflected in the water. As Amsterdam and Bruges demonstrate, this is a requirement for a spacious and picturesque effect. The architects were held strictly to Soeters' masterplan. They did not have to copy the Zaan-style houses literally, only keep to their spirit, and preferably in identical materials and colours: in wood, and in blue and green.

The climax of this acknowledgement of the past is the *Inntel* hotel by Winfried van Winden, which has probably surpassed the *Zaanse Schans* (a picturesque neighbourhood) in popularity. Van Winden has assembled all the Zaan building styles and forms of decoration into a mass of wood that makes the nearby *Rabobank* melt away like a Japanese nuclear power station. Hordes of foreign tourists flock in, and those who have the time stay in one of the hotel's period rooms, which were also inspired by Zaan interiors. This includes flowery curtains, a box bed (of course) and crocheted valances over the windows to ward off the curious. In fact all Van Winden has done is to stack up a dozen overlapping Zaan houses. We recognise the wooden joinery of course, and the ridge boards with their swans and weathervanes.

The brutalist station from the high-tech period of the 1980s is camouflaged by giant houses with ridge roofs. Once again they have red tiled roofs that contrast sharply with the vivid green. Criticism might be levelled not so much at the size of the buildings as at the cladding. Plastic planks have a flattening effect, unlike wood. Of course they are more easily maintained because no painting is needed, but there is no grain to catch the light with its fine texture.

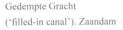
Gedempte Gracht
('filled-in canal'). Zaandam

Soeters' most important change was in the traffic situation. On leaving the station, one descends by a gentle slope towards the centre. In this way no one has to wait any longer for the traffic lights on the provincial trunk road that passes in front of the station. And the *Gedempte Gracht* has been transformed into a pleasant pedestrian area thanks to a proper relationship between public space and buildings.

Proud of the town again

Whatever else though, the architecture of Zaandam can be put in the 'laugh-or-I'll-shoot' category, based on the pursuit of quick effects as seen in soaps. How long does a joke remain funny? In Dubai or Las Vegas it does not really matter, because the settlements are in the sand, where visitors come only to be entertained. The Taj Mahal and the previously built pyramid in Dubai are there for no other purpose. It's different when you allow the copies, enlarged to giant proportions, in a historical town like Zaandam. They will soon become an irritation. The laugh gradually fades once you have grasped the double meaning in the joke.

Yet one can in a certain sense be positive about the changes. They have polished up the town's image and brought new life to its centre. The inhabitants can be proud of their town once again (to prove this, they are flaunting the biggest *HEMA* shop in the Netherlands, which has occupied one of the retail premises). One will have to get used to the idea that a centre is built for 30 years – and no longer – and after that will be renovated or changed. It's not necessary in cities like Amsterdam and Bruges, because they have been cherished and pampered for centuries. For new and spoiled inner cities there is no other way: an XL transformation, but one with character. ■

Translated by Gregory Ball

High Stakes

The Photographs of Erwin Olaf

[TINEKE REIJNDERS]

It is as if Erwin Olaf is navigating the River Styx and, in passing, captures something of the silvery darkness from the underworld. He has a penchant for draping the panoramas of life in funeral weeds. Several times he has based a photo series on the complex symphonies of blacks and greys. But rarely has he drawn out so many colourless nuances from the photographic process as in his recent series *Berlin*. Every one of the 13 photographs in this eponymously located series exudes an unadulterated melancholy, and even the colour photos have been tinted with a muted palette. We are just one remove from decay and death here. Erwin Olaf has always been a man of extremes, an *ensceneur* of extraordinary beauty and intense experiences, usually based on intimacy. In some of the photographs in this series, he has penetrated the unfathomable rhetoric of black more deeply than ever before. The series *Berlin* (2013) speaks volumes in this regard.

Berlin is a city which exerts a strong pull on artists to this day. It is a city for the new, but also a city to which history clings like ivy to a brick wall - several histories, in fact, with the fall of the Berlin Wall in 1989 perhaps being the one that has touched us most. German reunification and the years that followed saw freedom celebrated in every way imaginable. Erwin Olaf was a regular visitor in the 1990s and enjoyed the excessive celebrations. Now that, like others of his generation (Erwin Olaf was born in 1959), he is concerned about developments that threaten our existence on earth, he has gone back to Berlin with historical images in his head. 'I see correspondences between the present day and the interwar years', he says. 'We in the Western world are dancing on the edge of the volcano. You can feel that something ominous is coming; we read about it in the papers, but we carry on celebrating regardless. We are at a tipping point. That's the feeling I wanted to express in this series.'

Perhaps it is the element of reappraisal that is encapsulated in the idea of revisiting Berlin, this time with contemplative intentions, that imbues the images with a sense of sincerity, of wisdom, despite the fact that, as usual with Olaf, they are born of a wild theatrical fantasy.

The Berlin series is situated in the interwar years, a period when the people of Berlin nervously sought their entertainment in an elegant and avant-garde metropolitanism, and the locations also date from that era. But the voice of Johann Joachim Winckelmann, the 18th-century art historian, can also be heard

Erwin Olaf, *Portrait 05,*
9th July 2012, Carbon Print,
ca. 17 x 22.67 cm.

resonating in this series. His famous expression *Edle Einfalt und stille Grösse* ('noble simplicity and quiet grandeur'), his description of the true nature of the 'classical' Greek art, appear to have had an unintended influence on several photographs in the series.

Noble simplicity

Portrait 05, 9th of July 2012 is a small carbon photograph of a girl. She sits ramrod straight and gazes at us from her armchair, without giving away any hint of her feelings. Her blonde hair is drawn tight, two round plaits echoing her ears. Parts of the image remain swathed in shadow, contrasting with the details that are picked out by a Caravaggesque shaft of light: the left side of her face, the leather coat she is wearing, the row of leather buttons, the arms of the chair,

Erwin Olaf, *Berlin, Clärchens Ballhaus Mitte*, 2012, Lambda print, Fuji Chrystal Archive digital paper, 60 x 90 cm. and 120 x 181 cm.

the tops of her laced boots. Her hands are hidden in black leather gloves, resting on the arm of the 1930s chair. We see nothing more of this nameless girl but that one half of her perfect face. In the upper right quadrant, a sculpted head protrudes from the wainscoting, as round and well-defined as the head of the young blonde. There is also a second wooden head, that of an older person; we can imagine the slanderous whisperings between the walls of the old room. As usual in this oeuvre, however, the photographs reveal no meaning. They are full of references, but convey no message. That message perhaps lies in the atmosphere, the mood, the limbo of what is beautiful and perfect – and thus mortal, threatened. Surely a child like that cannot be sitting in this upper middle class interior simply in order to merge with the decor? To appear as implacable as the great aesthetic care with which the other objects are arranged? It is as if Erwin Olaf is trying to squeeze all liveliness out of the image in order to leave an exalted extract, a web of mystery that challenges viewers to project their own ideas onto the image. Is she wearing modified shoes? Perhaps she is disabled? Do her Aryan features and haughty gaze not arouse emphatically painful associations whilst at the same time her age exudes innocence? The viewer is invited by this exceedingly precise print to search long and carefully in the matt sea of blacks and greys. For this and a few of the other photos in the series, the photographer has used the 19th-century technique of carbon printing. With this technique, negative and print are exactly the same size, contributing to the feast of nuances.

At first sight, not all the photographs in the series match Winckelmann's description of 'quiet grandeur'. In the colour photograph *Clärchens Ballhaus Mitte, 23rd of April 2012*, the main subject is a young girl – at least she is the most highlighted subject, dressed in a pink top and light blue culottes. She is looking at the

camera, while behind her three older women sitting at a cafe table are watching her from their seats against the wall. They look as if they have stepped out of a Goya painting. Two of them are heavily made up and still fairly attractive; the third cares nothing about decorum, with her slipped shoulder strap and hostile gaze. She is just as authentic as the girl, but is at the other end of the spectrum of life. This photograph, too, has an alienating effect. The ease of the cliché, women of a certain age who can no longer recapture the image of their youth, is subordinated to the value of a philosophical observation that goes beyond time and place.

Equally timeless and sober is the photograph in which we see the artist himself ascending a staircase: *Olympia Stadion Westend, Selbstporträt, 25th of April 2012*. It is a broad staircase whose steps fill the bottom of the image and which narrows towards the vanishing point as it ascends. It is illuminated by daylight. The subject has his back to us. He is wearing a sober suit. As he climbs from the dark tunnel towards the light streaming in from above, the camera captures a tiny ray of light on his left hand, coming from an unidentifiable source. The picture is a perfect example of 'noble simplicity', but also of an over-orchestrated symbolism. Nevertheless, no one will deny that this is a masterful image, brimming with underlying intensity. Yes, this is Berlin; this is where the Olympic Games were held in 1938; there are echoes of Adolf Hitler here, of Leni Riefenstal. And at the same time this is also Erwin Olaf, a man whose creativity and career are in the ascendant. He is the man who shot a triptych self-portrait in 2009 with the titles *I wish, I am, I will be,* the last of which shows him hooked up to oxygen tubes. Just as Erwin Olaf has always been open about his homosexuality, so he has always spoken spontaneously about the pulmonary emphysema which will increasingly restrict his physical functioning in the future. Climbing the stairs is therefore a tremendous effort for his body.

Berlin, Berlin, *Olympia Stadion Selbstporträt,* 2012
Lambda print, Fuji
Chrystal Archive digital paper,
60 x 88.85 cm. and
120 x 177.7 cm.

Erwin Olaf, *Chessman* I, 1988, Lambda Endura
Print on Kodak Professional Paper, 100 x 100 cm.

Mythical, grotesque source

Berlin is a high point to date in a career spanning more than three decades. Erwin Olaf has time and again proved to be the indefatigable builder of new, completely original images. His signature is always present, and even the photographs with an unexpected twist are unmistakably recognisable as the work of Erwin Olaf. His work is characterised by oppositions (black/white, naked/clothed, young/old, successful/excluded) and by a deep aesthetic quality which embraces both the human figure and the decorative element. From the start, he has divided his free work into series and published them in books. His photographs are collected all over the world and exhibited in important places. The weighty tome *Own*, which contains his most important photographs, was published in 2012.

There are many photographers who focus on the human body, but none have sought out the extremes with as much passion as Erwin Olaf. He once said that the books of Gerard Reve had opened his eyes to possibilities that had previously been considered inappropriate. And his work is indeed not for the prudish. It is striking that the playful Groninger Museum organised a retrospective in 2003 to mark its 25th anniversary, entitled *Silver*, with eponymous catalogue, whereas the Stedelijk Museum in Amsterdam has to date not purchased a single photograph. And I myself must confess to quickly leaving an opening at a Paris gallery for his black photographs from the *Dusk and Dawn* series, because the darkroom-like atmosphere which dominated is not my natural habitat. His own mother, Olaf likes to recount, was initially very shocked by the photograph of her son in ejaculatory pose. Homosexuality is undoubtedly a driving force behind the far-reaching aesthetic of his work, and there is a clear thread of the gay sense of the theatrical running through his photographs. It generally does not dominate, however, though it initially seemed as if it would; Erwin Olaf made his debut with photographs for gay magazines and his name hit the headlines when naked photographs were removed from the Foto '84 exhibition in the Nieuwe Kerk in Amsterdam. However, his work is too rich in associations to label it purely sexual.

The book *Chessmen* was published in 1987, in which the 32 chess pieces were depicted in a series of bizarre compositions. Olaf moulded bodies and attributes for the pieces; children's wartime clothing from the dressing-up box is combined with vibrators, dildos and horns. The models are eccentric, while their faces and features are hidden behind veils or under helmets and funnels, focusing all attention on the bodies, the flesh of which is sometimes bound with thick ropes or hung with gossamer. It is a parade of naked bodies, originating from a world that is between Venetian carnival and a Mediaeval Underworld – with women fat and thin, large and very small, and with men in impossible poses, floating, hanging, kneeling. A couple of male arms stretching heavenwards support a real baby: the king. According to Olaf, the black-and-white chess piece series was inspired by the enthusiastic chess reports that were broadcast by chess master Hans Böhm on Dutch radio and TV. The photographer saw great battles in his mind's eye and tapped into his own mythical, grotesque source, a source which has never ceased flowing.

Olaf is an eloquent man who will never forget to thank his models for placing their confidence in him. Following the major photographic tableau *Leidens Ontzet* ('Relief of Leiden') which Olaf created in 2012 for Museum De Lakenhal in Leiden, a documentary was shown on the creation of the series. It shows how he draws people into his magic with his natural decisiveness and goes straight for the goal he is trying to achieve. The perfect composition is a question of a moment; if necessary, details can be altered later on the computer.

How far can I go?

Before becoming a photographer and taking the name Erwin Olaf, Erwin Olaf Springveld studied journalism at the Utrecht School of Journalism, being admitted on the basis of his school essays. His studies were not helped by his tendency to continue polishing a text *ad infinitum*. One day he interviewed the painter Marte Röling and, because the real photographer was ill, took some photographs too. One of his lecturers recognised their quality, and that is how Erwin Olaf came to bid farewell to his studies and become an assistant to the professional photographer André Ruigrok, in whose studio he learned all the tricks of the trade. 'Erwin worked for me for two and a half years', remembers Ruigrok, 'and we parted on very good terms. He wanted to become famous, and he's succeeded.'

There are very few Dutch artists who have made their drive so emphatically clear. Fame could not come too soon for Olaf, and he was not always able to hide his impatience. Already warmly embraced by an international array of followers, until recently he still complained about the lack of attention given to his work by museums of modern art. This was perhaps an understandable lament from someone who for a long time lived from commissions and whose reputation was also earned in the world of advertising. He worked for large companies such as Diesel and Heineken, and succeeded in exploiting his own style within the advertising codes, landing him a Silver Lion award in Cannes. He also carried out assignments for magazines and made an impression with striking posters for what was then the Zuidelijk Toneel theatre company led by Ivo van Hove. An important mentor in his early years was the choreographer and photographer Hans van Maanen, who Olaf claims taught him the philosophy of simplicity.

His commissions in recent years have been extensions of his free work, such as the impressive series of theatre sets that he created several years ago for the Nieuwe de la Martheater in Amsterdam. He was also commissioned to produce the likeness of King Willem-Alexander for the Dutch euro coin, which was revealed to the public on 31 October 2013. Unexpectedly, he produced a faceted rather than a flat portrait, in what experts commented was an Eastern Bloc style. In a TV interview, Olaf said: 'I wanted to see how far I could go with cropping the portrait without losing his recognisability.'

That 'how far can I go' sounds like a device. In 1991, not long after the publication of *Chessmen*, he was invited together with the painter of dreamlike images, Frans Franciscus, to make a film at the Oud Amelisweerd estate. The pair based the film on Thomas Mann's *Death in Venice* and for the title part in the film, a beautiful boy named Tadzio, they chose Aat Nederlof, a Dutch actor with Down's syndrome. In order to break away from the image of an endearing boy with Down's syndrome, they made his role rather mean. The film lasts half an hour and is an exuberant ode to the absurdities of life. Olaf, with his weakness for mavericks, dedicated his next photo collection to people with learning disabilities. *Mind of their Own* (1995) is a series of colour portraits set against a psychedelic background that celebrates the beauty that in their case is not uncommonly disregarded. In the epilogue he describes how the theme continued to occupy him after *Tadzio*. 'Aat and his single-minded mother taught me that people with learning disabilities are independent people, with their own emotions and their own external beauty.' 'It became a series of eyes', he wrote. 'Eyes in which the absolute surrender to the camera dominates.'

That makes this joyous series a total contrast to *Blacks*, a series of photographs that was published in 1990 as the Focus collection. Here, the eyes are covered with small objects and everything is painted black, including the models. They are shown either full or half-length, richly adorned with fetish objects, framed by a mandorla, a sort of laurel wreath in which all manner of objects have been

Erwin Olaf, *The Mother*, from the series Dusk, 2009,
Lambda Print / Dibond / Wooden frame, 121 x 229 cm.

Erwin Olaf, *The Soldier*, from the series Dawn, 2009,
Lambda Print / Dibond / Wooden frame, 121 x 229 cm.

incorporated, including the trumpet, the horn of Fama, or fame. Full of youthful exuberance, Olaf gave full rein to his creativity; later, he would revisit the theme of 'black' with more control, not just in the Berlin series referred to earlier, but also in *Dusk*, the second part of *Dusk & Dawn* (2009). Here, the scenes could have been taken from a film; styled with frightening perfection, scenes which are played out in prominent houses and in times gone by. In *Dawn*, the interiors and clothes are white; in *Dusk*, everything is dark. Their premiere in the Hermitage Museum on the River Amstel in Amsterdam, the 17th-century annex of its St Petersburg namesake, provided a fitting setting for the series.

Erwin Olaf, *The Ice cream Parlour*, from the series Rain, 2004,
Lambda Print / Diasec, 70 x 70 cm. and 120 x 120 cm.

The amazing thing about the excessive dedication to beauty is that it never detracts from the sense of urgency that marks out Olaf's oeuvre. All his work has this urgency, even where the subjects have their backs to the camera or give off a sense of lethargy and abandonment. He seeks out the extremes of these feelings in the series *Rain, Hope, Grief, & Fall*, which were created between 2006 and 2008 and which were exhibited together for the first time in Fotomuseum Den Haag in The Hague. With their perfect 1970s interiors, the photographs depict the 'green widows', prepared down to the last detail to greet the world outside, yet for the time being doomed to stay at home, waiting. The plot sounds simple, but the refinement with which the viewer is also led through a series of almost depressive moods is inimitable. Yet nothing is dictated, and the scenes smoulder with indeterminacy. It is probably for precisely that reason that the photographs remain so tenable artistically. And because they continually provoke us. Erwin Olaf without doubt celebrates the absurdity of life with so much energy in order to prevent the waters of the Styx from flowing over our feet too soon. He is playing for high stakes. Phenomenally high stakes. ▨

All images © Erwin Olaf / Courtesy Flatland Gallery (Amsterdam, Paris).

Translated by Julian Ross

Erwin Olaf, *The Hairdresser*, from the series Rain, 2004,
Lambda Print / Diasec, 70 x 99.3 cm. and 120 x 170 cm.

Deeper and Deeper into the Forest

On the Work of Oek de Jong

Before the publication of *Pier en oceaan* (Pier and Ocean, 2012), I asked myself once or twice whether it would be more accurate to refer to the work of Oek de Jong's 'pens' rather than the work of his 'pen'. After all, each new book bearing his name seemed to have been written by a different author also called Oek de Jong. *De wonderen van de heilbot* (The Wonders of the Halibut, 2006), the diary that he kept while writing *Hokwerda's kind* (Hokwerda's Child, 2002), contains an illuminating remark in this respect: 'I need to reinvent myself as a novelist.'

And this is just what he has done: his first novel, *Opwaaiende zomerjurken* (Billowing Summer Frocks, 1979), is a sensitive bildungsroman; *Cirkel in het gras* (Circle in the Grass, 1985) is an intellectual novel of ideas; *De inktvis* (The Octopus, 1993), a pair of novellas, is in its turn mystical; and the 444-page novel Hokwerda's Child is very earthy, and with it cruel and sensual. I have not included de Jong's debut, *De hemelvaart van Massimo* (The Ascension of Massimo, 1977) and his essayistic prose in this summary, this shard portrait, as it is not uncommon for these genres to deviate from the rest of a writer's oeuvre.

De Jong's magnum opus, Pier and Ocean, marks the culmination of his earlier creative prose spanning many years: all the shards fall into their natural place, so to speak. Is there an explanation for this? Indeed, there are several.

Firstly, in this semi-autobiographical family saga, with its protagonist Abel Roorda, de Jong (re-)uses the narrative material of his life and the lives of his parents. Several of the features contained in his body of work are taken from the same source. No wonder: Pier and Ocean ends with the birth of Abel's (adolescent) career as a writer. Hence too the similarity to Billowing Summer Frocks (in particular), so much so that the respective protagonists Edo and Abel seem to have a strong spiritual connection.

Secondly, over the course of his lapidary oeuvre, de Jong gradually develops into a pureblood novelist – the novel is his form. In Billowing Summer Frocks, he still seems to be working intuitively, but from Hokwerda's Child onward, he is more aware of his craft. Bearing in mind that the novel, as Milan Kundera might put it, is a ladder that leads down into the human mind, deeper and deeper.

Thirdly, he has learnt to control this mind. Yes, control, not restrain. One book that, mistakenly, seldom gets a mention in reviews and discussions is *Een man die in de toekomst springt* (A Man Leaping into the Future, 1997), but in this book de Jong thinks himself out of the personal crisis into which his descent into the

Oek de Jong (1952)
© Klaas Koppe

human mind has led him. He stared into the abyss and the abyss stared back. The decade between 1985 and 1995, when he walked through a deep valley, was in his own words 'a dark time'. During this period, he only published the vulnerable mythical-magical pair of novellas The Octopus, which was met with general derision and incomprehension by literary critics.

Whistling bullets

Very few authors have broken with their earlier work like this, have put their hard-earned status on the line in the same way as de Jong. The Octopus led to a complete reversal of esteem. In an article about the state of affairs in Dutch literature (*Maatstaf* 8/9, 1991), the literary critics Arnold Heumakers and Willem Kuipers came to the conclusion that A.F.Th. van der Heijden, Oek de Jong and Frans Kellendonk were the successors to W.F. Hermans, Harry Mulisch and Gerard Reve ('the Big Three'). This selection seemed to me at the time very premature: Kellendonk died in 1990, before his writing had fully matured. And hardly anything had been heard from de Jong, literarily speaking, since Circle in the Grass. Heumakers in particular must have deeply regretted his public statement of faith in de Jong. In his subsequent, negative discussion of The Octopus, he even declared de Jong's writing career 'dead and buried'. This was probably the harshest judgment at the time, although most of the other reactions did not beat about the bush either: 'woolly nonsense', 'mumbo jumbo', 'a mystical lucky dip', 'curiosities'. All at once, de Jong found himself in a Wild West scene, the sound of clarion calls replaced by whistling bullets.

If we calmly reconsider The Octopus, with which de Jong tried to take his hitherto more classically imbued writing in a different direction after eight years of silence, the author appears to be trying to find a clearer way of expressing the prevalent, archaic language of imagery rooted in the unconscious – and therefore a clearer way of expressing meaning too. Compared with his previous work, he sets off on an expressly apsychological path, and in so doing pulls the rug from under the reader's feet.

De Jong's A Man Leaping into the Future, a volume of essays written between 1983 and 1997, provides the necessary background to his creative quest. In these essays, he confronts things from the past that he finds fascinating, from Caravaggio's

The Raising of Lazarus to Frans Kellendonk's *Mystiek lichaam* (Mystical Body). He takes the reader along on a journey through time, from ancient Egypt to the chaos of postmodernity. The unspoken starting point for this self-examination is the question: which elements from human history shall I take with me into the twenty-first century? By revealing which influences from his predecessors he will keep and which he will discard, de Jong defines and legitimises his own writing. And after detailed essayistic examination of the differences between their ideas – or world views – and his, he presents the reader with a self-portrait at the end of the volume. A portrait in which all the mystical features accumulated over the course of centuries by like-minded artists have been combined and made into a one-off entity by the name of Oek de Jong.

The title A Man Leaping into the Future is taken from an essay on the poet Paul van Ostaijen, whose work de Jong appreciates in particular for its vitality. 'Van Ostaijen is a man who leaps into the future.' In an informative essay on mysticism, defined by him as 'the selflessness that is the essence of any creative activity, that which gives itself 'for nothing', the concept of 'leap' comes under closer discussion. In the language of the mystics, paradox is the ultimate trope, as this forces one to leap 'from one logic to the next, from acting to non-acting, from knowing to non-knowing, from self to non-self.' Van Ostaijen made this leap and for this reason he serves as a shining example.

But after shaking off the old world views and world forms, Oek de Jong can just as easily be considered a man leaping into the future. He says in his volume of essays that he is ready for the postmodern turmoil in which anything can serve as material. One sentence in particular reads as a credo: 'He must do his job, he must write well, and not be afraid to sink deeper and deeper into his art.' With this, the writer Oek de Jong announces his return.

Inching creeper

Yet his third novel, Hokwerda's Child, did not appear until 2002. A completely different de Jong than many foresaw. Many, because the frenzied de Jong-watchers never sleep. Shortly after the publication of A Man Leaping into the Future, I came across a story by him in an Amsterdam street newspaper. A short, threatening fragment that left me wanting more, about a young girl who goes home with a grubby man. Dark eroticism and leather, very unlike de Jong. Refreshingly concrete.

This adolescent girl – she is called Lin – turns out to be the key figure in Hokwerda's Child. Her relationships steeped in eroticism are central to the novel. With Henri, a rough-and-ready welder about ten years her senior, 'who fucked her, forced her open, left and came back'. And with the civilised lawyer Jelmer – a couple of years older – who, well-bred or not, respects her in bed. In the broad narrative of Hokwerda's Child, de Jong allocates a remarkable amount of space to sex – more than in his earlier prose. They are at it constantly: 'She felt his prick swell in her hand, she pulled the skin back and then turned her hand over, so that it lay on the inside of her wrist, on the throbbing vein. "You're going to do it with me aren't you, eh... horny bastard... hard-sweller... inching creeper."' De Jong's characters do not engage in foreplay; they penetrate, thrust and pound away quite merrily and free from inhibitions from one day to the next. The missionary position reigns, and corporality is the order of the day, whether it is the mechanical licking of an armpit, the mindless fingering of a sweat patch above the buttocks, or the noisy sucking of an Adam's apple.

In short, the characters in Hokwerda's Child are everyday run-of-the-mill men and women. No more tormented intellectuals or ethereal *NRC Handelsblad* correspondents in Rome. Meet instead twenty-four-year-old Lin Hokwerda, who has huge breasts and a jubilant libido. Lin spent her early childhood in the Frisian countryside, before her mother left her punch-throwing father, taking Lin and her sister Emma with her. Lin has lived in Amsterdam ever since, and at the start of the book we find her working in a shop that sells leather clothing. She has already been in one relationship, with the drug addict Marcus. Quick as a flash, she falls head over heels for the muscly Henri, who works as a welder on an oil rig. Their first date ends in rape, but that does not stand in the way of a passionate relationship. At one point, Henri goes too far even by Lin's standards. The fact that he beats her, even 'sells' her to an African sailor like a pimp, is apparently acceptable. But the frequent cheating does not have Lin's blessing. There follows her meeting and then relationship with Jelmer. Then an adulterous encounter with Henri. Then an argument with Jelmer. Then a relationship with Henri. Then murder and manslaughter.

In Hokwerda's Child, de Jong seeks to represent the psychology of the irrational, which he does in two ways. Firstly by showing the course of Lin's love life: she feels 'chained' to Henri, although Jelmer is undeniably a better choice for her. Secondly by allowing her tumultuous life, which we share for a few years, to end in an act of social self-ruin: murder. A crime of passion as an illustration of what the human being, like a keg of gunpowder waiting to explode, is capable of.

Anyone reading this description of Lin might think, 'What an irrational cow'. But however self-destructive her behaviour might be, once the reader has empathised with her for hundreds of pages, it just becomes an absurdity of life to be accepted rather than a mystery to be solved. The reader has little choice but to submit to the story, for reasons of willing suspension of disbelief and de Jong's seductive ability as a writer.

Hokwerda's Child is a naturalistic novel pure and simple. Lin's fate seems determined by her heredity, her upbringing and the concrete circumstances in which she finds herself. Take the title of the novel alone. In keeping with the old-fashioned genre that spotlights the pathology of the weak, The Unfortunate might have been an option – after all, this designation is used twice in the text. It is true that Lin's experiences have something of a symbolic story of suffering, just like several of the contributions in the street newspaper. But the title, Hokwerda's Child, retains the provincial smell of the regional novel, which de Jong's book is too in part.

Another curious leap forward, around one hundred years back in time to naturalism - but understandable given de Jong's previous history as a writer. One can certainly see in retrospect how, time after time, he struggles to gain control – of his material in the first instance. Hence the constant attempts to 'invent' a different genre for each new book, the jumps from floe to floe, always asking the same question about meaning. Circle in the Grass is too ambitious, dealing as it does with love, politics, art and cultural criticism all at once. De Jong is left intellectually stranded after this book, before being literarily stranded by the spiritual The Octopus. With the obvious consequence that he goes a long way to reinvent himself as a storyteller, witness Hokwerda's Child. And what better way than in such a traditional realistic form as the late nineteenth century novel?

A glimpse behind the front door

From Hokwerda's Child onwards, de Jong's ambition lies in (sensory) storytelling. His expression is never formulaic. He is a careful and effective writer with a sharp eye and a feeling for detail. Although he appears to shun metaphor, his great scene-setting abilities completely suck us into the story; indeed, from Hokwerda's Child on, de Jong is fully immersed in scene-setting in his art. He has a rare ability to create life-like characters that still seem real even after you have finished reading. Scene after scene is imprinted on your memory. Sometimes it just takes a simple sentence: 'Dina walked deeper and deeper into the forest.' He proves himself a master at evoking those feelings that often spring from relationships, such as desperation, melancholy and euphoria; those quick shifts between experiencing happiness and a solar eclipse brought on by sexual jealousy; darkness – something de Jong can penetrate like no other. Just as in Hokwerda's Child he sought to fathom the psychology of a murderess, Pier and Ocean is about providing a glimpse behind the front door, to show what really happens in families. Often this turns out to be hidden violence.

De Jong said in an interview that he was inspired to write Hokwerda's Child after reading Tolstoy. Pier and Ocean is noticeably Proustian in its conception. For around 800 pages, the reader is drawn into the story of Abel Roorda, his religious parents and even more religious grandparents. De Jong uses them to depict the changing Netherlands, from the Hunger Winter to the prosperous 1970s. He brings this history to life by focusing on the life choices of ordinary people down through the generations – we empathise with his characters as contemporaries. De Jong manages to achieve the constant and high intensity of the prose by bringing to life the facts of Abel's life through Abel's experience of events. This experience, in turn, consists of a meticulous evocation of both Abel's sensory perceptions and of what is taking place in his consciousness.

De Jong is still a writer who reinvents himself with each new book. Only now he does so within the context of the novel tradition: he strives for renewal within the novel genre. With Pier and Ocean, he measures up to his idols Simon Vestdijk and Proust. While these writers use alter egos in their semi-autobiographical *romans-fleuves*, Pier and Ocean focuses on four characters from three generations, thereby reserving a lot of past history for his protagonist Abel Roorda. The first one hundred pages – magisterial pages – of the polyphonic novel Pier and Ocean describe a day in the life of the pregnant Dina, Abel's mother-to-be. She lives in with a landlady in Breda while her husband is quartered as a soldier in a nearby barracks, and she cannot stand it anymore. Back she goes to her hometown of Amsterdam. And as she sets out on this undefined quest, her unfortunate past history passes before her eyes: the enforced choices, the missed opportunities, the pressures to conform. This as a prelude to Abel's existence, to explain how he came to be formed and deformed. So, alongside Abel's history, de Jong also depicts the marriages of his parents and grandparents, and shows how various characteristics and circumstances affect the generations.

De Jong uses details rather than historical events to bring to life the lost Netherlands of Abel's youth and his parents' and grandparents' generations. He describes the Netherlands of the forties, fifties and sixties, during which time profound changes occurred, from on the ground, from the everyday perspective of the citizens of the time. A woman with healthy teeth who is talked into having false teeth fitted by her dentist, a man who decides to stop wearing a hat, the sexual freedom afforded by the advent of the contraceptive pill – such signs of the times. This realism is de Jong's tool for boring deeper into reality – the reality of his character(s).

All the same, Pier and Ocean has an extremely symbolic title, in spite of this realism-as-device. It refers to a series of paintings with the same name by the symbolist Mondrian. Sitting on the dunes at Domburg and observing how the rows of groynes seemed to 'walk into' the sea, Mondrian identified the groynes as male and the sea as female. However, this is just one of the meanings of 'pier and ocean' in de Jong's novel.

Birth as a writer

The constant motion is that Abel is always seeking out extreme points, whether it is a beacon on the dike at Het Sas, the last groyne on the beach, the very tip of the bow of a tanker, or the outermost point of a rocky promontory in Finistère. This tendency is linked to Abel's birth as a writer, with which the novel ends. He has been brought up listening to Old Testament stories, and the story of Samuel has led him to believe that there is another, divine reality outside this one, one from which someone is talking to him. He expects (as in the story) to hear the voice of God, to have a vision. Filled with this desire, he keeps going to extreme points of the land. He senses that this is where it will happen. But no. In vain.

At the end of the novel, Abel realises that there is no 'other world'. Pier and Ocean is not least a novel about the loss of faith – in Abel's life and in the changed post-war Netherlands. Although to begin with Abel is still under the spell of the (faith-determined) notion of 'eternity', in the fifth part of the novel this is exchanged for the concept of 'concentration', which is discussed in several passages. Abel comes to realise that the other world he has been seeking has already been discovered. This world is inside him. It is the world of the subconscious, which uses images, not divine inspiration. The discovery of this wealth that he can draw on marks the birth of his life as a writer; he can set to work.

This marks the end of this semi-autobiographical novel. But we can be quite certain about what will happen to Abel, we only have to look at Oek de Jong's self-aware, authentic, active and above all vital writing. ■

www.oekdejong.nl

Oek de Jong's work is published by Uitgeverij Augustus and has been translated into several languages, although not yet into English.

Pier en oceaan (Pier and Ocean), novel, 2012.

De wonderen van de heilbot. Dagboek 1997-2002 (The Wonders of Halibut. Diary 1997-2002), 2006

Hokwerda's kind (Hokwerda's Child), novel, 2002

Een man die in de toekomst springt (A Man Leaping into the Future), essays, 1997

De inktvis (The Octopus), short story, 1993

Cirkel in het gras (Circle in the Grass), novel, 1985

Opwaaiende zomerjurken (Billowing Summer Frocks), novel, 1979

Translated by Rebekah Wilson

An Extract from *Pier and Ocean*

By Oek de Jong

Two days after his confession they had zipped their sleeping bags back together in the tent and made love. The first time fast and fierce, then again, this time quiet and slow. Abel didn't know if it had helped. Neither did Digna. She'd turned on her side, her back to him, felt for her insect repellent and rubbed some on, then fallen asleep.

Abel lay awake. He heard the waves breaking at the foot of the cliff, the water splashing up and cascading down onto the rocks, the sea withdrawing with a rattling of pebbles on the beach, the next wave breaking with the same dull drone. After his confession, Digna hadn't wanted to touch him for two days, even preferring not to look at him. The turning point had come this evening. Perhaps you needed it, with a girl like that, she'd said. A while later, after she'd put on her jumper, pulling her hair roughly out of the neck hole: and perhaps it's good for us in the end too. Her rage had flared up again as they made love.

He listened to the breaking of the waves, the rattling of the pebbles. Slowly the sweat dried on his body. Slowly the emotions ebbed away. He felt even more miserable, more guilty, now that he'd seen Digna's helpless love, now he'd felt her arms and legs around him again, now he'd heard her come. Digna.

Enraged and in love at the same time. He closed his eyes and saw Denise. She was still there. He pushed the memories away. But then – when Digna seemed fast asleep – he let her back in. Denise with her sorrowful eyes. His body had yearned for her. He could still feel that yearning. Come on, come on, oh jesusandmary, come on. Her husky voice. Twice he'd driven to the station to take the train to Vlissingen without actually going. The day before departure he'd gone home after dinner at the Maelcotes' and driven past the station again. The train from Vlissingen had just arrived, as if it was meant to be. It was just after a storm. Steam rose from the street, a damp warmth hung under the trees on the station square. He saw Denise emerge from the station, a baggy nylon jacket over her miniskirt, a shoulder bag, a shopping bag. An unknown girl he knew. She stopped a man and asked him for a light. The man gave her a light and made himself scarce, as if frightened by her. He saw her cross the empty, steaming station square and disappear slowly but surely under the trees of the avenue into town. He'd wanted to follow her, speak to her. But it was impossible.

Abel listened to the waves at the foot of the cliff. The dull drone. The water splash-

ing up and crashing down. He drifted further, thinking of his father and mother, his brothers and sisters in the bungalow far away, the boat he wasn't sailing, the white hull in the dark reeds. The new moon he'd seen rise this evening had risen there too... Toni, as he'd last seen him: lying on his stomach in the saloon of the sloop, a fat black fly on the blond hair at the back of his head. He'd heard nothing more from him... Dave, upper body naked, jeans sliding down. Mrs. Anja, strands of hair over a blanket, a piece of her harem trousers, two solid bare feet. Denise's warm body under the sleeping bag in the forecabin. It seemed long ago... Still the fear was there as he thought back to his journey over the dark shallows. Having just clambered on board, as he removed his muddy shoes, he'd seen the rising water flow around the ship, dead calm, glistening... Stop thinking about it... Stop thinking about it... Watse and Lena, at a campsite somewhere, lying around in their tent playing cards half the day... Job practised the cello eight hours a day... Danker was now helping his father on the land... He and Digna in a tent on a cliff in Finistère... Everyone far away, alone. Even Digna, lying just beside

him. Images of the sea drifted through his head: swirling between the rocks, splashing high in the glare of the evening sun. An unknown coast, but immediately familiar. A place where he wanted to be, and Digna too... Long strands of seaweed, washed up on the beach, stretching metres long. That's the ocean... A long train of seaweed wound around my body, a bunch of it on my head. That'd make me feel cheerful... Might it cure me? But what of? A bunch of seaweed on my head, my whole body wound up in it... A beautiful stone, found on the beach. That raises expectations, vaguely, for a second, less than a second. Especially when it's a stone she's found and given you... Despite her rage she still gave me a stone... Pubic hair spreads the scent of her excitement... You'd hoped your life would be different in another country, but it's the same... It'll be the same everywhere.

From *Pier en oceaan*,
Uitgeverij Augustus, Amsterdam, 2012

Translated by Anna Asbury

More of the Same?

The Changing of the Guard in the Monarchy

King Albert II announces his
abdication on 3rd July 2013

[PETRA DE KONING]

Many television-viewers may not have noticed it, but for the royal palaces it is a radical innovation: when they give their television addresses, the Kings of Belgium and the Netherlands, Philippe and Willem-Alexander, no longer sit at their desk, as Philippe's father Albert and Willem-Alexander's mother Beatrix did. Philippe of Belgium stood, while the camera moved slowly around the room and even treated viewers to a glimpse of the garden. The Dutch Willem-Alexander sat in an armchair next to an open fire, his legs crossed casually.

But that was as far as the changes went. The flower arrangements and Christmas trees were still there, as was the classical music (Brahms for Beatrix, Telemann for Willem-Alexander) and the Belgian national anthem – which for Philippe's message on the national holiday was played slower and more solemnly than a year earlier when his father spoke.

With the slight nervousness that befits a beginner, they uttered speeches that could just as well have emerged from the mouths of Albert II of Belgium or Beatrix of Orange-Nassau. Touching on a 'meditation on our existence', solitude, unemployment, cooperation and confidence.

Willem-Alexander (47) was installed in Amsterdam on 30th April 2013 and Philippe (54) almost three months later in Brussels. If there is any sign that their arrival has brought the monarchy in the Low Countries to a turning point, it is still only very tentative.

From clumsy to vigorous

For a long time, neither Willem-Alexander nor Philippe was considered a perfect heir in their respective countries. They were seen as not especially intelligent and perhaps even unfit. Willem-Alexander, known as 'Prince Pils' in his student days, was always tense when near cameras. He studied Water Management so as to have something to occupy him until he became King. The shy but also impulsive Philippe mainly led trade missions, during which he occasionally made awkward political statements about his deeply divided country. He sometimes also gave the impression that he had a 'mission' that he would launch into as soon as he was King. He wanted to keep his country together at

Queen Beatrix signs the Act of
Abdication in the Royal Palace in
Amsterdam on 30th April 2013 © ANP

all costs. From time to time, doubts were openly expressed: could the monarchy survive under their leadership?

Philippe and Willem-Alexander are now seen as kings who are doing their best, and their popularity is increasing. They have metamorphosed from two ill-at-ease crown princes who were capable of shaking the foundations of the monarchy into kings whom most of the population consider to be hard workers. 'Philippe fulfils his task as if he were in the scouts,' says the historian Marc Van den Wijngaert, an expert on the Belgian royal family. 'One good deed every day. But all with the best of intentions. And you can see that he really believes in it. A lot of people find that quite endearing.'

When he made the traditional visits to get to know his country as King, Philippe started out in Flanders, where support for the French-speaking royal family is weakest and where the largest political party, the N-VA, aspires to divide the country. He sometimes found himself the target of street protests.

Willem-Alexander also toured the provinces to get to know his people, in care homes, neighbourhood centres and schools. He was not confronted with a politically divided country. He was just as warmly welcomed in Friesland – which even has its own language – as in Southern Holland. In the Netherlands, republican protest has for some time remained limited to a few individuals in the crowd holding a banner saying 'I am not a subject' or 'Liberate the King'.

Willem-Alexander's image had been tremendously improved some years before his succession by his marriage to the Argentine Maxima Zorreguieta, who soon became very popular in the Netherlands. In Philippe's case, his marriage to Countess Mathilde d'Udekem d'Acoz did not have the same effect. It did help him at first, but it soon became apparent that Mathilde had actually adopted the same tense nervousness as Philippe, and the story was that he was jealous of her initial popularity.

Mathilde was also compared to Maxima, who had learnt to speak good Dutch very quickly. Mathilde, who had grown up in bilingual Belgium, continued to speak Dutch quite poorly. She was parodied because she did not always come across as very intelligent or empathic either. As the Queen she garnered more favour as a result of her enthusiasm in the stands at the football World Cup in Brazil, though she lost some of it again when she mixed up two Belgian players.

In Flanders, with all its sensitivity regarding language, an error King Philippe made when speaking Dutch was immediately picked up: on the evening of his installation he had made a mistake when expressing his pride in his country, what he said was a literal translation from French.

In the Netherlands, on one occasion Maxima caused quite an upset when, as a princess, she declared in a speech that she had not been able to detect any characteristic Dutch identity. Did she mean that the Netherlands had no distinguishing features? No, she said afterwards. It had been 'a great compliment': she had meant that the Dutch were easily able to deal with the differences and individual identities of the country's regions. She had met Limburgers who were very proud of their own province and its own products, and she said she had experienced exactly the same thing in Friesland. 'And I thought it was so agreeable that in the midst of all this I have found the space to feel Dutch.'

All this fuss did nothing to change her great popularity, some of which rubbed off on Willem-Alexander. In the last few years, support for the Dutch royal family has undoubtedly also been boosted by the 2012 skiing accident involving Willem-Alexander's brother Friso, who spent a long period in a coma and eventually died.

By the time Willem-Alexander became King, his suitability for the job was no longer seriously disputed. Much less was expected of Philippe as King. In Belgian government circles it was considered that Willem-Alexander and Maxima need not necessarily come to Belgium for their first foreign visit after the coronation. These first trips made by royal couples always attract a great deal of attention and it was thought that Philippe and Mathilde would be compared unfavourably with the Dutch couple. So they went to Luxemburg first and their later visit to Belgium did not generate a huge amount of interest in the media.

The Belgian government also helped Philippe by giving him a clever and extremely experienced Chief of Staff, the former diplomat Frans van Daele. He resolved to help Philippe for a couple of years and then let a younger advisor take over. He immediately helped Philippe through the first, potentially very complicated year, which was marked by elections whose main winner was the Flemish nationalist N-VA party. The previous government, formed following the federal elections in 2010, had lasted 541 days.

Van Daele, a Fleming, knows the new generation of politicians in Flanders and understands how they think and what they want. When it came to forming a government, King Albert tended to let the old generation of Flemish statesmen do the rounds every time attempts made by the party leaders had become bogged down. Philippe made a more vigorous impression: if one party chairman did not succeed, then it was the turn of the next.

King Philippe swears the oath in the Belgian Parliament on 21ˢᵗ July 2013

Maxima's tears

Politics in the Netherlands are far less complicated than in Belgium, and there is no party whose aim is to divide the country. So when it comes to forming a government, life was a lot easier for Queen Beatrix than for King Albert. But her successor is not exposed even to this mild political climate. In spring 2012 the Dutch parliament took the task of forming a government out of the head of state's hands. The government parties at the time, the Christian CDA and liberal VVD, did not want this change, but a majority, mainly of left-wing parties, voted it in.

This means that Willem-Alexander is now much less vulnerable than Philippe, though one could also say that it has made his job less interesting. But he is not complaining. In a television interview he gave just before becoming King, Willem-Alexander said he would also accept it if all that remained to him were ceremonial duties. 'It wouldn't bother me at all. That's what I'm the King for. And if I have to sign anything, I'll do it.'

When governments are formed in Belgium's regions – Flanders, Wallonia and Brussels – the political parties arrange everything themselves. When it comes to Belgium as a whole, the parliamentary Speaker could take the initiative (instead of the King) and himself appoint *formateurs* (individuals charged with forming a new government) and *informateurs* (individuals who examine whether a proposed government formation might succeed). But he will be *either* a French-speaker *or* Flemish, which may make him less acceptable to others. The Belgian royal family is not Flemish at all, but nor is it linked to any French-speaking political party. So Philippe is probably not yet rid of the complicated task of forming Belgian governments.

In a poll by the RTL television channel, Willem-Alexander scored 96.1% for popularity. But very few demands have so far been made of the new Dutch King. At the Winter Olympics he had a beer together with the Russian President Vladimir Putin, and that was considered 'possibly not very wise'.

A completely different light was shed on that glass of beer when, at the end of July 2014, supposedly pro-Russian separatists in Eastern Ukraine shot down a plane and in the process killed 298 people, 196 of whom were Dutch nationals. This took place on a Thursday. The Dutch Prime Minister Mark Rutte spoke to the Russian President on the phone several times a day, because he exerts considerable influence over the separatists. He gave press conferences every day. But it was only on the following Monday that Willem-Alexander spoke to the people on television.

This was thought to be rather late, but not a serious error. On the day of national mourning, when the bodies arrived back from Ukraine, Willem-Alexander and Maxima attended, together with politicians and ambassadors. Interest in the royal couple focused mainly on Maxima's tears, while Willem-Alexander himself shed none.

No research on the matter has been done recently, but in Belgium it is assumed that most French-speakers support the monarchy. The royal family is one of the last remaining symbols of the unity of the country that many French-speakers wish to preserve. Philippe's popularity is on the increase in Flanders: according to a poll by the Flemish television channel VTM, 64% think he is doing well, and 72% are happy with Mathilde.

Marc Van den Wijngaert, the expert on the royal family, thinks that support for Philippe has also increased because of people's incomprehension of his father's behaviour. It seems Albert does not intend to accept that his son is now head of the royal family. He gave an interview – in French – to a commercial broadcaster without previously consulting Philippe. When his other son Laurent was seriously ill, Albert and his wife Paola did not at first visit him in hospital. Later, again without consulting Philippe, they published a letter about their son's illness that was seen as excessively emotional and perhaps even

Philippe and Mathilde on the balcony of the Brussels palace on the day of the coronation on 21st July 2013

damaging to Laurent, who was already known to be the family's weak link.

Philippe and Albert never did have an easy relationship. Albert, involved in a long-term love affair, did not pay his children much attention. And now, by sacking Albert's Chief of Staff, Philippe showed himself – in the eyes of public opinion – to be no pushover. The Flemish too considered this a resolute action.

But when it is proposed that the kingship in Belgium could also be made purely ceremonial, the call almost always comes from the Flemish. The desire for a republic is also a Flemish phenomenon and is mainly associated with those more on the right wing of politics. But this is not the wish for a Belgian republic... only a Flemish one.

If the Belgian monarchy should one day come to an end, it will probably be to make way for a Flemish republic and a French-speaking neighbour.

You hardly ever hear left-wing Flemish politicians speaking against the monarchy: they evidently prefer to keep quiet so as not to be associated with

Flemish separatists. Things are different in the Netherlands: those who have left-wing ideas and vote for a left-wing party also tend to have greater doubts about the monarchy than those who think and vote on the right.

There are also left-wing Flemings who think that it is a matter of their national character: they say that the Dutch take a lot of things – including the royal family – more seriously than the Flemish. Nor do they think that Philippe can do much harm, and they say that his awkward behaviour simply shows that he is a man of flesh and blood. According to one Belgian psychoanalyst (with a Flemish mother and a French-speaking father), the Belgians see themselves reflected in their royal family: 'We find ourselves a little clumsy too, and belittle ourselves, not putting on any airs.'

In the Netherlands, the Meertens Institute, which collects and analyses expressions of Dutch culture, has examined the population's sense of 'Orangeness'. It turns out that this is by no means associated only with the royal House of Orange, but just as much with people such as the Dutch astronaut André Kuipers and Dutch sports stars.

Monarchs of the Low Countries

Ceremonial kingship?

The accession of the two new kings appears to ensure the continued existence of the monarchy in the Low Countries. There is still little to be said about the two crown princesses – the Dutch Amalia (11) and the Belgian Elizabeth (13). The fact that Elizabeth is first in line to the throne and has been going to a Dutch-speaking school since she started at the nursery says a lot about the effort Philippe wants to put into gaining the confidence of the Flemish and preserving the unity of his kingdom.

In his book *België en zijn koningen* (Belgium and its Kings), Marc Van den Wijngaert writes that in Belgium the substance of the King's role is diminishing de *facto* and is thus becoming more and more symbolic: as a result of state reforms, Flanders and Wallonia are increasingly deciding things for themselves. The Netherlands soon became accustomed to the head of state no longer being

Princess Beatrix and her granddaughters in
the Nieuwe Kerk in Amsterdam on 30th April 2013. © ANP

involved in forming the government. And, even without any appreciable pressure from republicans, the ceremonial kingship that Willem-Alexander has already mentioned may not be far off. As Van den Wijngaert says: 'From the fact that Willem-Alexander talked about it himself I had the feeling that the Netherlands may be moving nearer to this sort of ceremonial kingship than Belgium.' ▪

Translated by Gregory Ball

Princess Elisabeth of Belgium

Wonderful Mechelen

From Burgundian Grandeur to Media Lab and Malt Whisky

Je connais Malines, et, si Malines n'était pas en Belgique, et peuplée de Flamands, j'aimerais y vivre, et surtout y mourir. Combien de carillons, combien de clochers, combien d'herbes dans les rues, combien de béguines!

I know Mechelen and, if Mechelen were not in Belgium and populated with Flemings, I'd love to live there and especially to die there. So many carillons, so many bells, so much grass in the streets, so many Beguines!

Charles Baudelaire writing to his friend Narcisse Ancelle,
Mayor of Neuilly (2 September 1864)

There is no better way to get to know Mechelen than to gaze on it from on high and then to stroll around it. Within a radius of a square kilometre, the visitor can discover the many different faces of this provincial Flemish town juxtaposed between its big brothers Antwerp and Brussels: from mediaeval and Burgundian to arch-Catholic and modern, nay super-modern.

Mechelen from on high

But first we will climb the 15th-century tower of St Rumbold's Cathedral, the defining landmark of Mechelen, which can be seen rising towards the heavens long before the visitor arrives in the town. Up we go to the skywalk, a panoramic 'floating' walkway running behind and above a glass wall that lays out the entire landscape at our feet as we gaze around and down from the almost 100 m tall tower, like an all-conquering general. The tower can be climbed every day. And climbing is precisely what it is: five hundred and thirty-eight (538!) steps – no lift –will take you to pole position, from where far to the south you will see the Brussels Atomium glinting in the sunlight and to the north the contours of that other, competing spire of the Cathedral of Our Lady in Antwerp. Looking down, it is immediately obvious, as observed by Baudelaire in the fragment cited above, just how many clock towers adorn

this town. Only Prague may boast more churches. Today, Mechelen is still the official residence of the Belgian Archbishop, André Léonard, who tries to watch over his flock from his palace, with its superb garden that is sometimes open to the public.

The centre of Mechelen, which lies at your feet, is concentrically ringed by the River Dijle as it flows from Leuven, where it joins the Rupel and Scheldt rivers en route to Antwerp and the sea. Mechelen grew up within that circle as an autonomous administrative and judicial centre (*heerlijkheid*), one of the seventeen provinces of the Habsburg Netherlands. Mechelen was therefore an immediate political neighbour of Holland, Flanders and Brabant. It was to retain that autonomy as a small *heerlijkheid* surrounded by bigger, often hostile neighbours right up until the French Revolution in the late 18th century. The derived meaning of the word heerlijkheid, as a place of magnificence or glory, is completely apt: after Bruges, Mechelen contains more listed buildings than anywhere else in Belgium.

Within the radius of the old mediaeval and pre-modern Mechelen, two icons of modernity can be seen on opposite sides of the circle. On the southern edge it is difficult to see beyond the gigantic arms of the cranes towering above the railway station, which is to be completely rebuilt over the next decade. Mechelen, from where the first passenger train on the European continent departed in 1835, is giving its industrial heritage a complete makeover. Looking in the opposite direction, towards the north, a massive pentagonal white block comes into view, next to what was once the old Dossin barracks and the place where 25,484 Belgian Jews and 352 gypsies were assembled during the Second World War in preparation for transportation to the German concentration camps.

Skywalk on the Cathedral
© Aikon Producties

The pentagonal block, the Holocaust Museum (closed on Wednesdays), was opened in December 2012 and does indeed document the Holocaust in Belgium and Mechelen, but devotes attention to other excesses of genocide during the 20th century too. If climbing the hundreds of steps up St Rumbold's Tower is too daunting a prospect, taking the lift to the roof terrace at the Holocaust Museum also offers a splendid outlook, not only over Greater Mechelen and beyond, but taking in the nearby inner courtyard of the barracks where the deportees were assembled as well.

Eight centuries of history within two hours

Seeing Mechelen from on high is one thing. However, the only way to really get to know the town is to wander through its streets. Within the space of two hours you will saunter easily through eight centuries of history. At ground level, you immediately find yourself on the Grote Markt, where all the streets of the old town converge. The market square itself dates back to the Middle Ages, when it was used among other things as a stage for executions. The Cloth Hall (*lakenhal*), which previously served as the town jail, and the old Aldermen's Hall (*schepenhuis*), date from the 13th and 14th centuries. At that time, Mechelen was a prosperous town thanks to its textile industry and local artisan trades, including the production of tapestries and the famous Cordovan 'gold leather' (Cuir de Cordoue) which was used by the well-to-do to adorn the interiors of their homes.

But it was in 1473 that the economic boom in Mechelen really began, when the Burgundian Duke Charles the Bold founded the Court of Audit (*Rekenkamer*), the central financial authority of the Low Countries, in Mechelen. The Great Council (*Grote Raad*), the highest court of appeal in the Low Countries, came to Mechelen a year later, being housed in the old Aldermen's Hall. The member councillors of these central institutions built residences befitting their rank and status nearby. The most handsome building is that of Councillor Hieronymus

Holocaust Museum
© Stijn Bollaert

van Busleyden. In the Merodestraat, another street which gives onto the Grote Markt, you can visit the complex that now does duty among other things as the Municipal Museum (*Stadsmuseum*). Students from the nearby international carillon school are often to be found practising their bell-ringing in one of its charming towers. Mechelen is the undisputed centre of the carillon, something which enchanted Baudelaire – and Victor Hugo too (see below).

Van Busleyden played host to the greatest humanists of his day, including Erasmus. Thomas More made a diversion to Mechelen and wrote a number of verses in praise of the home and hospitality of his friend, to be sung in Latin. By this time, at the start of the 16th century, Mechelen had become the home of the Burgundian Court. Margaret of York, sister of the English Kings Richard III and Edward IV, will undoubtedly have recognised something of her home-town in Mechelen: the same modest scale, the same splendid Gothic cathedral. When Margaret lost her husband and consort Charles the Bold, she travelled with his daughter Mary of Burgundy to Mechelen. Her residence still stands in Keizerstraat, which begins on the Grote Markt next to the neo-Gothic town hall, its use transformed to that of municipal theatre (*Stadsschouwburg*).

Burgundian Mechelen

It was from here that Margaret arranged the marriage of the (15th) century between Mary and Maximilian of Austria. At a stroke, the Burgundians had become Habsburgs and world citizens. It is for this reason that the coat of arms and flag of Mechelen bear the double-headed Habsburg eagle. When Mary died fairly young, Margaret of York looked after Mary's daughter Margaret of Austria and son Philip the Handsome. Philip, the father of Emperor Charles V, also died very young. By this time, Margaret of York had passed on too: a plaque in the Minderbroederskerk church where she lies buried (now the Cultural Centre) commemorates her death, and above all the Burgundian stamp she placed upon Mechelen. Henceforth, it was Margaret of Austria who called the tune.

Margaret of Austria moved into a palace directly opposite her Yorkist aunt and, following the death of her brother Philip the Handsome, took care of his son Charles. Margaret's palace is today the courthouse. Visitors can wander in freely to enjoy the Renaissance gardens. If you are in luck, you may be invited in by the President of the Bar, whose office is in what was Margaret's bedroom. The downstairs reception room of Margaret's palace is generally freely accessible. It is striking how small in scale, almost intimate, the official rooms appear today. In fact, the same applies for the meeting room in the old Aldermen's Hall, where dozens of dignitaries from the Great Council had to sit side-by-side in a compact space. Not only were people smaller five centuries ago, as we know, but apparently they were content with less space than we are today.

Margaret of Austria was the incarnation of the glory of Burgundian Mechelen. Occasionally she wrote melancholic poetry (in French) and gathered the cream of intellectual and artistic life around her in Keizerstraat. Renowned botanists such as Rembert Dodoens (who wrote the first herbal) and Carolus Clusius (discoverer of the potato plant) were very regular visitors, but Anne Boleyn also spent 18 months there from 1513, learning to be a lady-in-waiting. Janus Secundus wrote the best humanist love poetry there in his Basia (Book of Kisses), and can be safely regarded as the predecessor of that other illustrious Mechelen poet, Herman de Coninck, who electrified the Flemish poetry world with his debut, *De lenige liefde* (1969).

The death of Margaret of Austria and Emperor Charles brought a definitive end to the Burgundian grandeur of Mechelen. In the second half of the 16th century, Brussels became the capital of the Low Countries, but the Burgundian heritage of Brussels can only be partially reconstructed and lies underground. By contrast, the visitor wandering around Mechelen can still admire the splendid residences of the humanist councillors and the palaces of the two Margarets.

Dossin barracks where Belgian Jews and gypsies were assembled during the Second World War in preparation for transportation to the German concentration camps © Kazerne Dossin

The religious wars in the last quarter of the 16th century prompted almost everyone of standing to flee Mechelen. The Dutch cities of Amsterdam and Haarlem were the main beneficiaries of the influx of these highly skilled Mechelen expats, such as the father of the painter Frans Hals, as well as Hals himself. Incidentally, the grandfather of Ludwig van Beethoven, likewise a native of Mechelen, would move to Bonn in the 18th century. The only consolation prize granted to Mechelen by the Spanish Catholic Habsburgs was the seat of Belgian Catholicism: Mechelen has been the home of Belgian archbishops from the time of Granvelle, in1561, to Godfried Danneels and Léonard today. Churches mushroomed. Authentic paintings by Rubens, who owned a small château in Elewijt near Mechelen, can still be seen hanging in the Church of Our Lady-across-the-Dyle (Onze-Lieve-Vrouwekerk over-de-Dijle) and St. John's Church (*Sint-Janskerk*). More work was carried out on the Gothic St Rumbold's Cathedral in the 16th century. Later, Beghards and Beguines would also come to live in Mechelen. The small beguinage and especially the larger one – also close by St. Rumbold's tower and Grote Markt – are as authentic today as they were in the time of Charles Baudelaire, who disparaged Brussels but embraced the quietude of Mechelen.

Its central location meant that Mechelen was preferred to Brussels and Antwerp as the site for the first passenger railway station on the continent in 1835. Many British railway engineers made their homes in Mechelen, and people came from far and wide to learn about the steam train. Victor Hugo alighted in Mechelen in August 1837, where he was ceremonially received by Leopold I, the first King of the Belgians, along with a massive crowd. Hugo was impressed:

> *Il y avait là dans la foule un pauvre cocher de coucou, picard ou normand, lequel regardait piteusement les wagons courir, traînés par la machine qui fume et qui geint. 'Cela va plus vite que vos chevaux', lui dis-je. — 'Beau miracle!' m'a répondu cet homme. "C'est poussé par un efoudre." Le mot m'a paru pittoresque et beau.*

> *There was a poor coachman in the crowd, with a crate of an old coach, from Picardy or Normandy, watching pathetically as the wagons ran along behind the smoking, groaning engine pulling them. 'That goes faster than your horses', I told him. 'What a miracle', the man replied. 'It's pushed along by a flash of lightning.' His words seemed picturesque and beautiful.*

Hugo, by no means blind to the dynamic, 'lightning' new age symbolised by the train, was nonetheless more charmed by the two 'admirable' Rubens paintings, and especially by the sounds of the local carillon (to which he devoted an entire poem) and climbing the tower of St. Rumbold's: 'almost twice as many steps as the towers of Notre Dame', as he remarked. In his wake came more French writers, such as Paul Verlaine, who in September 1872 passed through Mechelen on the train in the company of Arthur Rimbaud, and wrote about the experience in a poem dedicated to the town:

> *Malines: Les wagons filent en silence / Parmi ces sites apaisés. / Dormez, les vaches! Reposez, / Doux taureaux de la plaine immense, / Sous vous cieux à peine irrisés!*

Mechelen: The wagons fly by in silence / Through the becalmed landscape. / Sleep ye cows! Rest/ Gentle bulls of this immense plain, / Beneath your barely iridescent skies!

Like Hugo and Baudelaire before him, Verlaine preferred the quiet, pre-modern Mechelen to the busy, industrial hotspot of its pioneering railway – the Catholic, one might say: the ultra montane Mechelen, train or no train, was still very much alive. The Congresses of Mechelen, in which Catholicism was debated at great length, became a byword. In fact Baudelaire referred to them in the same letter that espoused his conditional love for Mechelen. Later, the Congresses were transformed into ecumenical conversations between the Catholic and Anglican Churches – the Malines Conversations – which were held between 1921 and 1927. Archbishop Désiré Mercier, who has a dedicated chapel in St. Rumbold's, was the initiator, and was also the man who ensured that Catholic Mechelen was noticed in Anglican England. During this same period many English girls came to the boarding school at the Ursuline Institute in the village of Onze-Lieve-Vrouw Waver, a few kilometres outside Mechelen. The school fees paid by these well-to-do English students funded the building of the finest (glazed) Jugendstil winter garden in the whole of the Mechelen area.

City of media and children

Mechelen has undergone a radical facelift since 2000, under the stewardship of Mayor Bart Somers. The façades have been cleaned up and water features and parkland have been added. Mechelen has more inhabitants today than ever before – 83,000 in total – and a highly diverse population. The policy has mainly targeted creative double-earners. This has helped Mechelen attract a great many media companies, large and small, in recent years. Sanoma, the Belgian lifestyle magazine publisher, is housed in a site near the station, while Telenet, the Flemish Internet and cable TV distributor, has its headquarters in a former barracks just across the River Dijle. A number of successful smaller TV production houses have also found their way to the city. In collaboration with the town of Vilvoorde, the arrival point for the first train journey from Mechelen, the ambitious Track 25 project has been set up – named after the historic 25 railway line that linked the towns in 1835. This partnership between the two towns' Chambers of Commerce, their media industry and the Thomas More Hogeschool college, is intended to create a 'triple-helix' cross-fertilisation structure from which each of the three partners benefits.

Mechelen is also trying to live up to its image as a child-friendly town. For the last ten years, the Mechelen-Zuid district has hosted Technopolis, a science and technology activity centre for children and teenagers. Long before it became fashionable in most museums, visitors here were able to discover the wondrous world of science and technology in an interactive way: racing against a horse, generating electricity by performing gymnastics on a trapeze bike, or making your own toothpaste. There is also the Toy Museum, near the old Nekkerspoel Station, where thematic exhibitions (devoted to Lego or to the artist Bruna, for example) add an extra dimension to the permanent collection of historical toys – lots of trains and railway stations, naturally, but also depictions of the Battle of Waterloo and Star Wars.

If you've had enough of all that history, there is always the option of taking a boat trip from the station, along the Leuvense Vaart canal to Planckendael open-air zoo with its colonies of bonobos, storks and penguins. But if, like me, you prefer to remain within the centre of Mechelen, when leaving the Groot Begijnhof beguinage you might pop into the Anker brewery, the home of Gouden Carolus, a dark Trappist beer which consistently wins prizes – and sometimes gold medals – at beer festivals all over the world. They recently began distilling their own single malt whisky there too.

Mechelen really is wonderful. ▪

Translated by Julian Ross

Residence of Hieronymus van Busleyden © Layla Aerts
Residence of Margaret of York © Koen Broos

More an Inventor than a Designer

Iris van Herpen's Needle, Thread and Three-Dimensional Techniques

[BREGJE LAMPE]

At the age of thirty, Iris van Herpen (born 1984, in Wamel) is already a fixture on the forefront of the international fashion and art world. Mid 2014 she won the Andam Award, a prestigious international fashion prize worth 250,000 euro and a year's coaching from François-Henri Pinault, the big boss of fashion group Kering (formerly PPR, the main competitor of LVMH). By then Van Herpen had already received three Dutch Fashion Awards and two Dutch Design Awards.

For Van Herpen the Andam Award is the umpteenth proof that her talent is being recognized internationally. The Dutch designer was up against a host of international designers like Yiqing Yin, Jean-Paul Lespagnard, Steven Tai and Fausto Pugli. The jury consisted of big international names like photographer Ellen von Unwerth, Angela Chung, the editor-in-chief of the Chinese Vogue, Sarah Andelman, the creative director of Colette, and some of the most important people at Kering.

Previously the prize had been awarded to Victor & Rolf, Martin Margiela and Giles Deacon – who all went on to establish well-known labels. And it looks very much like Van Herpen is set to become another famous brand name too. She is in fact already well on her way. She can count women like Daphne Guinness, Björk and Lady Gaga among her customers. Last year the New York City Ballet asked her to make costumes. At the end of 2013, Dover Street Market in London began selling her clothes.

Her solo exhibition, shown in Groningen two years ago, is now travelling the world. The influential and well-known fashion designer Karl Lagerfeld is a fan and regularly lets her know that he follows and appreciates her work. And influential fashion journalists like Suzy Menkes always attend her shows in Paris.

Umbrella spokes

Iris van Herpen had always wanted to 'do something with clothes'. Or dance. When she was about fourteen – 'at the time, you know, when you are starting to be preoccupied with what you are wearing' – she decided to study fashion design. In 2006 she graduated from the most respected art school in the Netherlands: the ArtEZ Institute in Arnhem, with a major in fashion design. During

her studies she interned with the world-famous Alexander McQueen in London and with Claudy Jongstra in Friesland, a Dutch designer who is especially well-known for the fact that she works a lot with natural materials like felt and wool.

While many designers choose a spot abroad after their studies, to gain more experience in the fashion world, Van Herpen was always determined to set up business for herself. Within a year of graduation she came out with her first collection at the Amsterdam Fashion Week, the most important platform for new Dutch talent. She immediately stood out: her complicated, avant-garde creations, with sometimes absurdly large shoulder pads, were *the* subject of conversation during the cocktail hour after the show. From then on she was a force to be reckoned with in the Netherlands. For her first few collections she used hardly any fabric. For her debut collection, *Chemical Crows*, in January 2008, inspired by a group of crows flying around her studio in Arnhem, she took apart more than four hundred children's umbrellas and used the metal spokes in her dresses and shoulder pads. For the same collection she designed close-fitting dresses made from thick braids of thread and leather, and leather strips combined with metal rings.

Her first show stood out because it was different. It wasn't a commercial collection inspired by daily wear, nor were there absurdly elegant or luxurious dresses. There was no colour; everything was grey, black or cream-coloured. The feminine, tight shapes, the preference for dark colours, the use of unusual materials, were all there already, at her first show. That Van Herpen had her own style right from the beginning of her career is extraordinary, for the designer was only 23 at that first presentation.

But at the end of it there was a pale, shy, frail girl hovering in the background. She moved graciously, thanks to her many years of ballet training – her mother was a ballet teacher. But she hardly dared to open her mouth to the press, while much of her face was hidden behind tangled red hair. As if she had no right to be there. That girl, who grew up in a small town in Gelderland, has grown into a woman. Now, when she receives the press at the end of a show, or in between shows at her studio, we see a self-assured lady. Her hair is pulled back, her back is straight. She looks you in the face and is not afraid to talk.

Letting go of gravity

In the eight years after her graduation Van Herpen has grown a lot: as a human being and as a designer. Nowadays she is headquartered in a spacious studio with lots of light in the Veem building, directly on the IJ in Amsterdam. Her style is still as recognizable as before. But the umbrella spokes and other unusual materials have been replaced by special high-tech materials. She is continuously researching new techniques and possibilities. And she is at the forefront in the use of 3D printers, a much-discussed technique that has nearly become synonymous with her name.

In 2013 she was invited to be the guest editor of A-Magazine, a magazine that portrays the world around a designer. With this she followed in the footsteps of hat designer Stephen Jones, Givenchy's Riccardo Tisci and designers Yohji Yamamoto and Haider Ackermann. Van Herpen made a bizarre but beautiful cover in collaboration with model Hanne Gay Odiele and photographer Pierre Debusschere. The job of guest editor was a perfect opportunity for the designer to explain her work. A show only lasts fifteen minutes at the most and the commentary afterwards is often summarized in four or five sentences. In the magazine there is an interview with choreographer Benjamin Millepied, with whom she has designed ballet costumes and an essay by Harold Koda, the costume curator of the Metropolitan Museum of Art, about the Charles James exhibition.

Van Herpen's work isn't easy to explain. She is not the kind of designer who finds inspiration in everyday life, or for whom comfort is the most important criterion. She doesn't fantasize about princess dresses with wide skirts reaching to the ground. No, when Van Herpen fantasizes it's about something as abstract as letting go of gravity and how it would look if models could float through space. Or about all the things that would be possible if she could combine 3D printing with 3D scanning.

A 3D-printed dress

Van Herpen collaborates with a small group of scientists, biologists and archi-tects from around the world. Among them Neri Oxman of the Massachusetts Institute of Technology, Rachel Armstrong of AVATAR (Advanced Virtual and Technological Architectural Research) of the University of Greenwich in London and architect Philip Beeseley, who often collaborates with CERN, the Euro-pean Institute for Nuclear Research. Together with them Van Herpen works on long-term projects like materials for which no worm or cotton plant would be required and which don't yet have a name.

She finds it important to be continually researching and to look further ahead than just the next show. That's why she immerses herself in the new-est technological developments, related to flying, invisibility and growing ar-chitecture. With this she has clearly found a niche. That's a clever move, for as a young fashion designer you do need a niche if you want to be a player in the international fashion world. The public at large needs to know what you stand for as a designer.

In 2009 she left the Amsterdam Fashion Week behind and went abroad. She began in London with shows during the London Fashion Week. This is the fash-ion week where many young designers with international ambitions start out. She debuted there in July 2009 with the collection *Radiation Invasion*, where with dresses layered with folds she showed the invisible electromagnetic radia-tion that surrounds us. The second collection she showed in London was called *Synesthesia* and dealt with the sensitivity of the body. She depicted this with clothes made from gossamer-fine fringes; the singer Bjork wears a piece from this collection on the cover of her album *Biophilia*.

In 2011 a 3D-printed dress she designed for the collection *Escapism*, about the emptiness of digital addiction, was named one of the fifty best inventions of the year by TIME magazine. That dress and the rest of the collection were the reason that the prominent French Féderation de la Haute Couture invited her to become a member. For Van Herpen acknowledgement by the most prestigious institute in the fashion world was the international breakthrough of which so many beginning designers dream.

Since 2011 she has been showing during Couture Week in the fashion mecca Paris. London was good for her name and a first foray into the international fashion world, but in the end every designer wants to go to Paris. This is of course also true for Van Herpen. For Paris is still the place to be.

There are enough clothes in the world

In 2011 she showed the collection *Capriole* during Paris Couture Week, evoking the feeling one has just before and during a parachute jump. And it was during Paris Haute Couture Week that she showed one of the most extraordinary collections, *Voltage*, for here, for the first time, she used flexible material from a 3D printer. For this collection, in which she examined the body's own electricity, she won the Dutch Design Award in 2013. Before that, material from a 3D printer was often hard and stiff, which made her clothing look like objects. Not for nothing were they so often exhibited in museums. But thanks to the Belgian company Materialise, where she had had her designs printed from the very beginning, she finally had the use of supple material from the printer.

Van Herpen had waited years for this moment. She had shown a whole congress hall full of 3D-print company directors the potential of flexible materials and what applications would be possible in fashion. For that is another side of Van Herpen, she is also an inspired speaker, who can make others believe in her dreams.

In the next collection, *Wilderness Embodied*, about wild nature, shown in 2013 during the Haute Couture Week in Paris, she continued with the use of flexible material from the 3D printer. She made impressive dresses and suits that surround the body and developed matching shoes in collaboration with United Nude, the shoe label of Rem D. Koolhaas.

Van Herpen has said for years that couture is enough for her; that she isn't all that eager to take the usual paths in the fashion world; that she doesn't want to just hurl more clothes into the world. And yet, in October 2013, she showed at the Ready-to-Wear Fashion Week in Paris for the first time. But that she now participates in the commercial variation of the Couture Week doesn't mean she is turning into a brand that just makes T-shirts for retail outlets. On the contrary, it is not her intention to dress as many people as possible. There are already enough clothes in the world, she finds. She wants to think up new materials and surprise the old fashion world with her ideas.

Clothes with a beat

That the press, in spite of the overly full program of the Ready-to-Wear Week, pays attention to her work became apparent at her debut there, in October 2013. At the first show of a relatively unknown designer who isn't part of a great empire like LVMH or Kering, no more than a handful of interested people usually attend. They are there because they have known the designer for some time, or are from the same country or because they are friends.

But influential fashion journalists like Suzy Menkes and Vanessa Friedman came to the Ready-to-Wear debut of Van Herpen. The well-known actress Tilda Swinton was also in the front row at Silencio, David Lynch's exclusive night club where the collection was being shown. On the runway was top model Saskia de Brauw, among others, who has also worked for big labels like Givenchy and Saint Laurent. That such big names were present at Van Herpen's show means that her talent is recognized internationally.

At her debut in Paris she immediately took advantage of the opportunity to introduce a new technique: clothes with a beat. *Embossed Sounds* is the name of the collection, which consists of close-fitting tops with Plexiglas bead work and short dresses with embossed tribal-like motifs of high-tech materials in which sensors have been incorporated that cause the clothes to produce sound when they are touched.

Her second presentation during Ready-to-Wear Week, called *Bioparicay*, was just as much a bravura act. The decor especially, created in collaboration with the artist Lawrence Malstaf, was unsettling: in the middle of the runway, three models were suspended in huge plastic bags that were slowly being vacuum-sucked during the show. Think of Van Herpen's dream of models free from the pull of gravity, floating through space. The decorations on the clothes were made from synthetic glass and the showpiece was a short dress consisting of loose and flexible parts from a 3D printer, coated with silicone.

The question is how suitable these pieces of her ready-to-wear collections are for retail outlets. For not everything Van Herpen invents is easy to produce. Let alone to wear. But indeed, she does not have to dress the whole world. 'And those who want to wear my clothes must be able to afford them', she says. At the moment her clothes are being sold through eight international shops, among them the famous Dover Street Market in London. The plan is that her unique couture collections and long-term research will continue to be the basis of her work, and that the ready-to-wear that is derived from that will be suitable for retail outlets. Van Herpen is only at the beginning of this process, but she has proven that there is room for her singular approach. ▪

All images © Iris van Herpen

Translated by Pleuke Boyce

Oddball Amazement and Restless Waywardness

The Polymorphous Work of Joke Van Leeuwen

[ANNEMIE LEYSEN]

Joke van Leeuwen's airy, apparently casual manner of bending language to her will is quite unparalleled. Time and again she comes up with new free forms, cast in a mildly absurd style, cleverly starting the reader or spectator off on the wrong foot and creating wilful characters who watch the world from the sidelines through their naïve, beady eyes. Over the years, Van Leeuwen's original, imaginative writing, drawing and performing style has set her signature on her oeuvre. Her books and poetry for children, young people and adults have won copious awards at home and abroad and are often translated. Her inspired, cabaret-type literary tours de force ingeniously interweave subtle humour and infectiously anarchic hilarity. She might as well have patented polymorphism. The prevailing tone is always funny, sometimes boisterous, with a somewhat melancholy light-footedness and mild subversiveness. 'I strip things of the obvious by viewing them in a different light,' she says in an interview. 'Writing children's books is a way of looking at the world from underneath, just as cabaret allows me to see it from the side. That view often has a humorous effect. Hilarity turns things upside down.'

Her books for young readers observe the world through intriguing characters, perfectly combining illustration and text, disarming humour and stunning virtuosity of language. Over the years, Magnus, Deesje, Viegeltje, Bobbel, Kukel, Kweenie, Slopie, Toda and most recently Frederik and Frommel have become friends and allies to a couple of generations of adults as well as children. Van Leeuwen observes the world and the madness which prevails there with disarming humour.

Crooked noses and messy, spiky hair

Joke van Leeuwen was born in 1952 in The Hague. Even as a child she wrote stories for the household newspaper of the church minister's family in which she grew up. When she was fourteen the Van Leeuwens moved to Brussels, where her father became professor of theology. There she studied graphic design and history. After several years in the Netherlands, she has long lived and worked in Antwerp. Her years in Belgium have given her a strong sense of con-

Joke van Leeuwen (1952)
© Klaas Koppe

nection with Flanders and its inhabitants. She sometimes struggles with Dutch respectability and trend sensitivity, she once conceded in an interview. Border crossing defines both Van Leeuwen's life – she sometimes refers to herself as a 'Netherbelgian' – and her work, where she navigates effortlessly between the vague boundaries of literature for toddlers, children and adults. Setting one above the other strikes her as nonsense. Alternatively, as Nelleke Noordervliet put it when awarding her the Gouden Ganzenveer (Golden Goose Quill) literary prize in 2010, 'She turns adults into children and takes children seriously.'

In 1978 Van Leeuwen debuted with *De appelmoesstraat is anders* (Applesauce street is different), a black and white picture book, strikingly non-conformist for its time, about a new resident who wants to break through the uniformity of the street. Right away this was unmistakeably a Van Leeuwen book.

The author consciously avoids conforming to the hype around the realistic children's book, in fashion in the 1970s, in which readers were burdened with the world's big social problems. Humour and cabaret-type hilarity have always been important ingredients of her work. Misery and sadness are not avoided, but are implicitly given their place, without pedantic emphasis. A philosophical undertone is never far away. Recurring themes such as loneliness and lack of understanding are subtly handled in her stories, an approach which heightens their impact.

In her second book *Een huis met zeven kamers* (A house with seven rooms, 1980), a girl makes a journey of discovery through her 'Nice Uncle's' house. Each room is associated with its own funny story, accompanied by songs, poems, puzzles and handwritten letters. Language virtuosity comes up trumps: from then on word games, fitting names for people and objects, and unique use

of language and dialogue, along with Van Leeuwen's own peculiar illustrative style, became her trademark. 'Some things are simply easier to draw and others to write,' she explains. Her scratchy drawings and paintings offer a special interpretation of the narrative and are often a substitute for the text itself. The characters she draws do not belong in a woolly-minded children's world. No Barbie cheeks or cute snub noses; instead there are crooked noses, strange, beady eyes and messy, spiky hair.

Van Leeuwen repeatedly succeeds in constructing perfectly composed stories from what at first glance appear to be chaotic associations.

In *De metro van Magnus* (Magnus's metro, 1981), for example, the storyline is determined by eight metro stations. By chance Magnus turns up in his own drawing of the underground. At each stop he withstands tests, undergoes strange adventures and meets unusual characters. At the last station he visits his granny, who lives in an old people's home called the 'Warm Waiting Room'.

Candid and articulate

In almost every book, even her novels for adults, Van Leeuwen's heroes go on a journey or quest. The characters are always on their way somewhere, to a place of safety. The journeys are like lessons in life and, on closer inspection, are all models for life itself. Every journey is also full of absurd meetings and witty coincidences. The children she introduces into her stories are surprisingly emancipated and articulate, in spite of their childish naivety. The young heroes look at the world around them with a candid, non-conformist gaze, withstanding unusual situations with surprising energy. The adults tend to come across as less heroic in the children's books, often appearing washed out and wrapped up in their own affairs, with little interest in the children entrusted to their care.

Only the rather strange, marginal adult characters are granted a reprieve. They are generally odd, sidelined personalities who, by dint of not fitting in themselves, are sensitive to the young heroes.

In *Deesje* (1985) a rather unworldly girl is sent by her father to stay with her 'half aunt'. It is another sparkling journey full of intrigue and peculiar meetings. Here again, loneliness and lack of understanding are recurring themes. The same theme emerges in *Het verhaal van Bobbel die in een bakfiets woonde en rijk wilde worden* (The story of Bobbel who wanted to be rich, 1987). Again the heroine is different, struggling to fit into an orderly society.

De wereld is krom maar mijn tanden staan recht (The world is crooked but my teeth are straight, 1995) is a kind of comic strip about 'the light and dark sides of the beginning of a woman's life'. That beginning is revealed in a perfect combination of text and illustration with snappy, often poignant humour. Once again, a book about the many questions of a girl who understands nothing about adults.

Iep (Eep, 1995) at first appears to be a hilarious story, but there's more to it. It is a moving book about deprivation and loss, about the drive for freedom and emancipation, about loneliness and alienation. The little bird-girl Viegeltje redefines reality for everyone she meets, literally watching and experiencing the world from the air. The lively word games, tender observations of the *comédie humaine* or adult world, boundless imagination and disarming illustrations make the book one of Van Leeuwen's masterpieces. *Iep* unites all the trump cards of her writing, playing on language and emotion like no one else can.

A carefully balanced combination of humour and seriousness in word and image makes her poems, stories and novels unique in their class. As in *Kukel* (1998), for example, where Van Leeuwen introduces a rootless little boy, left to his fate by his seven singing sisters. In his great longing to belong to someone he makes a gift of himself to the childless queen. The queen's manner of speech is magnificent and particularly amusing.

In *Wijd weg* (Far away, 1991) and *Dit boek heet anders* (This book is different, 1992) the author experiments with symbolic narrative material, less accessible perhaps, but still intriguing, another virtuoso piece of writing. *Bezoekjaren* (Visiting years, 1998) is intended for an older readership, a novel inspired by stories told to Van Leeuwen by Malika Blain. The girl Zima narrates the story of her family during the politically turbulent 1970s in Casablanca. The impoverished but warm suburban existence of a large family is thoroughly shaken up when

first the eldest son, then the second, is arrested and imprisoned for 'dissident activities'. Years of uncertainty, long trials and endless strings of prison visits are slipped almost nonchalantly into accounts of everyday life. Viewing everything through Zima's guilelessness, the reader can only guess at the political machinations behind the events.

In *Toen mijn vader een struik werd* (The day my father became a bush, 2010) and her latest book *Maar ik ben Frederik, zei Frederik* (But I'm Frederik, said Frederik, 2013) the adult world is portrayed with sharp irony. The pointlessness of each war in the former and almost Kafkaesque misunderstandings in the latter are thought-provoking.

Kweenie (2003) is another experimental book, different from usual. In her earlier children's books Van Leeuwen wove fairly consistent, gripping stories around her illustrations. In this book *the story* is the protagonist and narrative art is the theme. A strange story about strange stories, how they come into being and how they work. A story also about what was, is and will be. Colourful illustrations, collages, photo arrangements, excerpts of comic strips, paintings and inventive typographic effects surprise us on every page. A feast for the eyes!

The books for 'novice readers' are often hilarious. The limited language resources such stories impose tend to result in boring reading material. In *Sus en Jum* (Sus and Jum) and *Fien wil een flus* (Fien wants a flus), Van Leeuwen again proves her boundless inventiveness, making a treat of learning to read.

Two non-fiction books are equally surprising. In *Waarom een buitenboordmotor eenzaam is* (Why an outboard motor is lonely, 2004, commissioned by Ons Erfdeel), 'a book for children and other people', Van Leeuwen answers twenty-one language questions. It's never boring, even if the book is all about the origins of languages, sound changes, spelling rules, difficult conjugations, rhymes, etymology, synonyms and proverbs. With her different take on the world, Van Leeuwen succeeds in making all that rather dry, academic information easily digestible and exciting. She does so by immediately putting each serious, documented account in its place with language jokes and gags, virtuoso verse or lively illustrations and hilarious comic strips. *Een halve hond heel denken* (Thinking a half dog whole, 2008) is about looking, manipulation of images, the golden ratio, the way advertising wins us over, and how imagination plays tricks on us. Instructive, crystal clear, and as always disarmingly funny.

Hopping in my head

Adults are also generously served by Van Leeuwen - and not only by her children's books for any age. From 2008 to 2009 she was the city poet of Antwerp. She used the city as a 'vehicle' for her poetry, immediately showing involvement in the ups and downs of her Flemish home. A particularly ingenious work was her 1100 metre long poem which, with the help of designer Bob Takes, she mounted on the wall of the Antwerp pedestrian tunnel under the Scheldt river, as a gift to the residents.

In four novels and four collections of poetry for adults she gives her readers the freedom to enjoy her masterful inventions in their own ways. Her poems are full of the same exuberant, playful and highly individual manipulation of language, giving words a life of their own. The sound games and linguistic quips of the children's poems in *Ozo heppie* recur in her poetry for adults. Anecdotal poems, pure language games and interesting observations abound in *Vier manieren om op iemand te wachten* (Four ways of waiting for someone), *Laatste lezers* (Last readers), *Wuif de mussen uit* (Wave goodbye to the sparrows) and *Grijp de dag aan* (Seize the day). She repeatedly starts out from small, everyday words, fanning out to grander distances, like sparrows rising into the air. Sound sometimes takes over from meaning. Here, too, text and image are peculiarly integrated. The intriguing scratchboard illustrations set viewers free to make their own interpretations.

In the novel *Vrije vormen* (Free forms, 2002) Van Leeuwen penetrates the clichés of the art world. The tone in which she observes the hyped-up art scene, bureaucratic society and the relationships between people is gently ironic and contrary once again. Dok (an acronym for 'Door Oefening Kunst', meaning 'art through practice') is a talented artist who finds herself in an artistic and emotional impasse after a relationship break-up. She takes in a foreign woman to fill the gap, but communication with Mara is awkward. One way or another, things get dramatically out of hand. The neologisms, imaginative as always, sound funny and succinct, but there is a melancholy behind them.

Alles nieuw (Everything new, 2009) returns to the theme of *Vrije vormen*. Here again the story centres on an elderly landlady (Ada) and her young tenant (Lara), and once again artistic experiments come into play. A couple of characters even pop up again. Van Leeuwen's two main characters take it in turns to speak. Young Lara wants 'to artistically manipulate reality', doctoring old pictures and photos. An old photo of Ada's missing daughter receives a new face. Misunderstanding, incomprehension and crippled communication are important themes in this book too. This powerfully composed story is about young and old, memory and future, reality and falsehood. The many drawings and graphic inventions make it a typical Van Leeuwen product.

With her latest novel *Feest van het begin* (Celebration of the Beginning, 2012) the reader tumbles into the eighteenth century. The setting appears to be that of revolutionary Paris, but Van Leeuwen has opted for intimate stories of the little people behind the history, and that produces an overwhelming world. With her perfect eye for detail and impressive empathy she introduces four main characters of flesh and blood living through the first two years of 'the new freedom'. A wonderful book about beauty and truth.

Van Leeuwen sees what we do not. Like Catho from *Feest van het begin* she can stand on her head, continually viewing the world differently. 'It has to be hopping in my head,' she says; and so it does, 'hopping' in her special sentence structures, graphic work and springy tales. She writes just as she talks and draws. Whether she is on stage, writing a story or drawing, the same unique voice emerges, the voice of Joke van Leeuwen. Time and again she surprises her readers with her uninhibited view of people and the world; she succeeds in enduringly enthusing readers of all ages, piquing their curiosity about what might happen. ▨

Translated by Anna Asbury

An Extract from *Celebration of the Beginning*

By Joke van Leeuwen

On an October Monday in the first year of the new freedom rain pours down uncompromisingly on the capital city. It beats a multitude of tiny pits in the water of the river, which runs through the city like a crooked spinal column, drawing twisting rivulets in the mud of still unpaved streets. The open gutters can no longer cope with the flow, and water spurts from drainpipes, which only reach halfway across the house fronts, pouring down onto shivering horses' flanks and flimsy carriage roofs. Passersby attempt to avoid splashes from the wheels, which throw up dirt and remnants of nitric acid that could burn holes in their clothing. Sparrows and cats hide in spaces too small for humans.

The rain gushes past the severe façade of an orphanage in one of the faubourgs, where for fifteen years, alongside other children with lost parents, a foundling girl has lived who can stand on her hands. The nuns who clothe her and set her to prayer have named her after two holy women.

That afternoon she looks through one of the few windows free of the ridged stained glass which distorts and discolours the outside world. She knows from hearsay what is happening and looks out on the silent street outside the orphanage. However little she sees, she is not permitted to continue looking, for there is cleaning to be done and new words to be learnt in a dead language that must be kept alive.

The water drums on a wallpaper manufacturer's damaged house, where everything has been smashed to smithereens by workers who came to take what was rightfully theirs, making off with the excellent wines from the cellar while they were at it. In gloomy attic apartments women and children of tanners' assistants and water carriers put down buckets and pans to catch the drips leaking in.

The rain soaks a young woman with a black patch in the skin of her upper lip. She came to the bakery expecting long queues at the door again, but the shop is closed and she returns to her mistress without bread.

The rain drums on the low house of a painter who remains indoors. He heard the alarm bells this morning, saw children pass by violently swinging hand bells, as if trying to call everyone out of the house, but he does not go to see what is happening. He avoids the unknown masses, although he wishes they all knew who he was and what he did.

Grey pools form on the roof of the workshop where an instrument maker is working on deepening the keys of a new pianoforte. It is a rectangular upright model. This smaller format sells better than the more beautiful, richer sounding grand.

The executor of court orders listens in his drawing room to the noises outside, then continues to play his cello, while his wife comes to sit with him, tucking a stray lock of hair behind her ear.

The rain falls on the cafés where men drink coffee with milk and discuss the general will and their own, and it soaks the long skirts of market women who have already been out and about for hours, that morning a good thousand of them went to the town hall to demand that the king come to the capital city, as it was promised that he would return in person from his palace, a short twenty kilometres away, where he lives with his foreign queen and small children, as if they prefer to have nothing to do with the frenzied capital and are grateful for the road around it, enabling them to circumvent its heart.

The women have thrown piles of official documents into a heap in the town hall lobby, for no bread can be baked from all that prattle on paper, they have found pikes to wave proudly in the air when they go to collect the king, as they need to make an impression, and their cheap clothing will not suffice for that. A couple of cannons will be needed too, thick tubes on wooden carts, even if no one has the cannon balls for them.

The deluge soaks the tens of thousands who have gathered to march on the palace. The water trickles down the leather apron of a saddler who has armed himself by fixing a handle to a block of wood, it saturates the white cap of an auctioneer woman with a professional scream. She screams an opening in the curtain of rain. The drips slide down the cheeks of the seamstress who has brought a broom to wave and the young actress who strikes up a simple song with just one line about what they will do today. Her words are taken over and transmitted through the throng, who like to be handed tailor made texts. No one thinks of hiding, everyone wants to be visible and remain so, shouting and singing about the arrival of the great baker of the fatherland, their national bread supplier, for his corporeal presence, his entire royal embonpoint, will improve the situation and bring the bread within reach.

The rain soaks the curious, who approach the bridges en masse to watch the demonstrators set off, eight drummers at the front, all here thanks to whispered rumours and peeling alarm bells. They see a number of women grasp the long pikes they have obtained while others take up cutlery, the cannons coaxed along, the flags that were meant to fly proudly clinging to their poles, and sashes in the approved colours hanging around shoulders and bellies as if their bearers were making gifts of themselves. The drumming, shouting and monotonous singing rises high into the air, letting off thick clouds of rage and ingrained timidity, stale and dark, the crowd becomes one enormous buzzing creature, radically christened in the name of something in need of a new name, the mud spatters on skirts and aprons, dirty clogs, worn out jackets and new uniforms.

A long avenue leads like a length of carpet to the palace, where the rain forms pools between the stone legs of symbolic women. The water gushes down the stone necks of prestigious men, turning as it hits the secret part of the roof, where the king sometimes withdraws when he wants a little peace and quiet, to think of the ingenious mechanisms of locks and shotguns rather than the realm.

The man is grieving with his wife for their little heir, who died of consumption, his emaciated body buried for a sum that would buy bread for tens of thousands. Now their house seems even more roomy and they are never alone, constantly surrounded by servants to dress and undress them, open doors and bring bouquets, beggars of favours, portrait painters, masseurs, wine pourers and whisperers, guards, cleaners, revellers, flatterers, lovers, seers and diviners, and the surgeon who succeeded in making him potent.

The endless procession of devotees walks out of the city, into the woods, through a village where there is insufficient food for so many passersby, and along the straight avenue towards the palace. Most of the women participating do not yet have children, or their children are grown up, they can afford to make the march, in their increasingly heavy skirts, their legs underneath fiercely striding forth. All afternoon they keep on thinking that they belong together, on their way - muscles aching, thirsty and red cheeked - to a better future.

Before darkness falls they reach the National Assembly building, not far from the palace. A chance delegation finds its way inside on tired feet clad in muddy shoes or clogs like sunk boats. They sit down on the platform, some staying below to take over the remaining empty benches. When they hear that the esteemed representatives are talking about compensating the lapsed rights of nobles, they become impatient, for the matter in hand is false grain speculation and the coming of the king to the heart of the capital, they have a petition to hand over, but is a rain soaked petition enough, will a petition result in food.

The clergy who try to hush them into deference are met with a mouthful of abuse, those who think they can calm the ladies present with a kiss to the hand are pushed away, they did not come for kissing of hands, what can they buy for a kissed hand. Some remove their coats and lay them on the floor to dry, there lie the coats on their bellies, sleeves spread out, as if wearier than the bodies that wore them.

Outside the impatience grows, what is going on, where can they find a dry place to sit, it rains on and on and darkness has long fallen. The guards are coming, it is said, latecomers, what do they want.

A small, wet group of protesters is permitted to enter the palace to demand that the king accompany them to the capital, for everyone wants to be certain, wants their delegation to hear it from his full lips in person, to hear the voice of their saviour who struggles to speak in public, from their inspiration who likes to eat large chunks of game, but they are a weak bunch, those allowed through the two gateways, who cross the large square and are received among mirrors and onlooking images of ancestors. A girl of seventeen among them faints, how can their demands impress when they are conveyed by such a young thing, who collapses at the drop of a hat, how can such a child make demands when she receives smelling salts and is embraced by those she came to speak out against.

They return without guarantees, without promises written in black and white.

Those who have not fallen asleep on the benches of the National Assembly, on the chairman's seat or somewhere outside under a shelter, who do not think enough is enough now, but want to press on in the dark, find the royal gates locked, but they will get through, they are cold, their clothes stick to their skin.

The rain is less fierce, but still has not stopped.

Guards on horseback come to drive them back, the nervous beasts snort and the guards become unsettled, they do not have their fear of this gigantic crowd under control, one of them begins to shoot, he would have said it was in self-defence, had he had the chance – and it was not the protesters wielding cutlery who deprived him of that chance.

His bullet hits the son of the saddler who has been carrying a block of wood with a handle for hours to defend himself. Now he sets the heavy implement aside, kneels down and tries to scream his son back to life.

The crowd transforms into a maul, forcing an opening, the man who fired the shot is pulled from his horse, someone has an axe, someone hacks his head off, it goes crosswise through the thin flesh of the throat, through blood vessels, muscles, windpipe, oesophagus, thyroid. Others hang his headless body upside down on one of the gateposts. He would have been four or five years' older than the saddler's son. His blood thins in the rain.

Finally, in the early morning, while it is still dark, the squalls disappear above the restless throng, now forcing their way into the palace, as many as can press through the doors on either side, they tear upstairs to the royal quarters, trailing mud on the white marble, spattering the walls, they strike out at the vases, cast a quick glance at the medieval stone statues towering unmoved above the caps and hats, richly decorated little tabourets stand in their way, a couple of women throw open a window onto the garden as if inviting the rest of the world along. The advance guard forces the door to the chamber of the bodyguards, who have retreated for the sake of self-preservation. They push on through to the queen's bedchamber. Her four-poster bed is empty. Curious hands tug at her bed linen, the absent queen is cursed with everything that has already been said about her, so often that it has begun to resemble truth: that she is a whore, that she orders hearth fires lit with banknotes, that she is the cause of all misery, the devil who came from elsewhere, and should have stayed there.

They stand there in their muddied clothes amidst the gilding, shouting and singing and cursing.

In panic the queen has taken the secret route to her husband's quarters, Open up, open up. The multitude storms into the hall of mirrors and multiplies. The royal family barricaded in the bull's eye salon is rescued by the guards, the king will appear on the balcony, if everyone goes back outside he will appear on the balcony, he will promise that they will come to the city, yes he will do what he can, he loves his people, they must just dress appropriately and have their trunks packed, but the whole family will come.

The rain has passed, but the road to the capital is still covered in puddles, through which the many thousands wade, barely capable of putting one foot in front of the other. In stiff clothes they reach the capital, shivering with cold, but burning with pride at their own unexpected prospects. Among them a carriage carries a sleep-deprived family, and behind the carriage follow carts full of sacks of flour found in the stores. Loaves of bread weighing four pounds are speared on pikes like umbrellas. The participants of this victory march wave branches they have pulled from the trees on the way, young women hang on the arms of guards. Along the side of the road stand the onlookers who slept in their own beds last night, and are now present because they realise that history is being written and that sidelines have their place. A child looks out of a first floor window to see two dead heads on pikes going by. The image is branded on his brain to remain there seventy years.

The victors are weary, they have not slept, they have not had much to drink and have barely eaten, they want to continue to be lifted up, but time moves on, the crowd breaks up, empty space opens up between the bodies once again.

Some seek to prolong the flush of excitement in a café. Others crawl into their own bed or amble back to work, open their front door, grab a pan to piss in, sink down onto a chair and lay their head in their arms.

From: *Feest van het begin* (Prologue),
Querido, Amsterdam, 2012

Translated by Anna Asbury

Two Poems

By Joke van Leeuwen

Four Ways of Waiting for Someone

1 Sitting. Thinking of lying. Hands
   smoothing the tablecloth around a dish
   that's difficult and much too much for two
   and not like the picture, but smells
   fantastic, out through the windows,
   doing its best not to collapse, like
   a sucked-in tummy trying not to
   bulge – inversion too is simile.

2 Walking. To the window and back,
   perhaps, then back to the window again,
   because sound confounds the brain with
   what you hope to hear, but isn't there.
   A procession dances past, people in fancy dress
   who call a scrawl of words and know each other
   all by name, certain by the look of things
   that someone must be looking.

3 Standing. At an exit, entrance where
   you said you would, but there are three,
   and you're not sure if this or that.
   Standing still won't get you there, but moving
   might mean missing what you'd almost had.
   Forgot to mention who's to stay and who's
   to move, who sees who again and when,
   and from how far.

4 Not.

Vier manieren om op iemand te wachten

1 Zittend. Denkend aan liggen. Je handen
   strijken rimpels in het tafellaken glad
   rond een gerecht dat moeilijk en te veel
   voor twee en niet als op het plaatje is,
   maar ruikt, het ruikt de ramen uit, het
   doet zijn best niet in te zakken, zoals
   een ingehouden buik niet bol te zijn -
   ook andersom is vergelijken.

2 Lopend. Bijvoorbeeld naar de ramen
   en terug en toch weer naar de ramen,
   omdat geluid zich buigt naar wat je
   horen wilt, maar het niet is. Er danst
   een stoet voorbij, verklede mensen die
   iets onverstaanbaars juichen, van elkaar
   goed weten hoe ze heten en te kijken
   dansen dat je kijken moet.

3 Staand. Bij een ingang, uitgang waar je zei
   dat, maar er zijn er drie, je weet niet meer
   of die of deze. Van blijven staan komt
   niemand tegen, maar met bewegen
   wordt haast bereikt wat net verdween.
   Zeker nog niet gezegd wie blijft en wie
   beweegt en wie dan wie wanneer
   en van hoe ver weer ziet.

4 Niet

From: *Vier manieren om op iemand te wachten. Gedichten*
(Four Ways of Waiting for Someone. Poems),
Querido, Amsterdam, 2001

She Said

She said, we'd ordered new compassion,
we had, they were going to deliver
the new compassion on Friday.
On Friday they say, is Saturday okay.
We say yes, but only in the morning.
They say, not on, that's not on,
the morning. My husband says, fine,
I'll come and pick it up myself,
Saturday in the morning, okay?
Okay, they say. He gets there
Saturday, they say, no compassion.
He says, how come, it's supposed
to be here? No, sorry, all out, come back
Friday. He says, what do you mean,
Friday, I need it right now. They say,
sorry, it's not in yet. He says,
but you said you had it already.
They say, are we supposed to say
we haven't, is that what you want
to hear, us saying we haven't?

Zei ze

Zei ze hadden we nieuwe ontferming
besteld wij, ze zouden die brengen,
de nieuwe ontferming, op vrijdag.
Zeggen ze vrijdag kan het op zaterdag.
Zeggen we ja, maar dan wel in
de morgen. Zeggen ze gaat niet,
dat gaat niet, de morgen. Zegt mijn
man goed, dan kom ik die zelf halen,
zaterdag dan in de morgen, dat kan?
Ja dat kan, zeggen ze. Komt hij daar,
zaterdag, nergens ontferming. Zegt hij
hoezo niet, die zou er toch wezen?
Nee nee, die is er niet, komt u maar
vrijdag. Zegt hij wat vrijdag, ik moet
die meteen. Zeggen ze gaat niet, die
is nog niet binnen Zegt hij u zei toch
dat die er nu was? Zeiden ze
moeten we zeggen van niet dan,
wilt u dat horen,
van zeggen van niet?

From: *Wuif de mussen uit. Gedichten en beelden*
(Seeing Off the Sparrows. Poems and Pictures),
Querido, Amsterdam, 2006

Translated by David Colmer

Mystical White Images of Man

On the Work of Johan Tahon

[ERIC BRACKE]

His hybrid plaster sculptures with human features now attract the attention of the international art scene, but until the mid-1990s they had to make do with the love their solitary creator gave them. In his tormented sculptures, Johan Tahon (Menen, 1965) links the sculpture of Rodin, Brancusi and Lehmbruck to the present day. He also keeps the mystical flame burning.

Between Michelangelo and Rodin

In spring 2012, two sculptures by Johan Tahon stood in the middle of the former, now tumbledown, Cordonnier stocking factory in Wetteren (East Flanders) as part of a group exhibition called *Aangeraakt/Touché*. The light that entered at an angle through the saw-tooth roof caressed the crumbly white skin of these plaster sculptures. The artist inspected the result with a half-smile on his face and then took an approving look at the puddle on the grimy floor and the knitting machines languishing a short distance away. Photos and paintings by other artists were also on display amongst this evidence of the miserable conditions the employees until recently had to work in.

With hindsight, it was no surprise that Johan Tahon enjoyed the sight: he cherishes disordered workshop spaces as biotopes for his works of art. It is not without reason that he calls his studio his greatest work. And his sculptures are not in the first place independent objects. This artist has the urge to let his sculptures communicate by making them relate to their surroundings, the space and the other objects to be found there. In the book *Johan Tahon, Observatorium* (Ludion, 2008), which the artist gave me as a gift there in Wetteren, Wim Van Mulders observed that 'Tahon's successful exhibitions are like a life-saving re-creation of the conditions in the studio'. The works belong there like weeds on a verge, just as fundamental and natural, but more puzzling.

Before the sculptures were installed in the old stocking factory, I had become acquainted with the artist's pragmatic attitude towards his work. Tahon's sculptures are often unstable, fragile constructions with heavy round heads – and sometimes two heads – or outsized arms that move the centre of grav-

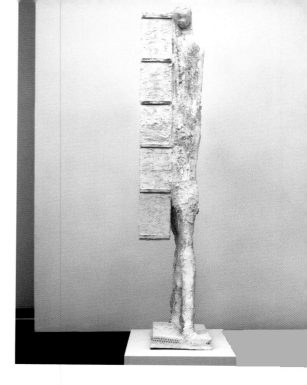

Fin (2014), plaster and wood, 64 x 100 x 340 cm.
Exhibition: *Adorant* at Gerhard Hofland, Amsterdam, 2014.
Photo by Gert Jan van Rooij.

ity dangerously far from the middle of the base. This is why the transport firm had received instructions to handle the works with care. Yet the most imposing plaster sculpture still emerged from the lorry in pieces. But then Tahon and his assistant appeared with buckets of plaster and water and started putting the delicate pieces back together again. They seemed not to be bothered that the result was not entirely identical to the original work. This was not a technical reconstruction of a sculpture intended to stand the test of time, but a healing operation by which the sculpture was reanimated in its new surroundings.

While they were plastering away uninhibitedly, I was reminded of August Rodin. The expressive surface of Tahon's sculptures, with or without drying scar tissue, displays a kinship with Rodin's unpolished works. Furthermore, some of the French sculptor's works also lean backwards dangerously, such as the bronze statue of Honoré de Balzac, one version of which is at the Middelheim Open-Air Museum in Antwerp. Rodin abandoned the traditional, superficial imitation of nature and tried to give his sculptures a dynamic, vitalist tension that was intended to illuminate some of its essential qualities. To achieve this, he usually asked his models to keep moving. In Tahon's work we also see a comparable urge to penetrate to the heart of the human condition, but he takes an even more unconventional approach. Tahon uses plaster body parts that he finds standing or hanging here and there in his studio and intuitively makes a composition out of them. He tries, even more than Rodin, to evoke man's tormented and wavering nature by means of extreme tension in the form. The distortions of his hybrid plaster beings with their unmistakably human features and the sporadic influence of African art are above all an expression of the state of the artist's own soul. In a 1998 conversation Tahon said: 'What takes shape

Adorant I & II (2013-14),
glazed ceramic, 32 x 29 x 78 cm.
Exhibition: *Adorant* at Gerhard
Hofland, Amsterdam, 2014.
Photo by Gert Jan van Rooij.

in my sculptures is the existential question. I don't like using the word existential, but I don't know how else to express it. My sculptures are a mirror-image; when I talk about them it's as if I'm talking about myself. It's all about doubts and fears that gnaw at me deep inside. At the same time, there is something universal about the sculptures because they express fundamental questions with which I think everybody struggles.'

At the same time he said of the unruly traces of the modelling of the sculptures, which is also so typical of Rodin: 'My sculptures are not finished. If they had a smooth finish I would experience them as a lie. I want to express vulnerability and fragility.' It was this unfinished state that led the curator Jan Hoet (1936-2014) to make comparisons with Michelangelo.

Father

Johan Tahon was still very young when he became acquainted with the work of Auguste Rodin, Wilhelm Lehmbruck, Constantin Brancusi and Alberto Giacometti, four sculptors who have clearly influenced him. Yet artistic aspirations were not encouraged in the Tahon household. His forefathers were rugged fishermen from Northern France, but his father had climbed the social ladder and became a headmaster in Menen, where Johan was born. While he was growing up, the young and uncertain Tahon was burdened by his father's alcoholism. At the age of fifteen he started making sculptures, which he saw as gifts to himself. He later gave an indication of the personal significance of these pieces: 'They have an almost ritual significance in my everyday life, like totems and masks among primitive tribes.'

He sought refuge at the drawing school in Menen, more specifically in the sculpture workshop in the cellar of that dignified mansion. For this lonely, over-sensitive adolescent it was a magical place with a 'spiritual atmosphere' where the drawings of Rodin and Brancusi made a deep impression on him. Under the inspiring guidance of his teacher, he forgot the rest of the world while shaping clay.

There, in the cellar in Menen, where no daylight penetrated, Tahon learned to love traditional sculpture and has remained true to it to this day. On this subject, he said, in the book *Fragmenten, Johan Tahon in gesprek met Bart De Baere* (Art Box, 1997): 'To me sculpture is the only art form where a certain complete-ness is required, both physical and psychological. It takes you over completely, because you truly practise sculpture with your whole body. Dragging materi-als, working with weight, going almost to physical extremes. And psychologi-cally and philosophically too. In fact a human can't give any more than that. That is why I find sculpture more interesting than other art forms.'

The first sculptures Tahon made were of modest proportions. In an open-hearted interview for the weekly magazine *Humo*, Tahon confirmed that the premature death of his alcoholic father, who would have preferred to see his son become an engineer, also signalled a turning point in his sculpture. 'I mourned, and tried to cope with his death, and I noticed that my sculptures had suddenly become completely different: they outgrew me, they became more monumental. All at once my relationship with my sculptures was like a child to its father. As if I had created father-figures, but not deliberately. Those sculptures were also reminiscent of images of ancestors, and one could even imagine they had a religious import – they became proto-sculptures.'

Grigory (Balm) (2012),
glazed ceramic, 47 x 47 x 95 cm.
Photo by Kari Decock.

For a long time the artist continued plodding along in his studio, living out the romantic cliché of the poor artist who lives only for his art. These were meagre years in which he clung to his sculptures like loved ones and read the writings of Carl Gustav Jung, the founder of analytical psychology. During that time he also knocked together a bronze-casting installation in his garden. He got up at night to maintain the temperature of the furnace. It was there, worn out by a lack of sleep, that he cast his first bronze sculptures: 'It was precisely at such moments that I almost physically experienced the link, a sense of solidarity across the centuries, with such Renaissance artists as Donatello.'

It was meeting the museum director and curator Jan Hoet that was decisive in the international development of his career. Tahon recalls this meeting in his studio in late 1995 as if it were yesterday: 'It was ice cold, and it was just as freezing inside my studio as outside. Jan was extremely enthusiastic and very much impressed by my huge sculptures in plaster. We drank red wine that was too cold. ... A few months later I was invited to take part in an exhibition, *The Red Gate*.'

Mediaan (2009), bronze, H 5 m At Central Commission for Statistics in Heerlen, The Netherlands. Photo by Judy Saget - van Aken.

This exhibition was held in 1996 in the new depot next to the future Museum of Contemporary Art (SMAK) in Ghent, which was only to open three years later. Tahon's participation in *The Red Gate* brought him out of his isolation. All at once the art press in Flanders became aware of his existence and gradually he made a name for himself in the Netherlands, where Queen Beatrix revealed that she was an admirer, and in the rest of Europe too.

Partly thanks to Jan Hoet, Tahon was subsequently able to exhibit his work at international galleries and leading museums. Ten years later he had an exhibition in Istanbul. Getting to know this historical place, a crossroads between Oriental and Western culture, was a revelation to him and led to new technical developments in his oeuvre.

Turkey

In Istanbul Tahon was captivated by the renowned Iznik ceramics, and also by the ancient Sufi writings and rituals. In recent years he has spent longer periods in Iznik, a small town just outside Istanbul, where he also has a studio. The book *Observatorium* contains a section of photos that Stephan Vanfleteren took in Iznik at Tahon's request. In the most important centre of ceramics in the Islamic world, Tahon experiments by trial and error with the age-old techniques and with his kiln. What is unique about the ceramics of Iznik is that quartz is mixed into the clay. Quartz is said to have a beneficial, healing and sound-proofing effect.

Tahon initially made mostly small sculptures, often of children's heads with a white glazed surface. Later he also experimented with ceramic tiles that he fired himself. 2010 saw the inauguration of the renovated 'Palais de Belgique', the present Belgian Consulate General in Istanbul, whose entrance hall now boasts a mosaic by Johan Tahon. It is a narrative work inspired by Willy Spillebeen's historical novel *Busbeke, of De Thuiskomst* (Davidsfonds, 2000). The book recounts the life of the sixteenth-century Flemish humanist known as Ogier Ghiselin de Busbecq, who was an ambassador at the Ottoman court. His native village of Busbeke (Busbecq) is close to Tahon's own native town of Menen.

Ich (2000), clay, plastic and insulation foam,
25 x 20 x 40 cm.
Photo by Bruno Cornil.

Most recently Tahon has been trying to create life-size sculptures using ceramic techniques. A foretaste of this was shown at the Istanbul Biennale in autumn 2011. This large sculpture was set up at the entrance to the Tiled Kiosk, a fifteenth-century pavilion with historical earthenware just outside the walls of the Topkapi Palace. Tahon also placed his own work amongst the antique Iznik and Sejuk ceramics, the first time anything like this had been done at the museum. In the meantime he has achieved major status as an artist in Istanbul. Turkish art magazines, newspapers and television channels regularly report on his work. He also attracted attention with a solo exhibition in the ancient Byzantine church near the Topkapi Palace during *Istanbul 2010 – European Capital of Culture*.

White is always nice

His experiments in Turkey have of course also had an effect on the oeuvre that takes shape in his studios in Flanders and the work we see there. At the exhibition in the old stocking factory in Wetteren two years ago, he installed a glazed white child's head in a cellar that stank of fuel oil and whose lights flickered on and off. The glaze looked as if it were dripping off the head, and the eyes seemed blind. This had a particularly odd and almost painful effect. The smothered emotion of this silent, gleaming sculpture had obvious associations with the choking present-day dramas of child abuse.

Yet the evolution in Tahon's oeuvre remains rather limited. For the sake of completeness it has to be said that he also briefly experimented with polyester. The choice of this material was more a matter of chance, when he had to transport works by plane and they had to be as light as possible. But regardless of the technique and material, the artist wrestles in all his work with the same great restlessness and emotions that had previously also occupied the great sculptors of early modern art. And whatever form his figures take, the one thing that always recurs is the human face. And the radiant white.

Map of the Universe (2009) and First Perseus (2008),
plaster, H 234 cm & 110 x 95 x 290 cm.
Exhibition: *Hemisphere* at Hagia Irene (Topkapi Palace), Istanbul, Turkey, 2010.

Tahon also remains an artist with a pronounced predilection for mysticism, so his interest in Sufism, which one could call Islam's mysticism, is no coincidence. During our conversation at the old Cordonnier factory in Wetteren he also admitted that the text the artists at the exhibition had been given by way of inspiration, called *Aangeraakt/Touché*, had definitely appealed to him. It made a connection between a line from *The Internationale*, the song of the socialist struggle, the Dutch version of which was written by Henriette Roland Horst in 1900, and the word 'touched', referring to a sensual experience of the overwhelming divine love that has featured in mystical literature from Augustine to Hadewych.

White, which symbolises light, fits well with the mystical nature of Tahon's sculptures. In *Observatorium*, Wim Van Mulders wrote: 'White is the wispy sigh of materiality as it dissolves into a reanimated dream. Tahon's white shows a higher state of being because it is the lightest breath of matter. A white sculpture primarily displays oblivion and solitude.' Tahon is known not only for his penchant for mysticism, but also his aversion to strategic career planning. 'A lot of artists nowadays are concerned above all with strategy: they work out rationally how they can achieve one success after another, as in sport. That's something I have never spent my time on,' he claims. I believe him. ▪

www.johantahon.com

Translated by Gregory Ball

Semen (2010), plaster and glazed ceramic, 53 x 50 x 221 cm. Exhibition: *Der Traum des Bildhauers* at Gerhard Marcks Haus, Bremen, Germany, 2010. Photo by Rüdiger Lubricht.

Learning the Lessons of History?

Scientific Fraud in the Low Countries

[VITTORIO BUSATO]

'If the researcher first strives to the best of their ability for objectivity and pure reasoning, and secondly adheres to the prescripts of honest research and open publication as described in this book, then there is no room for confusion. Others may then repeat his work if they wish and/or may identify where, despite his best efforts, influences from ideologies other than that of objective science have crept into the researcher's definitions, or where he has committed methodological errors.'

This quotation is more than fifty years old and comes from the book *Methodologie. Grondslagen van onderzoek en denken in de gedragswetenschappen* (Den Haag, 1961) by Adriaan de Groot (1914-2006). The book was translated in 1969 as *Methodology. Foundations of inference and research in the behavioral sciences*, but all quotations in this essay are translated from the Dutch original. De Groot spent a long time as a professor at the University of Amsterdam, and a shorter period at the University of Groningen. Many still see him as the most influential Dutch psychologist of all time. His 1946 doctoral thesis, *Thought and choice in chess* (1965), is regarded as the intellectual precursor of cognitive psychology. Another significant, more national contribution was his encouragement of social scientists in general and psychologists in particular to provide empirical support for their theories. In *Methodologie* – more than fifty years ago, remember (the Dutch-language edition dates from 1961) – he set out in crystal clear fashion how that could be done as fairly as possible.

Generations of social science students have been educated with his empirical cycle and related research maxim: 'If I know something, I can predict something; if I cannot predict anything, then I know nothing.' This empirical cycle begins with *observation*: the systematic collecting of empirical facts and the formulating of hypotheses. The second phase is *induction*, in which the hypotheses are formulated more precisely. Next comes the phase of *deduction*: the formulation of specific predictions based on those hypotheses. These predictions are then empirically *tested* using new empirical material. In the fifth phase, the results are *evaluated* for their theoretical validity, after which the cycle starts again from the beginning.

De Groot argues that it is crucial during this process to draw and maintain an explicit distinction between exploratory and verification research. Hypotheses, he argued, must be formulated *in advance* and tested using *new* data. 'Anyone who imagines exploration in reporting as verification research by acting as if the hypothesis had already been formulated precisely before the research began – something which is sadly all too easy to do – is guilty of a serious infringement against the social ethics of science. In the 'open' communication between scientists, it is expected that such misrepresentations will not occur.'

The purpose of exploratory research, De Groot stresses, is to build hypotheses. Hypotheses are not tested during exploratory research; as with verification research, they are not precisely formulated in advance, but are simply explored in order to formulate more precise hypotheses in line with pre-existing theoretical findings. 'The notion of 'exploration' too often turns out to be a euphemism for unnecessary contamination in a piece of research which would have been far better if it had had a systematic, objectively descriptive design. (...) The consequence is that what was initially intended as verification research, but in reality is a poorly executed project, is presented as 'exploratory research' as a last remedy for methodological shortcoming.'

According to De Groot, exploratory research is *preliminary research*. If it is not followed up by precise theory and/or hypothesis formulation and testing, then it is virtually useless. 'Mixed', theoretically based investigations must be subjected to the requirement cited earlier, namely that the researcher *maintains a clear separation between the different forms and procedures*. The meaning of the level of significance, for example, depends greatly on whether we are dealing with verification or exploratory research. For example, if we continue to explore until we find something 'significant', the preselection means this is no longer significant in a statistical sense.'

The fraudulent inventor

Do we really learn the lessons of history? Judging from a number of recent cases of scientific fraud in the Low Countries, there is some cause to doubt this. If 'researchers' such as Diederik Stapel (Tilburg University), Dirk Smeesters (Erasmus University Rotterdam), Don Poldermans (also Erasmus), Mart Bax (VU University Amsterdam), Peter Paul Rijpkema (University of Amsterdam), Patrick van Calster (University of Groningen) and a Flemish professor of rheumatology at Leiden University have studied *Methodologie* at all, it is clear that they have paid scant regard to that empirical evidence base and to prescriptions relating to honest research and open publication – to say nothing of the explicit distinction between exploration and verification research.

What were their transgressions, again? The social psychologist Stapel turned out to have invented much of his oeuvre; he climbed rapidly into the international top ten of the greatest scientific fraudsters. His Flemish colleague and professor of consumer behaviour Dirk Smeesters, also a social psychologist, was caught out manipulating data in three articles that have since been withdrawn.

The internist and university professor Don Poldermans fabricated data for around two hundred patients. Mart Bax, a professor of political anthropology, was charged with scientific misconduct long after retirement (though without consequence, as if his fraudulent inventions had passed their statute of limitations); among other things he was accused of citing non-existent publications, falsified achievements and distinctions that had never been awarded in official documents, and basing his publications on unverifiable source references.

Law professor Peter Paul Rijpkema was accused of plagiarising large sections of a book published in his name from a book written by his predecessor, without crediting him; unlike Stapel, Smeesters, Poldermans and Bax, Rijpkema's actions were ultimately not classed as infringements of scientific integrity, but as extreme lack of care. The transcriptions by Professor of Criminology Van Calster, by contrast, did cost him his job; in 2005 the Vrije Universiteit Brussel stripped him of his doctorate because large tracts of his thesis had been taken without citation of sources from a widely used management manual; this proved to be the hair that broke the camel's back for his Groningen employer.

And what of Annemie Schuerwegh, the rheumatologist? She was dismissed after colleagues discovered fraud in her laboratory research. It turned out that A.S. had been creeping into the laboratory at night in order to manipulate patients' blood samples so as to disguise the fact that a test she herself had designed was not fit for purpose. Fortunately her patients, like those under Poldermans, were never in danger.

Pressure to publish

What motivates scientists, who know that they are at great risk of being unmasked through the self-cleansing power (at least that is its intent) of peer review, nonetheless to commit fraud? Is it the constant pressure on academics to publish, as Stapel himself stated in a bid to explain his fraud? Should the cause of this fraud perhaps be sought in too much vanity, egotism or narcissism, prompting those concerned to use fraudulent means if necessary to secure a presence in journals with the highest *impact factor*, those magic words in the world of science today?[1]

This pressure to publish, the rat race it engenders and the emphasis on quantity is sometimes lamented, for example in the Flemish newspaper *De Morgen*, by a large group of scientists as a response to the fact that the Flemish government distributes funding to academic institutions primarily on the basis of the numbers of publications and numbers of students and doctorates (the notorious output funding). This, it was argued, increases the temptation to put empirical reality in a slightly more favourable light in order to increase the chance of publication – all the more so because journal editors are much more inclined to publish 'significant' results.

This pressure, or perhaps more accurately the market-based thinking of academic institutions, can also give rise to perverse incentives. If universities are funded partly on the basis of the number of graduates, the danger of academic inflation is not far away; it is easy to adjust the standard of an examination. If universities receive more money for producing more publications, we should not be surprised that management will focus on raising the number of publications. One professor, who had been invited to apply for a professorship – at Tilburg, ironically – told me for example of being tempted 'by bonuses of € 5,000', on top of the salary, for every publication that appeared in a top journal – though it must be said that the party in question regarded this practice as unique to that university.

It is kitchen sink psychology, of course, but it seems equally likely that narcissism cannot be ruled out as a potential (partial) cause of scientific fraud.

The scientific philosopher Sir Karl Popper (1902-1994) – a close acquaintance of De Groot, as it happens – once said that science is not so much about *who* says something as about *what* is said; that appears to be less and less the case in today's scientific judgement-by-results culture. Take a quick look on the Internet at CVs of academic psychologists; many of them report the impact figures of the journals in which they publish, as well as the number of times their articles have been cited – figures which naturally change over time. Is this kind of self-congratulation the way to express the fact that one 'counts'? Is it the best way of expressing the real impact in relation to the task of psychology and psychologists, namely to understand and help others?

Wherever the truth may lie, pressure to publish or excessive vanity can never be a single explanation for scientific fraud. There are after all very many scientists, vain or otherwise, who struggle under the perceived pressure to publish but who are not tempted into fraud. The reality is that people in general, and therefore also scientists, are prone to cheating, to engage in dodgy business, to make mistakes, to lie, and in some cases to cross the line.

Grey area

Different categories of infringements of integrity are recognised in the world of science. Inventing data stands firmly in top place, followed by plagiarism and extensive manipulation of data. Below this, however, is a much greyer area.

Practices such as omitting data that do not fit the researcher's purpose, adjusting statistical analyses so that the results turn out more favourably, recycling or splitting research results purely in order to reach more publications, adapting and 'sexing up' hypotheses retrospectively in order to obtain results that are significant – did I already mention that De Groot highlighted such practices more than fifty years ago? – are all today regarded as questionable research practices.[2] It is by no means always clear how deliberately these practices have been applied. For example, if a researcher freely admits that they have eliminated an outlier from the data set (say, for example, a subject who deliberately sabotages a research project) then, unlike a researcher who does this 'clandestinely', they are not guilty of any wrongdoing at all.

How common are such questionable research practices? According to a recent study by Harvard Business School, one in ten psychologists may at some time have improperly forged data.[3] According to a more recent doctoral thesis, half the scientific publications in the field of experimental psychology contain statistical anomalies, ranging from rounding data up or down to sanitizing data to obtain a more favourable outcome. Earlier research led by Jelte Wicherts, currently senior lecturer at the Department of Methodology and Statistics at Tilburg University and initiator of the recently founded *Journal of Open Psychology Data*, suggested that psychologists who do not publish their data may also have something to hide. By way of illustration, a few years ago he and colleagues published a report of a remarkable survey in the journal *American Psychologist*.[4] Of the authors contacted who had published in the last two issues in 2004 of the high-impact journals *Journal of Personality and Social Psychology*, *Developmental Psychology*, *Journal of Consulting and Clinical Psychology* and *Journal of*

Experimental Psychology: Learning, Memory, and Cognition, only a quarter (!) made their data available for reanalysis. That is interesting, because the ethical guidelines of the *American Psychological Association* (APA) impose a requirement on researchers to make their data available to colleagues for at least five years. Even more remarkably, in another study Wicherts et al. found that researchers who do not make their data available also make noticeably more statistical errors.[5]

It remains unclear how systematically psychologists fiddle with the statistics. Would those psychologists admit their unfair play if they were not allowed to remain anonymous? How many of them apply their unfair practices or even commit fraud in a cleverer and more subtle way and so slip through the net? It is difficult to establish precisely how often fraud occurs in psychology, even though the public at large may think that since the Stapel scandal the incidences of fraud are piling up and strict controls are absolutely essential. But in a profession that is characterised more than many others by mutual trust, it is not possible to exercise total control, as if researchers were potential drug mules on a flight from Curaçao to Amsterdam.

Back to square one

This does not alter the fact that journals of psychology are increasingly filled with calls to restore transparency and fair play in research, among other things by encouraging replication, sharing and publicising data and pre-registering experiments (where scientists state in advance what they plan to research, how they intend to do so and which conclusions they do and do not wish to be able to draw from their research). It is however questionable how new these initiatives are and whether devoting much more attention to the work of an old master in the profession such as De Groot might not be a much simpler remedy.

As stated earlier, journals publish far more significant than non-significant results. Replication studies have virtually no chance of being published. This is strange, because a replicated effect strengthens the effect originally found and a non-replicated effect places that effect in empirical perspective. The Open Science Framework is currently setting up any number of replication initiatives which are intended to form part of the scientific cycle with the aim of delivering more robust knowledge; one study does not after all constitute a body of research. This is indisputably laudable, but more than fifty years ago De Groot was already expressing surprise at how sporadically replication studies appeared: 'And if they are carried out, the results – entirely without justification– are often not published, especially if they are negative.'

De Groot also had something to say long ago about that transparency and sharing of data which Wicherts et al., among others, so laudably and loudly proclaim; read the opening quotation in this article once again. And fair is fair, researchers who call for pre-registration will also (yet again) need to turn to De Groot: 'The most detailed possible advance description of the verification (or experimental) design is in any event strongly advisable.' (De Groot, *Methodologie*)

Fair play in research also has to do with giving credits to those who historically deserve them; that is without doubt the best way to genuinely learn from the lessons of history. It is therefore time in the world of science, and definitely in the world of psychology, to pause for a moment. The kind of artisanal professionalism that De Groot described more than fifty years ago in Methodologie should once again become compulsory reading in scientific training. Compulsory *Methodologie* refresher courses should also be organised for doctoral students, postdoctoral researchers and professors (and unquestionably also for all social psychologists).

Once this is all solidly in place, there will be a significant reduction in the current excessive variation in knowledge about methodology and statistics among psychologists. I would then venture to predict that not only will questionable research practices become a thing of the past, but that it will also become clear that psychologists still know very little indeed. Much of the knowledge in the world of psychology, partly because of this unfair play, is based on theoretical quicksand. Making the study of *Methodologie* compulsory would help ensure that solid foundations are laid before erecting new structures.

And I would also dare to predict that a side-effect will be that the emphasis on quantity in science (at least in psychology) will decline automatically. Because if I know anything thanks to De Groot's masterful book, then it is that measurement may provide knowledge, but simply counting adds up to nothing.

Postscript

A brief final word about impact. A friend of mine is a widow; her son and daughter lost their father at the ages of six and eight, respectively. Her daughter is now fourteen. It recently struck me that she was so changed, as if her shyness and uncertainty had suddenly given way to an almost adult self-awareness. What had happened? It transpired that my friend's daughter had been to a bereavement counselling weekend for children who had lost a parent or sibling. That weekend was led by a psychologist from whom she said that she had learned an enormous amount about coming to terms with her emotions concerning the loss of her father and sharing that with others. *That* is impact. Would that counsellor also boast about it in his or her CV? ∎

NOTES

1) An impact factor is calculated based on the average number of citations of all articles published in a journal within a period of two years. The higher the impact factor, the higher the scientific prestige of a journal. Better journals are read by more scientists. That increases the chance that articles from that journal will be cited. That in turn increases the impact of the journal – and so on, and so on.

2) L.K. JOHN, G.F. LOEWENSTEIN & D. PRELEC, 'Measuring the Prevalence of Questionable Research Practices with Incentives for Truth-Telling', in: *Psychological Science*, 23, 2012, pp. 524-532. See also: M. Bakker, *Good science, bad science. Questioning research practices in psychological research, academic thesis*, University of Amsterdam, 2014.

3) See first reference in note 2.

4) J.M. WICHERTS, D. BORSBOOM, J. KATS & D. MOLENAAR, 'The poor availability of psychological research data for reanalysis', in: *American Psychologist*, 61, 2006, pp. 726-728.

5) J.M. WICHERTS, M. BAKKER & D. MOLENAAR, 'Willingness to share research data is related to the strength of the evidence and the quality of reporting of statistical results', *PLoS ONE*, 2011.doi: 10.1371/journal.pone.0026828.

Translated by Julian Ross

A Poor, Inspired and Melancholy Poet

Willem Bilderdijk, a Calvinist Celebrity

[RICK HONINGS]

On December 18, 1831, the Dutch poet Willem Bilderdijk (1756-1831) drew his last breath. This brought to an end the life of one of the most colourful, influential and versatile figures of the early nineteenth century in the Netherlands. Bilderdijk didn't just write poetry, he was also a jurist, linguist and all-round man of letters, a historian, philosopher, theologian, botanist, mathematician, architect and portrait artist. Nowadays he is mainly seen as a romantic and forever complaining poet, who expressed his *Weltschmerz* in overblown poetry, with high-minded lines like 'For me, for me, is nought to crave / In this punishing life, except the grave.' Bilderdijk wrote constantly and about everything under the sun: life and death, love and hate, religion, politics, a child's death, the King's birthday, the cooking of eggs. He was even inspired by the flies in autumn. His distaste for tobacco and German stoves was also expressed in verse.

His contemporaries regarded Bilderdijk as the greatest living poet, on a par with Homer, Dante, Shakespeare and Goethe. There wasn't a genre he didn't practise; in total he wrote more than three hundred thousand lines of verse. His collected poems fill fifteen hefty tomes, full of mythological, political and religious verse, and a lot of occasional poetry. Most of it is no longer very accessible to contemporary readers. His lyrical and autobiographical poems and his poems about death are the most appealing to us. Bilderdijk expressed his longing for death in many verses, with titles like 'The Misery of Earthly Existence', 'Body's Decay', 'Death Bed', 'On the Edge of the Grave', and 'Burial'. But he also wrote prose, for example his *Short Account of a Remarkable Journey Through the Air and the Discovery of a New Planet* (1813). With this work, fifty years before Jules Verne, he became the author of the first Dutch science fiction novel.

His contemporaries didn't just admire his work, they were also fascinated by his life. Bilderdijk was born in Amsterdam in 1756 and grew up as a prodigy. His debut, *My Lusty Delights*, filled with erotic verse, appeared in 1781. After studying law in Leiden he settled in The Hague as a lawyer. As a fervent supporter of the Orangists, the adherents of the Prince of Orange, he became an icon of that party. His marriage to Catherina Rebecca Woesthoven wasn't a happy one. Because Bilderdijk didn't know how to handle money, his debts piled up. When the French invaded the Netherlands in 1795 and William V had to flee to England, Bilderdijk haughtily refused to swear the oath of allegiance to the new

government. It resulted in him being exiled. This not only relieved him of a bad marriage, but also of his towering debts.

In England he began an extra-marital affair with Katharina Wilhelmina Schweickhardt, twenty years his junior, whom he taught Italian and who achieved renown as a poet herself. In 1797 she followed him to Germany. Because Bilderdijk was still married, living together was initially out of the question. He lived in Brunswick, while Wilhelmina resided in Hildesheim and later in Peine, together with the children she bore. In Germany Bilderdijk made a meagre living by giving private lessons. At the weekend he visited his lover. Those rides on horseback through the German swamps were hard on him. When the divorce from his first wife came through in 1802, he was able to start living with his beloved. In March 1806 he returned to the Netherlands. In June Louis Napoleon ascended the throne. He named Bilderdijk his language tutor and court librarian. After the defeat of Napoleon and the return of the house of Orange, Bilderdijk hoped to obtain a professorship at last. That was not to be. But he continued to write poetry, up till his last breath. After the death of Wilhelmina in 1830, Bilderdijk didn't want to live any more. He died a year later, at the age of seventy-five.

Bilderdijk as a melancholic poet by Charles Howard Hodges, 1810. Collection Rijksmuseum Amsterdam

Der Arme Poet
(*The Poor Poet*)
by Carl Spitzweg,
1839. Collection Neue
Pinakothek, München

Bilderdijk the celebrity

Bilderdijk can be regarded as an early Dutch example of a literary celebrity. His contemporaries were intrigued by his eccentric appearance, his long robes and the Turkish wrap or turban to alleviate his headaches. It gave him very much the appearance of an eastern prophet. Many people were also fascinated by his excessive use of opium, which was seen as most unusual. And his infatuation with his supposed noble origins added to his unique status. Bilderdijk even maintained that he was related to the mythical Knight of the Swan, from the famous medieval tale. Many wondered if he himself believed in this background or if it was just one of the mystifications with which he tried to astound people, his urge to differentiate himself from the common herd.

In the eighteen-twenties Bilderdijk emerged more and more as an orthodox Calvinist culture critic with prophetic aspirations. He began to air opinions that many regarded as reactionary and that caused great commotion. He was, for example, against democracy and the sovereign power of the people and for an absolute monarchy; he was against relief for the poor and smallpox vaccination, but for slavery and the inherent inequality of people. With this Bilderdijk rubbed many the wrong way. At the same time he became a figurehead in the movement of what is now called the 'Réveil': the orthodox Calvinist revival movement that put feeling at the centre, waged war with the spirit of the Enlightenment and called for conversion and piety.

There is something special about Bilderdijk's case. He can certainly be seen as an example of a Calvinist celebrity. But such a characterization contains a remarkable paradox. According to the teachings of John Calvin, with predestination as a basic principle, man is but an insignificant creature compared to God – nothing more than a worm. It would therefore befit him to be humble. Yet Bilderdijk continually presented himself as an exceptional and exalted poet, someone way above the common herd. How can this paradox be explained?

Before we can answer this, we have to look at Bilderdijk's public image. Like Byron, who is often called the first literary celebrity, Bilderdijk had a 'branded identity'. A big difference, however, was that Bilderdijk wasn't just a poet, but also an orthodox Calvinist prophet. That fits in with Thomas Carlyle's remark in *On Heroes, Hero-Worship, and the Heroic in History* (1841): 'Prophet and Poet, well understood, have much kindred of meaning. Fundamentally indeed they are still the same; in this most important respect especially, That they have penetrated both of them into the sacred mystery of the Universe'. Shakespeare especially combines both qualities, according to Carlyle: 'I feel that there is actually a kind of sacredness in the fact of such a man being sent into this Earth. Is he not an eye to us all; a blessed heaven-sent Bringer of Light?'

This could also be applied to Bilderdijk.

A brilliant melancholic

If there's one thing Bilderdijk is known for, it's his gloom and longing for death. It's an image he was himself responsible for, as he repeatedly promoted this attitude in his work. There can be no doubt that Bilderdijk must often have been truly unhappy. And he had reason to be. When he was five, a boy from next door stepped on his left foot. This brought on a painful case of periostitis and resulted in him spending the greatest part of his childhood indoors. In later life he never managed to obtain a professorship and he was much weighed down by the deaths of his children.

Even so, his melancholy can't just be explained by biographical facts. His gloom can also be seen as an integral part of his image as a poet. He was following in a tradition. Since the late eighteenth century, hypochondria, complaining about real or imaginary ailments, had been thought to be a sign of genius. Lots of authors fell prey to fits of gloom, or pretended they did. Leo Braudy, in *The Frenzy of Renown* (1986), connects this phenomenon to a growing 'urge for fame'. In the eighteenth century it became widely accepted that insanity, melancholy and genius went hand in hand. The idea was not new. In the fourth century B.C. a disquisition had been written which is generally attributed to Aristotle: *About Melancholy*. It starts like this: 'Why is it that all men who have been exceptional in philosophy, politics, literature or the arts have turned out to be melancholics?'

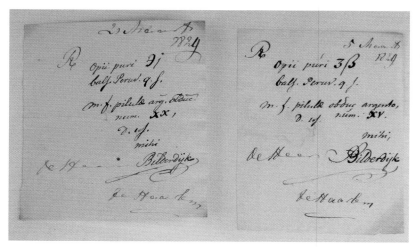

Personal opium recipes of Bilderdijk. Collection Bilderdijk Museum Amsterdam

Title vignette of *De voet in 't graf* (One Foot in the Grave) by Willem Bilderdijk, Rotterdam, 1827. Collection Bilderdijk Museum Amsterdam

According to Aristotle melancholy was connected to a surplus of black bile. A genius ran the risk of being plunged into melancholy, but that disposition was also a condition for achieving greatness. After 1750 melancholy became a fashionable ailment.

It's against this background that we must also interpret Bilderdijk's dejection. The theory of temperaments remained influential until late into the nineteenth century. From an early age Bilderdijk seemed very much taken by melancholy. When he was older he began to exploit it more and more as an artistic attribute. Nearly all of his letters are full of complaints about an endless list of physical and mental discomforts. He is either suffering from a 'buzzing' in the head, is short of breath, dizzy or confused, or complaining about a softening of the brain. At other times he sighs about insomnia, rheumatism, coughing, spitting blood, or pain. Bilderdijk rarely missed a chance to emphasize how ill, sad and miserable he was.

To describe his condition Bilderdijk uses ever changing metaphors. One time he calls himself a worn-out soldier, whose stiff joints prevented him from following the troops. In 1780, when someone wished him a Happy New Year, he stated that this would be impossible. One wouldn't wish an oyster good luck with his flying, or a cripple with his tightrope walking? Another time he presented himself as a miner, unable to lift a spade. In 1805 he called himself a crippled horse that would never prance again at the sound of the trumpet. Three years later he saw himself as a cat that had tumbled down from a wall. In 1810 he compared his feelings to the pain caused by a dog bite in which wasps were rooting around. And in 1825 he described himself as a cracked teapot. Bilderdijk was also fond of the images of the dehydrated cricket, the truncated tree and the trampled plant.

His longing for death flowed directly from his unease about existence. He continually made it appear as if he did not have much longer to live. His poetry greatly contributed to the image that he fostered of the nearly-dead poet. And it was also expressed in the portrait that Bilderdijk had painted of himself, in 1810, by Charles Howard Hodges. Leaning on his right arm, he sadly gazes into space.

The pose in this portrait is reminiscent of the pose in Albrecht Durer's *Melencolia I* (1514). This picture shows a winged, pondering woman, who is resting her chin on her left hand: the melancholic temperament personified. Bilderdijk was portrayed in a similar pose. It presented him the way he liked it: as a chosen one, a melancholic who had been elevated above the common herd.

The myth of poverty

A real poet is poor and lacks the basics. This has been the traditional image since the romantic period. The German artist Carl Spitzweg immortalized this image in his painting *The Poor Poet* (1839). It is remarkable to what a degree Bilderdijk managed to put this cliché into practice. But where Spitzweg meant to be ironic, Bilderdijk was deadly serious. There had, of course, been times in Bilderdijk's life when he was short of money. When, with the arrival of the French in the Netherlands in 1795, he was exiled, he was several thousand guilders in debt; in 1811 he declared bankruptcy. But this is only one side of the story, for Bilderdijk also complained about poverty when he had plenty of money coming in. In 1798, when he was living in Germany, he claimed he had been living on dry bread and water for months. His young daughter had to go barefoot, because he couldn't afford shoes. 'So what do I have to look forward to? To die of hunger.' According to him the girl was now unrecognizable, thin and dehydrated because of lack of food. That this was a pose is obvious from the letters Bilderdijk meanwhile wrote to his beloved Wilhelmina. He was continually showering her with presents: chocolate, coffee, a fur coat, a set of silver cutlery and even a pianoforte.

Bilderdijk also often complained about the cold: 'In deepest winter, with no wood in the house [...] when I can stand it no longer I leave the house and walk the circumference of the town two or three times, come home and am warm again, and continue writing my lectures. On some evenings I have to do this three or four times in order to get warm.' When you know that he gave about fifty private lessons a week, for which he was well paid, it's impossible to believe these statements.

According to him, his wife only wore 'a little cotton dress', just like his children. He claimed he had never been able to offer anyone a cup of coffee. He didn't own stockings, only pieces of cloth that he tied around his knees and that reached into his boots. At the same time we know that he ate a piece of beef or lamb every noon, with a glass of wine. The daily consumption of meat and wine was regarded as a luxury. So the poverty can't have been all that bad.

After his return to the fatherland, in 1806, Bilderdijk had nothing to complain of most of the time. King Louis Napoleon gave him an ample stipend. Nevertheless, he wrote in 1807: 'Here we are again, in a damp, dilapidated and in every respect uninhabitable hole of a house, where one can't escape the wind or the cold.' How could this be, seeing that Bilderdijk received an annual salary of more than three thousand guilders? In 1809 this amount went up to six thousand guilders even, more than a professor earned at the time! Still there are continual complaints about poverty, in his poetry as well. According to him he was living on dry bread and barley water, while his wife and child fed themselves with potatoes dipped in vinegar. During this time, Bilderdijk wrote to a friend on a Friday: 'Since

Monday I have had to take opium because I didn't have any bread.'

In later years, too, Bilderdijk kept the image of the poor poet carefully intact. While living at the fashionable Rapenburg in Leiden, between 1819 and 1823, he complained: 'Everything is old and run-down, there are cracks between the boards and even between the bricks.' So he moved, but the new house wasn't satisfactory either. It was cold, the walls were crumbling and he was troubled by smoke, draughts and dampness. But the English poet laureate Robert Southey, who in 1825 stayed for three weeks with Bilderdijk in Leiden, had a different impression: 'The house is a good one, in a cheerful street, with a row of trees and a canal in front; large, and with everything good and comfortable about it', he wrote in a letter to his wife. Apparently Bilderdijk's account wasn't entirely truthful.

This mythologizing of his poverty shows that it was an important feature of his celebrity; in this way he emphasized the image of an artist who stood outside of society. Bilderdijk turned his own life into a myth.

Divinely inspired

Bilderdijk made a name for himself as a poet with the literary societies in the second half of the eighteenth century. To that end he conformed to their views about literature and adopted the classical way of writing. He even let the members 'civilize' his work to their heart's content. Later he disdainfully distanced himself from this practice. Around 1806 Bilderdijk began to push the image of the inspired poet. 'The Art of Poetry', which he recited in 1809, is generally regarded as a milestone in this process. In it he criticized the pedants from his youth, who 'with pumice, plane and files' had ruined poetry. The true poet is a visionary. When he gets into a trance, he proclaims higher truths. In 1808 he described what happened when he was inspired. He would rise up like an eagle and see himself surrounded by lights. It should be noted that this rising up to higher spheres had a metaphysical dimension for Bilderdijk. An aesthetic experience was also a religious one for him. Bilderdijk literally believed that he was in touch with God.

To the outside world Bilderdijk made it appear that when he wrote poetry he found himself in a higher dimension, one that wasn't accessible to normal human beings. He didn't write what he wanted himself, but what a higher power dictated to him. He would be nervous and feverish and feel his heartbeat accelerating and his blood coursing faster through his veins. At such moments he felt he was inspired by God and that the poetry was coming by itself, like water from a fountain. This outpouring was comparable to an orgasm. To a friend he once graphically likened it to the way a woman in childbed pushes out the afterbirth.

The writing of true poetry was the outpouring of an overwhelming feeling, as involuntary as weeping or laughing: 'An outpouring of feeling that demands air, that has to expand, that has to communicate, that has to multiply or the heart would burst.' A real poet didn't write poetry in his armchair. That was the image Bilderdijk wanted to project. He liked to present himself as the inspired poet who spoke in verse for nights on end. But this was undoubtedly also a pose. His rough drafts tell a different story. They make it clear that Bilderdijk's poems didn't just flow faultlessly onto the paper. They are full of deletions, scribbles, underlining and corrections. They only reached their final form after lots of sanding and editing. In short, Bilderdijk also mythologized the way he wrote his poetry.

A chosen worm

Being famous would seem to conflict with Bilderdijk's Calvinist principles, with values like humility and modesty at their core. How can we explain this paradox? Although as a Calvinist, Bilderdijk might declare that he was a worm, with his public image he made it appear that he was a messenger from God. For did he not suffer from the melancholy that was typical for a genius, did he not experience poverty the way a real poet should, and did he not receive divine inspiration? Man might be sinful and small, but this didn't really apply to Bilderdijk. He was a chosen one, who had to show his fellow men the way. And that required a special image. That's why Bilderdijk is regarded as one of the most eccentric poets in Dutch literary history. ▪

Translated by Pleuke Boyce

Bilderdijk on his deathbed by Gerrit Jan Michaëlis, 1831. Collection Bilderdijk Museum Amsterdam

Two Poems
By Willem Bilderdijk

Tobacco-Smoking (1828)

    He did with Godforsaken hand
Break his old father's neck indeed
Who first that fatal stinking weed
    Imported to the Fatherland.
He gave the loathsome worm-like brood
Of weak and filthy languor food
    With this brain-drugging magic dust:
He smothered muscle-power and zeal,
Robbed poor mankind of life's appeal,
    For this drunken and swooning lust. –

Where am I? In what hell of need?
    At every footstep that I take,
I breathe in horrid clouds of weed
    That make my chest and airways ache.
How my heart and my innards turn,
When all these stinking oils now burn
    And the poison spreads through the air,
Round the body with a painful sting
And does this count as catering,
    Festive greeting and kindly care? –

Oh Golden Age old folk adored
    When the traditional good cheer
New strength into the bloodstream poured
    With such tasty and wholesome beer!
Yet, France, with your poisonous brews
That both palate and taste confuse
    This poison's firm place is allowed.
Let those who like it smoke with wine;
For me that incense will not shine
    For me, I need no noxious cloud.

'Het tabakrooken'

    Die heb met Godvergeten hand
Zijns grijzen vaders nek gebroken,
Die 't eerst dat heilloos stinkend rooken
    Heeft ingevoerd in 't Vaderland.
Hy gaf 't verachtlijk wormgebroedsel
Der laffe en vuile luiheid, voedsel
    In breinbedwelmingstooverrust:
Hy was 't die vlijt en spierkracht doofde,
En 't menschdom's levens waarde roofde
    Voor dronkenschap der zwijmellust. –

Waar ben ik? in wat Hel van rampen?
    Op ieder voetstap waar ik treê,
Omwalmt my 't walglijk onkruiddampen,
    En doet my borst en longen wee.
Hoe keert my 't hart en de ingewanden,
Wanneer dit stinkende oliebranden
    Zijn gif door heel de lucht verspreidt,
In 't lichaam om met pijnlijk wringen!
En geldt dit voor versnaperingen,
    Voor feestonthaal en lieflijkheid? –

ô Gouden tijd van onze Vaderen,
    Toen de ouderwetsche goede sier
Vernieuwde krachten stortte in de aderen
    In 't smaaklijk voedzaam garstenbier!
Doch, Frankrijk, ja by uw venijnen
Van aangezette valsche wijnen
    Heeft ook dit gif zijn rechte plaats.
Welaan, het moogwien 't lust vermaken;
Voor my zal nooit die wierook blaken;
    Voor my geen stinkend dampgeblaas!

Funeral (1827)

No muffled drum
Nor mourners' hum
Must rattle rum tum
Before my bones;
No bells that thrum
From minster dumb
Must cry 'well come'
To my grave's stones;
No throng dense, glum
Walk stiff and dumb
No garland or plum
Crêpe's creases rum
Round me keep mum
My scanty bones.
My years have come
To their full sum,
Eyes dim with scum;
Age's bared gum
Calls blind and numb
To what death owns.

What should I, though,
Robbed of the glow
Of heaven's rainbow
Want here in earth's bower?
No courage or show,
No lance or bow,
No soldiers' row,
Can avert death's hour.
No dance, hoho,
No dice's throw,
No wreath or bow,
Or ruling power.
Sand may go,
Grave winds blow,
It's useless so,
To honour ash sour.
His teeth below,
Archpriest we know,
Of mankind's woe,
Will overpower.

What's this to me,
Who from chains set free,
Hope eagerly
For my faith's plea,
Calamity
May defeat in state?
I combat with glee,
Though slips we see,
HE'll sustain me,
Who can stem this spate.
No tyranny,
No raging sea,
No hellish she
Of Sophistry,
No need, if we
In Jesus' lee
Don't dare demonstrate!
His angels free
He groups to be
Guardians round our head.
No doom can desolate.

'Uitvaart'

Befloersde trom
Noch rouwgebrom
Ga romm'lende om
Voor mijn gebeente;
Geen klokgebom
Uit hollen Dom
Roep 't wellekom
In 't grafgesteente;
Geen dichte drom
Volg' stroef en stom;
Festoen noch blom
Van krepgefrom
Om 't lijk, vermomm'
Mijn schaamlekleente!
Mijn jaartal klom
Tot volle som,
Mijn oog verglom;
En de ouderdom
Roept blind en krom
Ter doodsgemeente.

Wat zoude ik thands,
Beroofd der glans
Van 's hemels trans,
Op de aard begeeren?
Geen moed des mans,
Geen spies of lans,
Geen legerschans,
Kan 't sterfuur keeren.
Geen spel of dans,
Geen dobbelkans,
Geen lauwerkrans,
Of Rijkbeheeren.
Een handvol zands
Des grafkuilrands
Is 't nietig gants,
Dat de asch mag eeren:
De beet des tands
Des Aartstyrans
Des menschenstands,
Zal 't lijk verteeren.

Doch wat 's dit my,
Die bandenvrij,
In 't uitzicht blij
Dat ik belij,
Op 't noodgetij'
Mag triomfeeren?
Ik juiche en strij';
Wat glippe of glij',
HY staat me by,
Die 't af kan weeren.
Geen dwinglandy,
Geen razerny,
Geen Helharpy
Van Sofistry,
Geen nood, dien wy
Aan Jezus zij'
Niet stout braveeren!
Zijne Englenrij
Verordent Hy
Tot wachters om ons hoofd.
Geen onheil kan ons deeren.

Translated by Paul Vincent

Three Letters

W. Bilderdijk to K.W. Schweickhardt
Brunswick, 19 February 1800

My only dearest!

I have only time to tell you I am somewhat better, and convey my-self this letter to the post: yes I sufferd these three days unspeakeably with heathache attended with some delirium. I am impatient of your intelligence. As for the present I am nearly well. Adieu, my dear all of bliss. Love me as tenderly as I love and adore you. Adieu.

W. Bilderdijk to K.W. Schweickhardt
Brunswick, 6 December 1800

My soul's beloved!

Your dear longed for letter was a balm to my sad, wounded heart. Surely, my dearest, I am in the wrong torturing my-self with melancholy thoughts, which avail nothing, and which are unworthy a soul penetrated with thankfull adoration of God's all-gracious Providence; but it seems, these days of darkness of mind are the effect of that debility and illness I am fallen in and which did not leave me wholly. – As for the eruption, my beloved, I do n't perceive any more, and what was left on my hands dryes up under the use of the salve. Yet I am plagued with a terrible itching, more than before; and I want opium in order to rest a few ours at night. I continue also taking daily purgatifs: and as I am sure these are indispensably wanted in our cases, I pray do n't cease the use of them, my alldearest, as well for you self, as for the dear Julius. A long time we shall be obliged taking such remedies; for there's no great probability that the body will be cleaned sufficiently before the spring, when the changement of air and food, and convenient motion, easely will restore us to a perfect health. But till then, we ought to be carefull on our-selve, that not some neglect may cause us some relaps.

My head is so embarrassed, my dearest, that I can n't write. Therefore I will conclude and bid you adieu! Embrace our lovely child for us both, and love me as fervently and tenderly as I love you, my only bliss on Earth! Adieu a thousand times!

W. Bilderdijk to K.W. Schweickhardt
Hamburg, 13-15 March 1806

No, nobody suffered what I am deemed to! I can n't hold the pen, nor withhold myself from crying aloud! – Heaven, see down, see down, and at least make an end of such an ill-fate! No, a life in the utmost happiness, this world could afford, would not compensate one hour of what I feel of distresses.

My fever encreased violently yesterday at the lecture of your letter, and continues. Yet I had some rest to night. Heaven give, your next letter may rejoice my soul as this depressed and accabled me. – Every fingertop is me wound and open with apostema's [abscesses], so that I can n't hold the pen. – Adieu my soul's only delight, my heart's only love! God be with you and our dear Children! Be quiet and love your tender and unhappy

Bilderdyk

From: *Mr. W. Bilderdijk's briefwisseling 1798-1806.*
Ed. M. van Hattum. Utrecht 2007.

Alors On Danse

Twenty-Five Years of Dance Music in the Low Countries

[MATTIAS BAERTSOEN]

The renowned music magazine DJ Mag annually ranks the hundred best DJs in the world. In 2014 the Dutch DJ Hardwell was in first place for the second time and, moreover, all of those in the top five were for the first time from either Belgium or the Netherlands. This is not by accident, as over the last twenty-five years the Low Countries have helped shape electronic dance music and have been the source of numerous evolutions and revolutions.

The sound of Belgium

For Europe, the late seventies and early eighties were a miserable time. The Cold War was at its peak, the depression led to economic decline, and in some countries ultra-conservative governments came to power. The anarchic and subversive punk and the darker new wave pushed aside the frivolous disco music that had brightened up the seventies. By experimenting with heavy, impassive beats, such Flemish groups as The Neon Judgement and Front 242 made this darker new wave music a touch more danceable.

Several years later the sound of The New Judgement and Front 242 formed the basis of a new movement that unfolded in Belgium: 'new beat'. This genre took shape by chance when the DJ Marc Grouls had some fun with the speed at which he played Flesh, a disk by the Belgian electrowave group A Split Second. Instead of playing it at 45 rpm he used 33⅓. His night-owl listeners found the sluggish, monotonous sound of the music hugely intriguing. Grouls was a DJ at the Boccaccio, a club in Destelbergen, near Ghent, where new beat made its breakthrough; a place that appeals to the imagination. Grouls stuck to the same slow tempo all night. In 1988, the British pop magazine *i-D* wrote that walking into the Boccaccio in Ghent was like entering a distorted version of life in slow motion. 2500 people were dancing round rigidly, moving their limbs like robots at half speed. Every weekend the Boccaccio filled up with party-goers from all over the country, and from France, Germany and the Netherlands too. There is no statutory closing time for clubs, so at five in the morning you often still had to queue up for hours to get in.

But what exactly was this new beat? In *The Sound of Belgium*, a 2012 documentary by Jozef Deville that charts the history of dance music in Belgium, one party-goer offers a very telling definition of the genre: 'It is more like a manufactured sound than a true musical genre. The music is made more by technicians than musicians'.

New beat was born in unlit attics and sounds as pitch-black as the night, perfect for the night owls who only come to life in the dark. The heavy synthesizers and repetitive nature of new beat were a blueprint for the techno music that was to follow. Clubbers were mad about this new sound, but it also had a great many opponents: several magazines scoffed at new beat, and the national broadcaster refused to play the music and considered it scandalous that such a thing should be shipped abroad. New beat was nevertheless a huge success, and sales of some records easily reached 60,000. Flemish DJs were hot property in England and 'Mixed in Belgium' was printed on the record sleeves to stimulate sales. New beat went beyond just the music, and expanded into a real subculture with its own style of dress; the ingredients of the look were black boots, Volkswagen badges and devotional pictures and smileys printed on T-shirts.

As a genre, new beat vanished as quickly as it had appeared. In 1989, barely three years after its breakthrough, the pursuit of profit had completely swamped creativity. New beat acts drove from club to club in a minibus, and landed up to a thousand euro for a mimed show lasting barely twenty minutes. The crude number *The Sound of C* by The Confetti's – named after a discotheque in Brasschaat – was the kiss of death for new beat. The barman in the nightclub served as the band's mascot, the number was recorded in just three hours, and it was outstanding in its senselessness. The fans from the early days gave up on it, calling it 'nougat beat' by analogy with that sickly-sweet confection. The advent of Ecstasy (XTC), the perfect party drug, also helped new beat to its doom. The police raided nightclubs in search of drugs, and in barely six weeks seven of the largest clubs had to close down, including the Boccaccio.

Yet in the course of its short life new beat laid the foundations for the future. In Ghent, only a few kilometres' drive from the Boccaccio, Renaat Vandepapeliere and his wife set up R&S Records while new beat was at its height, and it grew

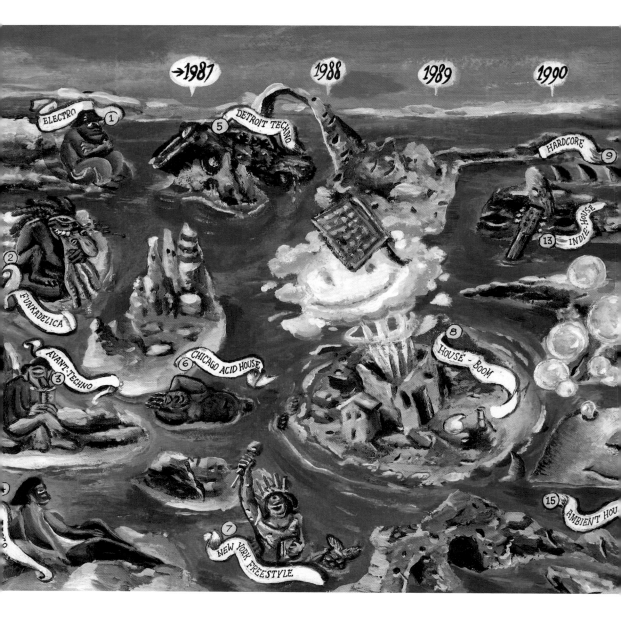

Land of a Thousand Dancers, an illustration by Typex for an article about dance, published in the Dutch music magazine *Oor* in 1993. At the time the picture was cut up and scattered throughout the article. This is the first time the original picture has been published whole. It was also the very first illustration Typex ever made, Mutsaers Collection / © Typex.

into one of the world's best and most well-respected labels for electronic music. It was internationally-oriented from the very beginning. It gave the American techno pioneers Derrick May and Joey Beltram and the British innovator Aphex Twin the opportunity to launch their first numbers. Vandepapeliere set up his own studio at his home, filling it with equipment the artists could use. When it got late, or if they came from overseas, he offered them overnight accommodation. Another label that appeared during the glory days of new beat was Antler-Subway, the brainchild of Maurice Engelen. He approached it as a businessman and producer, but also as the founder of the dance bands Praga Khan and Lords Of Acid. Through these groups, Engelen exported new beat to America and Asia. With success. Lords Of Acid gave hundreds of sell-out concerts in America and Japan, with such leading acts as The Prodigy and Rammstein as their supporting act. In his home country, it was only years later that Engelen received recognition for his pioneering work.

The terror of nothingness

Dance music also established itself in the Netherlands at about the same time as the breakthrough of new beat. After visiting the dazzling nightclubs of New York, the Flemish DJ Eddy De Clercq wanted to create the same atmosphere in Amsterdam. He was the first to play American house music numbers on the European continent. He opened the RoXY nightclub in Amsterdam and himself took to the turntables every Friday. In 1988 it was he who created *Pay the Piper*, the first house number in the Netherlands. Like new beat, house – commonly known as 'acid' – met with plenty of criticism. Journalists referred to 'the terror of nothingness'. De Clercq put a large part of its success down to this criticism. The more intense the opposition, the better the movement. That was also one of the major reasons for continuing, as he told the Dutch music magazine *Oor*.

Another Dutch metropolis, Rotterdam, focused on techno, the cool, hard counterpart to house music. Under the name Speedy J, Jochem Paap issued records on such renowned international labels as Plus 8 and Warp Records. He sold more than a million copies of his biggest hit *Pullover*. Dance was hot, and parties – legal and otherwise – were held in clubs, squats and warehouses. But, just as in Belgium, drug use flourished in the Netherlands and the police closed down a great many nightclubs, often with a considerable show of force. They brought a heavy-handed end to club culture, but not to dance culture. On the contrary. In 1989, the DJ Paul Jay, a member of the Soho Connection that united British and Dutch DJs, spoke the following prophetic words: 'I believe that house has opened a lot of Dutch eyes and is only the beginning of the establishment of a lasting dance culture in the Netherlands.'

In the early 1990s, producers in both Belgium and the Netherlands substantially increased the tempo of the music. The public wanted its music faster and louder: 'harddance' and 'hardcore' made their appearance. In Belgium, Christian Pieters, aka DJ Fly, set up Bonzai Records in 1992. One of its first releases was Thunderball's *Bonzai Channel One*. The number's rapid rhythms and high tempo meant it was labelled as harddance. The Bonzai Sound conquered dance floors all over Europe in no time at all. The tempo of the numbers rose to 140 beats per minute (bpm), a huge difference from new beat, which remained at about 90 bpm. The Dutch variant of harddance was called hardcore, and here the tempo went even higher. In the book *Mary Go Wild*, an overview of 25 years of dance music in the Netherlands published in 2013, DJ Dano, one of the pioneers of hardcore, says: 'How far could I take my audience? The answer turned out to be 370 bpm, beyond that they just stood still, ha ha! On one occasion I was the opening act at the Hemkade, but funnily enough the room remained empty. It turned out that the First Aid room was full, because people had started shaking *en masse*. The tempo was too much!'

Champagne, caviar & groupies

With hindsight, hardcore is not the most refined product the Netherlands has ever come up with, and the marketing and merchandising machine that was set in motion was possibly even more important than the music. The caps, T-shirts and mousepads printed with the Bonzai logo were at least as lucrative as the records. DJ Fly talked about this success in the Flemish weekly *Humo*: 'One day we received information from customs that in Antwerp they had intercepted a container from Asia that was full of T-shirts, half hardrock and half Bonzai, all fake.' In the Netherlands, 'hardcore' suddenly turned into 'happy hardcore', which gave the genre a more positive allure. This was followed by compilation albums, parties, T-shirts, magazines and its own programmes on radio and TV. Three Dutch friends, Irfan van Ewijk, Duncan Stutterheim and Theo Lelie, set up the ID&T events agency and in 1992 launched the all-embracing Thunderdome concept, which was the foundation of their success. ID&T expanded into the biggest party organisation in the world. For the first time champagne, caviar and groupies all appeared on the scene.

By 1998 hardcore was on the way out. Just as with the decline of new beat, the initial fans turned up their noses at its extreme commercialisation. Dance music split up into all manner of subgenres and the Netherlands concentrated on a melodious offshoot with lots of catchy, stirring synthesizer phrases; it was called 'trance'. The roots of this genre lay in Germany, but it was three Dutchmen who put trance on the world map: Ferry Corsten, Armin Van Buuren and DJ Tiësto (later to become simply 'Tiësto'). When Ferry Corsten issued *Out of*

The Blue under his alias System F in 1999, the joint really started jumping. As Corsten tells us in the book *Mary Go Wild*: 'Suddenly every door was open. I was called by the Ministry of Sound [a trendsetting London dance empire with several clubs and a record label, MB] to ask whether I wanted to mix *Trance Nation* [an acclaimed compilation album, MB]. Note that I wasn't even a DJ! But you can't refuse an offer like that. That first compilation immediately sold 400,000 copies. ... Then I heard from all the major English clubs. ... *Out of The Blue* sent everything into overdrive. One request after another came in. ... And then Bono called. At that moment it suddenly dawned on me: wow... here I am just talking to Bono of U2 on the phone!'

In 2002 *DJ Mag* for the first time proclaimed Tiësto the best DJ in the world, an honour he was later to receive twice more. Van Buuren and Corsten followed in fifth and ninth place. DJ Tiësto's success reached its peak in 2004, when he performed before the eyes of the world at the opening ceremony for the Olympic Games in Athens. The Dutch DJs turned into the pop stars of their generation.

The trance that Corsten, Van Buuren and Tiësto produced sounded quite euphoric; it was music that was 'bigger than life', too big for the smaller clubs. In addition, after the turn of the century we started experiencing music in a different way: party-goers shared photos and film clips via the internet and social media to show how much enjoyment they derived from going out. ID&T understood this and started up a number of impressive events both indoors and outdoors. The visual aspect became more important than ever: huge sets were custom-made for the chosen theme. Then there were circus acts, laser shows, fireworks, side stages and delicious food. ID&T made Mysteryland the biggest dance festival in the Netherlands, with 60,000 visitors a year. This was followed by Innercity, launched by DJ Tiësto, and Sensation, a dance party in the Ajax football stadium in Amsterdam that pulled out all the stops to create an all-round spectacular. In 2011 no less than 1.5 million dance-lovers attended one of the major festivals in the Netherlands. ID&T is also the driving force behind Tomorrowland, which is held in Flanders and, since the first one in 2005, has grown into the biggest dance festival in the world, with no less than 400,000 visitors in 2014.

Dirty Dutch

ID&T exported its open-air festivals all over the world, and Sensation has so far been organised in 22 countries. In 2013 140,000 party-goers turned up in the Chattahoochee Hills in the American state of Georgia for TomorrowWorld, a smaller version of Tomorrowland. Over there they are currently crazy about the European beat offered by the Frenchman David Guetta and the Swedish Avicii. Though it is the Dutchmen Afrojack, Hardwell and Nicky Romero that respond best to the wishes of American dance fans, who like their dance music on a large scale. This has led to the term Dutch Big Room House, Dutch House for short, or else Dirty Dutch. This is dance music suited to huge festival sites, with several climaxes in each individual number. The melodious nature of trance as played by Tiësto and Van Buuren was combined with the hard beats of house music and the cool of hip hop. Dirty Dutch caught on: Coachella, the major American rock festival, acquired a separate dance stage where the performers were almost all Dutch. It is as if they were minting money: in its list of the best-paid DJs of 2014, the American business magazine *Forbes* put Tiësto in third place (28 million dollars), with Afrojack at six (22 million dollars) and Hardwell at eleven (13 million dollars).

In another list, of the hundred best DJs in the world as drawn up by *DJ Mag*, Hardwell is right at the top. The Flemish brothers Dimitri Vegas & Like Mike, and the Dutchmen Armin Van Buuren, Martin Garrix and Tiësto complete the top five. At the time Martin Garrix was barely eighteen years old and was one of a new generation of Dutch youngsters who, as adolescents, uploaded a number onto the net and, before they knew it were travelling the world and being asked to perform as DJs in the most renowned clubs. They have benefited from the success of their predecessors and can rely on professional organisational structures.

Yet in the Netherlands people are also worried. In 2013 ID&T was bought by SFX, the dance empire headed by the American media mogul Robert F.X. Sillerman, though ID&T retains the decision-making in the creative process. Donald Stutterheim, one of the founders, emphasises that money is necessary to continue exporting their mega-concepts, and he has become the CEO of SFX Europe. When SFX also bought Awakenings, another of ID&T's showpieces, for millions of dollars in 2014, reactions were very harsh. ID&T defends itself by saying that in the meantime it is more the rule than the exception to be bought up by SFX.

A new standard

Questions are also being asked about the present state of the dance scene in Belgium. The pioneer Renaat Vandepapeliere gave vent to his feelings on the *Clash Music* website: 'When I go out, it's not the same vibe anymore. I see the kids and I think they're missing something. Now you get a list of very expensive DJs, big lights, and a big sound system, but when you walk in you can smell the money.'

In recent years Belgium has fallen substantially behind the rest of Europe. There is no organised scene as there is in the Netherlands and the centre of European electronic music has shifted to London and Berlin. There are some noteworthy success stories, however, such as the Ghent brothers Stephen and David Dewaele (2 Many DJ's) who in 2002 set a new standard with their compilation album *As Heard on Radio Soulwax Vol. 2*. The brothers cut up existing hits and then ingeniously pasted them back together again. This yielded daring combinations that had never previously been heard: the vocals from Destiny's Child were superimposed over Nirvana's hard guitar work, and those of Salt-N-Pepa over Iggy & The Stooges. *The New York Times* declared the album record of the year; David Bowie and Kylie Minogue are fans and 2 Many DJ's play for dancers at the hippest parties in the world.

The young Flemish drum-and-bass producer Boris Daenen, aka Netsky, is also an international success and, in addition, young Flemish producers are occasionally able to issue their records on a foreign label or supply a remix for an international star such as Beyoncé. In Belgium, though, all eyes are currently focused on the phenomenon called Paul Van Haver, aka Stromae. In 2009 he achieved a number one hit in more than ten countries with *Alors On Danse*. This was followed by *Papaoutai, Formidable* and other hits. Stromae performs at European venues and is gradually conquering the United States. In late 2014 no less a figure than Madonna invited him to her New York apartment to talk about possible collaboration. In interviews he declares that he is influenced by Jacques Brel, but also by Technotronic, the successful group headed by Jo Bogaert, who actually took his first steps as a producer during the 'new beat' period.

I mention this simply to show what things can lead to, things that started about twenty-five years ago in squats and small clubs and were dismissed as crude and repugnant. In this quarter of a century, dance music has expanded into a billion-euro business. The Flemish and the Dutch played a part as international pioneers: the ID&T party organisation developed into a market leader and the youthful producers on the Dirty Dutch scene nowadays fly straight from their classrooms to America, where they perform for tens of thousands of party-goers. And Belgium is home to Tomorrowland, the biggest music festival in the world.

Not bad at all for a movement which, according to the Netherlands' leading pop journalist when the first reports of house music appeared about a quarter of a century ago, would never amount to anything. 'None of it's worth any more than a postage stamp,' he said in 1988. How could he have known that in 2014 the faces of the Dutch DJs Tiësto, Hardwell, Armin Van Buuren, Dash Berlin and Afrojack would be immortalised on... a postage stamp? ▪

Translated by Gregory Ball

Tomorrowland, Boom, Flanders

Foreign Language Learning in the Low Countries

[LUDO BEHEYDT]

The situation regarding foreign language learning has changed considerably in the Dutch-speaking region over the last ten years. In the first place, this has to do with changing social realities. The language landscape in the Low Countries has undergone rapid change. Urban areas of Flanders and the Netherlands have in fact quickly become multilingual. For example, we only have to look at official figures for home languages in Flanders for 2011-2012 to be confronted with a number of surprises: in urban areas in Antwerp, 46% of the children do not speak Dutch as their home language. For Ghent the figure is 37% and for Mechelen 33%. Almost one child in eight in Flemish primary education speaks a language other than Dutch at home. This means that Flanders, like the Netherlands in fact, can now be characterised as linguistically super-diverse, for not only is cultural diversity increasing yearly, language diversity is as well. Likewise, more than a hundred different home languages are spoken in the Brussels Capital Region. This means that more or less half the children begin school speaking a language other than the official language of instruction. As far as foreign language instruction is concerned this implies that for many children regular education is actually foreign language instruction from the very outset.

In addition to this, as a result of increasing demographic diversity, globalisation and internationalisation both in Flanders and in the Netherlands, there is a growing need for an international lingua franca designed to serve both the present Babylonian internal diversity and the mobility of the youth and the employed. Much more frequently than before, speakers have to rely on another language or lingua franca to survive in various situations in our multilingual and multicultural society.

Moreover, a new attitude has arisen with regard to languages. In traditional foreign language teaching, languages were linked to their respective nations. French was the language of France and was considered a normative and monolithic standard language and its classically correct use deemed to be followed and respected. The same was the case for English, Oxford English being the ideal. Times have changed and in the meantime common language varieties and their usage have become much more acceptable. In multilingual environments, the varieties used by second language speakers have come to be considered as genuine varieties. The normative use that was required ten years ago,

along with its grammar book and dictionary, has since made way for tolerance for 'understandable varieties'. A multilingual speaker is no longer expected to be lexically and grammatically perfect and this is also clearly visible in foreign language education. The formerly strict, code-oriented foreign language education with its exclusive emphasis on grammar and vocabulary has given way to communicative language instruction along with an explicit shift in focus towards language use and mutual comprehensibility. The mastery of form is no longer the first requirement, communicative efficiency being more important.

European language policy and the Low Countries

These social changes have also had an influence on European language policy and will surely change European foreign language instruction in a profound way. Following the conference on *Multilingualism in Europe* in 2006, the European Union formulated the recommendation known as 'the one plus two principle', i.e. that besides providing mother-tongue instruction schools should also place instruction in two other European Union languages on their curriculum in order to promote European diversity and intercultural understanding and combat the dominance of any single language. To quote their 2006 recommendation literally, 'Multilingualism is an important part of our European identity which should be cherished and nurtured. If one lingua franca is allowed to predominate there is a risk that other national languages will suffer a loss of function (for example fewer written texts). To avoid this it is essential to increase our efforts to promote multilingualism.' In the meantime, the fear expressed here has increasingly become reality. The dominance of English has become considerable in the Low Countries. In his now notorious book, *Words of the World. The Global Language System* (2001), Abraham de Swaan remarked that the third language is no longer necessary. His advice was the following: 'Learn the national language as well as possible, then learn English as well as possible and only then learn a third language if it proves useful, advantageous or pleasing.' The Dutch government has obviously taken this advice to heart for, according to Article 9 of the Law on Primary Education, only English is mandatory as the

second language in Dutch primary schools. The situation for Flemings is some-what different, because besides Flanders, which is a monolingual region, there is also the officially bilingual region of Brussels. In the Brussels Capital Region, French is the first mandatory modern language for all pupils attending Dutch-medium primary schools, which means they receive instruction three hours per week from the second year on and five hours per week in the third and fourth grade (Art. 10 of the 1963 Language Law). In Flanders, French is still manda-tory as the first foreign language from the fifth year on in primary schools, but English can also be chosen as one's first foreign language in secondary school. Since 2011 introductory courses in English and German are also allowed in primary education. We also notice a gradual shift to more English instruction in Flanders. In June 2014, the Rector of Ghent University, Anne De Paepe, made a plea for more English medium programmes at Bachelor level 'to attract more international students and scientists'. Her Dutch colleague, Rector Magnificus Carel Stolker, is of the same opinion. He wrote the following in the 2014 re-view *Neerlandia*: 'The Anglicisation of academia cannot be stopped. Our 'own' MA students receive an increasing number of lessons in English and that will soon be the case for many bachelor students'. The stealthy changeover to the dominant language of English in higher education in the Low Countries will of course not be without consequence for foreign language instruction.

Bilingual education

If fluency in English is expected at the beginning of an academic programme, schools will necessarily have to take this into account. And we can already see this happening both in Flanders and in the Netherlands. One of the most striking changes in foreign language instruction is undoubtedly the adoption of bilingual immersion methods. Flanders is rather hesitant in this respect. As a result of the 2011 *Language Policy Document* schools may, as of 2013, start providing CLIL (Content and Language Integrated Learning) in which parts of the curriculum (factual subjects such as biology, mathematics, history, etc.) can be taught in a foreign language. CLIL schools are now appearing in Flanders – exclusively in secondary education for the time being – at which a maximum of one fifth of fac-tual subjects are taught in French, English or German. For this a CLIL standard has been developed that sets conditions which a school must satisfy in order to offer CLIL. In comparison to the Netherlands, Flanders is only reluctantly get-ting started with bilingual education. The situation in the Netherlands is more drastic. Of course, the reticence in Flanders is to some extent understandable. In a social environment in which Dutch is still on the defensive, the introduction of bilingual education is felt as being language and culture threatening, cer-tainly in Brussels, where French is felt to be the dominant language in society.

This fear is absent in the Netherlands. There, in 2008, the Board of Education suggested without further ado in its *Foreign Languages in Education* advisory document that 'English be partly made an official medium in primary education for a maximum of 15 percent of school time'. In the meantime, the immer-sion method has really taken off in the Netherlands. An increasing number of schools have begun experimenting with bilingual education and, in places where bilingual education was originally limited to the more difficult sections of secondary education intended to prepare students for university, it is now spreading to the mid-range sections and even vocational training. Of the more or less five hundred schools that offer a pre-university section, almost one in twenty have a bilingual stream providing factual subjects such as history, biology and physical education in a language other than the mother tongue. In September 2014 the following major step will be taken: twelve Dutch primary schools will commence a full bilingual programme. From infant school onwards, children will be instructed half of the time in English. The State Secretary for Education, Culture and Science, Sander Dekker announced this already in January 2014 and his reasons for doing so are significant: 'Dutch children will later on earn their crust in a world in which it will be more important than ever before to be able to speak English well, in addition to speaking Dutch. It is exactly when they are young that they can pick up a language with playful ease. Indeed, what's learnt in the cradle lasts till the tomb. Moreover, offering a foreign language early on in school makes education more challenging for talented pupils that have a gift for languages.' This is only in the experimental phase at the moment. In 2015 another 8 schools will be able to join this pilot scheme for fully bilingual education. If by 2019 the experiment carried out in these 20 primary schools should prove successful, the decision can be taken to allow more schools to convert to bilingual education. Only then will the Anglicisation of Dutch education really begin. Of course, this will call for a complete transformation of foreign language teaching, for the simultaneous provision of school subjects along with a totally new language will require a specific approach. But the Dutch have been preparing this for a long time. The Ministry for Education, Culture and Science have handed over the coordination and supervision of bilingual education to the European Platform, which set up a network for bilingual education back in 1994 and has even developed a set of bilingual education standards. Furthermore, this education system is being scientifically supervised and followed very closely. A team of researchers from Groningen University have already conducted research into the design and results of bilingual education in the Netherlands. They have published a detailed report on the research bearing a title that cannot be misunderstood: *A sustainable advantage. The findings of a study into bilingual education.*

One thing is immediately clear, bilingual education has the wind in its sails and the question now is whether traditional foreign language instruction will be able to handle the increasing competition from bilingual education. This explosive success is nonetheless somewhat surprising as there are as yet insufficient guarantees concerning the results of bilingual education and immersion methods. Even the research carried out by the team in Groningen does not justify the uncritically jubilant title of its report. The report only covers schools offering pre-university education that have opted with unqualified enthusiasm for bilingual education and that provide it, moreover, only for a target group of students that are amongst the strongest part of the school-going population. For students like these with this type of motivation, bilingual education does indeed seem to be an unqualified plus. But whether such elitist results can be extrapolated to education in general is very questionable. More specifically, there is the issue of whether children who speak another home language – Berber, Turkish, Polish, Chinese, etc. – will benefit from Dutch English bilingual education or whether English may not form an extra threshold for those who are still struggling with the first language threshold. Moreover, it is doubtful whether children who do not have above-average school skills will be able to handle the extra pressure of bilingual education. In a recent report in *Mens en Maatschappij* (September 2014) Inge Sieben and Nathalie van Ginderen from Tilburg University actually show that the risk of increasing social inequality caused by the introduction of bilingual education is clearly present.

Traditional foreign language instruction

Anyhow, the vast majority of pupils will still receive traditional foreign language instruction. But that too has undergone a number of changes. Firstly, two major changes have been introduced as far as the objectives of foreign language instruction are concerned. Attention to the code aspects of language, i.e.grammar and vocabulary, has given way to communicative skills. The learner has now primarily to be able to carry out a number of efficient speech acts, such as the expression of wishes, requests, orders, needs, advice, apologies, etc. But these objectives no longer suffice. The huge influx of migrants, the globalisation of culture and the rise in the number of international contacts over the internet or through exchange programmes, among other things, have added one essential task to the objectives of foreign language instruction, i.e. the fostering of intercultural relations. The 'intercultural speaker' is a learner who is aware of the culture specificity of language use and has some knowledge of cultural background, and based on this has developed the skill to analyse and interpret unknown cultural phenomena, thanks to which he/she is better able to understand the other. The ultimate goal in this case is the development of intercultural competence that allows the learner to function as a mediator between his/her own culture and the target culture.

Given the super-diversity in which the Low Countries find themselves, this has now become the central goal. And because the learner group has become so diverse, a set of teaching methods has to be found that can address and make use of such diversity. The fact that homogeneous Dutch-speaking classes are becoming a rarity should lead us to deal consciously with linguistic heterogeneity in multicultural classrooms. Pupils from very different cultural backgrounds, who speak different home languages, who are also used to very different culture-specific learning methods are now sitting next to each other in class and have to take on the same task, i.e. learning a foreign language. The solution to the problem that is being increasingly put forward is the introduction of task-based language learning. Task-based learning is designed to get pupils in heterogeneous classrooms to participate together in a shared task – each at their own level, using their own cultural resources – by drawing on their own specific language skills. In task-based learning, pupils no longer receive language lessons in the traditional sense of the term but have to complete a task together in which they use the target language both receptively and productively, while paying more attention to meaning than form. Such tasks are complete in themselves and have to be accomplished together by the pupils, using the foreign language and with the aid of the language teacher as an obliging coach. The teacher does not follow one or other orthodox teaching strategy but adapts creatively and flexibly to the pupils' learning styles and levels of language skill.

This does not mean that there are no final goals to be achieved. For such final goals, both Flanders and the Netherlands have unanimously agreed to use the same common European frame of reference. The *Common European Framework of Reference for Languages* (CEFR) is a descriptive framework that sets out various levels of functional language competence for all European languages. In the meantime, this CEFR, which was put forward by the Council of Europe in 2001, serves both in Flanders and the Netherlands as a standard guideline for education, educational methods, examination boards, and courses. All new methods and courses use it as a model and all universities and colleges of higher education use it as a threshold description for their language requirements. The framework distinguishes three traditional language users: basic users (A1 and A2), independent users (B1 and B2) and proficient users (C1 and C2). All foreign language instruction in the Low Countries is now based on this European descriptive framework. It is striking to note, however, that the framework provides no clear guidelines for testing and yet it is used as a placement test in schools and companies in the Netherlands and Flanders. It is also disappointing to see that this framework as yet contains no intercultural dimension, which means it cannot be used in intercultural language instruction.

We conclude here by mentioning the latest development in foreign language instruction, a development with which teaching methods have difficulty keeping up, and that is the technological revolution. Of course, there is no language course without a CD or a DVD nowadays, but as far as the use of ICT is concerned, it is very much a matter of paddling one's own canoe. How can we make the most of tablets, iPhones and apps? Is there a place for language teaching games? What didactic possibilities can Facebook, internet forums and voice recognition technology offer us? It is vital that technologists, linguists and teaching experts sit together and steer all this innovation.

Narrowed down to Basic English

It is probably clear by now that foreign language learning in the Low Countries is developing at a very fast rate as a result of social change. Increasing globalisation, explosive diversity and economic expectations all heighten the need to learn English as quickly as possible. The other languages are being pushed into a corner and the European wish for a 'mother tongue plus two' is steadily becoming a fantasy. And now that Flanders and the Netherlands are undermining language diversity in their language programmes, the fear that the once so-praised and valued foreign language skills of the Flemish and the Dutch will be narrowed down to *Basic English* is legitimate. ∎

All illustrations show details from Brueghel, *Tower of Babel*,
Kunsthistorisches Museum Vienna.

Translated by Peter Flynn

Vigsø, Denmark
Atlantic Wall
© Stephan Vanfleteren

Chronicle

Architecture

The Rediscovery of the Public Library
Birmingham Library by Mecanoo Architects

© Mecanoo Architects.

In this digital era, many people will find it incomprehensible that a library costing almost two hundred million pounds could be an asset to a city. But anyone who visits the new library in Birmingham designed by the Mecanoo architectural firm will soon change their mind.

Birmingham, the United Kingdom's second city in terms of population size, is best known for its industrial past. It has remained at the forefront of science, technology and economic development since the start of the Industrial Revolution. Numerous innovations have been developed there. Some even claim that the foundations of modern industrial society were laid in the city's plentiful craft workshops with all their creativity and innovation. The image of Birmingham is still that of a production city, although most of the workshops have vanished and the heart of the city is filled with modern office buildings. To rid itself of this persistent industrial image, Birmingham City Council has taken action in several ways, the most ambitious undoubtedly being the new library designed by Francine Houben of the Mecanoo architectural firm. The aim of the city council is to become one of the 'world's top 20 most livable cities' in the not too distant future.

In 2008 the Dutch firm Mecanoo won the international competition for which more than a hundred firms had submitted designs. Under the guidance of the Royal Institute of British Architects, a shortlist of seven architectural firms was drawn up: Foreign Office Architects, Foster and Partners, Hopkins Architects, OMA (Rem Koolhaas' firm), Schmidt Hammer Lassen, Wilkinson Eyre and Mecanoo. It was the last of these that received final approval. Mecanoo had previously designed the Technical Library at Delft University and in Birmingham, in close collaboration with the British engineering firm Buro Happold, they once again created a library that far transcends the notion simply of a collection of books under a roof.

Houben claims that 'libraries are the new cathedrals'. In addition to being a place for study, a library is above all a place for encounters. With an average of about 10,000 visitors a day, the building offers numerous opportunities to meet other people, but also to be alone. An agreeable spot can be found for every target group, calm or dynamic, study area or coffee bar, lounge or roof terrace. According to the designer, the library of the future will be active (and interactive). Encounter and interaction are focal points. For this reason, the new style of library is designed entirely as a social meeting place. It is an extension of the street, a true public space. Its lay-out is flexible, so that in the course of time its use can easily be adapted to changing needs and desires.

The library has been built on a former car park between the 1962 Repertory Theatre (REP) and the 1936 sandstone Baskerville House. The guidelines laid down that the REP could be demolished to make way for the new building. However, the design team opted to integrate the old REP into the new plan. In this way, the composition of the various existing volumes and the new building leaves open an old route leading from the neighbourhood behind it to the city centre. Mecanoo also provided the interior design for the renovation of the REP and the lay-out of the renewed outdoor Centenary Square. This enabled the complex to create strong links between past, present and future.

Although Birmingham is a reasonably green city, asphalt and concrete dominate the city centre as designed by the city planner Sir Herbert Manzoni after the Second World War. In this context, the roof terraces at three levels are agreeable oases where readers can relax or become absorbed in their studies.

The composition of the volumes is the result of the organisation of the programme of requirements. The rectangular volumes contain eight circular atria, arranged for the best possible distribution of natural light and the enhancement of natural ventilation. These circular spaces, surrounded by curved walls of books, were undoubtedly inspired by Mecanoo's earlier project in Delft. The atria also make it easy to view the building as a whole.

The library, 35,000 square metres in size, houses a study centre, a music library, a community health centre, rooms for multimedia, meetings and offices, exhibition areas, cafés, lounges and an auditorium. To limit the volume, a large part of the programme of requirements has been housed below ground around a circular sunken open-air amphitheatre.

The building is equipped with the latest technology so as to reduce energy consumption, and has thereby acquired the much-coveted BREEAM 'excellent' label. The circular metal ornamentation of the façade refers indirectly to the industrial crafts of the past, specifically gold- and silversmithing. It filters out harsh direct sunlight but retains transparency. The materials chosen for the floors - stone, ceramics and oak - mean that the building does not have the feel of a terminal or shopping mall. It assumes a domestic air, partly due to the unusual light entering through the facades.

This library houses several major collections. The undisputed highlight is the Shakespeare collection in the Shakespeare Memorial Room, originally built in 1882. When the original building was demolished in 1974, this interior by John Henry Chamberlain was moved to the old Central Library. Now it has once again been transferred to the new library. It is housed in a 'golden' volume in the upper half of the building.

This building has in the meantime won several prizes and is currently the largest public library in the United Kingdom. Some sources even claim that it is the largest public cultural space in Europe. Whether this is true or not, the building is indisputably a marvellous acquisition for Birmingham, and for lovers of architecture and culture it puts the city firmly on the map.

HARRY DEN HARTOG
Translated by Gregory Ball

Flanders' Films Go Hollywood

Let's begin by qualifying the title because it is slightly misleading, albeit intentionally so. 2014 saw the release in Belgian cinemas of new films by two talented and successful Flemish directors: *The Drop* by Michaël R. Roskam (° 1972) and *The Loft* by Erik Van Looy (° 1962).

These are English-language films and they were both filmed in America. Even before the films went into production, the Flemish newspapers were already giving wide coverage to both projects. Their respective cinema releases also attracted great media interest. It was in that context that the word 'Hollywood' regularly cropped up, often in titles and captions, for the combination of 'Flemish', 'film' and 'Hollywood' has a seductive ring, or at the very least it arouses the reader's curiosity.

For both directors this was their first American adventure. In the case of Erik Van Looy, also known for the thriller *The Memory of a Killer,* it was a remake of his 2008 box-office hit *Loft,* which attracted 1.2 million cinema-goers, a record for a Belgian film and one it will not be easy to break. Michaël R. Roskam, on the other hand, is a rather late-bloomer. He made his cinema debut in 2011 with *Bullhead*, which was an overnight success. Accolades were heaped on the film at home and abroad and, as the icing on the cake, it won an Oscar nomination for Best Foreign Language Film.

Flemish film directors who make a film for the big screen on the other side of the Atlantic are few and far between, even a touch exotic. And adventurous. Tintin in America as it were. But these two films have relatively little to do with Hollywood, if only because *The Drop* was filmed in New York and *The Loft* largely in New Orleans.

And why would a director want to produce a remake of a film he has already made? For Van Looy the answer is clear: 'I have always believed that Bart De Pauw's fantastic script deserves a global audience and the best way to achieve that is still an American remake. *The Loft* is a mainstream film, not a festival or art-house film'.

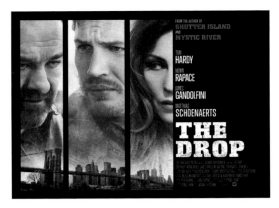
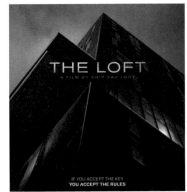

As *Loft* had been such a huge box-office success, some large Hollywood studios were interested in a remake. But then on their terms. Van Looy cites an amusing and telling anecdote in this regard: 'In the first exploratory talks there was a large Hollywood studio where they said: "Yes, we want to make the film and we don't want to change much. Only you can't have five men cheating on their wives. Can't we have them share that loft with two coming to watch basketball, two hockey and one cheating on his wife?" That's effectively what they said, but we didn't think it was a good idea.' So to retain as much control of the project as possible, *The Loft* was made as a coproduction between the Flemish production house *Woestijnvis* and the American independent film company Anonymous Content, known for (among other things) Alejandro González Iñárritu's *Babel* and Michel Gondry's *Eternal Sunshine of the Spotless Mind*.

Filming of the whodunit *The Loft* went off pretty much without a hitch, but the search for the right American distributor proved more problematic, even to the extent that the Belgian press began wondering out loud if Erik Van Looy's Hollywood adventure would ever get off the ground. But get off the ground it did, and at the end of January 2015 *The Loft* was released and on no fewer than 2,000 American movie screens.

Naturally, Michaël R. Roskalm's Oscar nomination for *Bullhead* had attracted the attention of American film studios. From the many offers that came his way, Roskalm chose *The Drop*, a contemporary crime drama set in Brooklyn and based on Animal Rescue, a short story by the famous American crime writer Dennis Lehane, whose novels *Mystic River* and *Shutter Island* had already been filmed by Clint Eastwood and Martin Scorsese respectively. *The Drop* is an atmospheric thriller set against the background of organized crime's use of local New York City bars as money-laundering 'drops'. Hence the title.

The project was financed by Fox Searchlight Pictures, the art-house sister company of the legendary Hollywood studio 20th Century Fox. Whereas in Europe the 'art-house' description is a sort of hallmark that can (still) be gaily bandied around, Fox Searchlight Pictures is less keen on it because to them it sounds arty-farty and so not commercial enough.

Before agreeing to the project, Roskam had stipulated his own terms: he wanted the cast of his American film debut to include Matthias Schoenaerts, the lead actor in *Bullhead*. He also wanted the Flemish director of photography Nicolas Karakatsanis back behind the camera. And so it was. By some remarkable coincidence, we also find the names of both Schoenaerts and Karakatsanis in the credits of *The Loft*. In fact, Schoenaerts is the only Flemish actor who also appeared in the original *Loft*.

Naturally, for the rest of his cast Roskam had to consult with his American partner, but apparently there was broad agreement on that score, including Roskam's suggestion of signing the English actor Tom Hardy for the lead role and engaging the Swedish actress Noomi Rapace. American actor James Gandolfini, now extremely popular as a result of the television series *The Sopranos*, was an obvious choice too. Gandolfini died shortly after filming. At the risk of sounding cynical, his death generated additional publicity for the American release of *The Drop*. And that is typically Hollywood.

JAN TEMMERMAN
Translated by Alison Mouthaan

History

Art and Culture in Times of Conflict

2014 was a year dominated as no other by commemorations of the First World War. Never before has the 1914-18 War generated so much public interest, a fact reflected in the exponential growth in the number of publications on the subject. One of those publications deserves particular attention: *Ravaged. Art and Culture in Times of Conflict.* It is the catalogue for the eponymous exhibition that was organised in 2014 at M museum in Leuven.

In thirty fairly short articles, the authors of the catalogue analyse an aspect of the history of war about which relatively little has hitherto been written, namely the ambivalent relationship between art and conflict. Throughout history, the destruction of art and culture has been an integral aspect of the prosecution of war. Plundering and destruction of cultural heritage during times of conflict is only very rarely regarded as 'collateral damage'; it is usually the result of deliberate actions which are intended to strike at the cultural and national identity of the enemy. The exhibition catalogue describes the symbolic value of such acts of deliberate military destruction throughout history. While the catalogue devotes special attention to the devastation wrought during the First World War, the reader will also find examples from all periods and from all parts of the world: from the destruction of the Library of Alexandria to the Protestant iconoclasm and the looting by the Spanish conquistadors in the sixteenth century, the plundering and destruction carried out by the French revolutionaries, the Maoists in China or, very recently, the Taliban in Afghanistan.

But the catalogue does not limit itself to the history of wartime destruction. Its approach is much more original, with the authors of the different articles also investigating the initiatives taken to protect national monuments, the importance of the art and culture that survives the ravages, and even the inspiration that several artists have drawn from these ravages since the sixteenth century. The book opens by addressing precisely this question. As the first two articles demonstrate, the destruction of art has regularly been portrayed allegorically. Until the French Revolution, many artists drew inspiration from the theme of the struggle between the god Mars and the goddess Minerva to remind kings of the disastrous consequences of war. Other artists were particularly fascinated by the legendary accounts of ravaged cities, such as the Homeric Troy or Rome in 1527, and portrayed these events on canvas in an extremely dramatic way. After the horrors of two world wars, however, it became ever more difficult to portray the ravages of war in a figurative manner. As an example, in his article on modern Beirut, a city tormented by an 'unendable war', Ghalya Saadawi refers to the work of Lebanese artists who turned away from clear and unambiguous portrayals of a war which they saw as being 'extended, unravelled and prolonged'. Later in the book, Yukie Kamiya tells us that the drama of Hiroshima was something that many artists were only able to interpret in a conceptual way. Their work is characterised by the way in which the events in Hiroshima, too horrific to portray, became a symbol for the hope of a rebirth.

If the catalogue begins with a question about the portrayal of the destruction of art in times of conflict, the articles on the protection and preservation of cultural heritage are found mainly at the end of the book. The articles in the middle section are more concerned with the various iconoclastic movements. Five of these articles discuss the ravages of the Great War. They recount the destruction of the Leuven University Library and Rheims Cathedral, but also describe the ideological debates between French and German intellectuals about who was to blame for these dreadful acts of destruction. In another striking article, Dominiek Dendooven demonstrates that the urban ruins left behind after the War quickly lost their value as tourist attractions in favour of the remnants of the battlefields. The populations of the ravaged towns and cities quickly set about restoring them and thus removing the visible war damage from the townscape.

American propaganda poster from the First Word War calling on citizens to join the army to fight the German enemy.

The recent past was too painful to allow tangible evidence of it to remain, something that is also highlighted by Mark Jarzombek for Dresden after 1989, with its strong desire to eliminate anything that recalled the Communist period.

The emphasis in the articles on the protection of national monuments is on the French Revolution, the Second World War and the colonial period. The idea of protecting national monuments arose during the Revolutionary Wars. Wessel Krul discusses the first calls by revolutionaries such as Henri Grégoire to protect France's artistic heritage, while Dominique Poulot draws attention to the founding of the first universal museum to stem from this movement: the Louvre. In the same article, Poulot also underlines the imperialistic character of the Louvre, akin to that of the British Museum in London. Throughout the nineteenth century, the discourse on the protection and conservation of national treasures prompted the transfer of works of art from the colonies to the newly founded museums. During the Second World War, the confiscation of Jewish property prompted plans to found a comparable *Führermuseum* which was to overshadow the nineteenth-century imperialistic museums. This megalomaniacal project was nev-

er completed, but nonetheless forms a symbolic breaking point in the approach to artistic and cultural heritage. From the 1950s onwards, accounts of the imperialistic and Nazi plundering raised new questions about the repatriation of the confiscated items and about the need for an amended international jurisdiction – topics which are discussed respectively by Bert Demarsin and by Sigrid Van Der Auwera and Koenraad Van Balen. The catalogue ends with two articles focusing on the propaganda surrounding the destroyed cultural heritage. Annette Becker and Peter Weibel show that destruction of art and culture is regularly employed as a means of dehumanising the enemy.

This exhibition catalogue has been compiled with great care and thought. The two editors have succeeded in shedding light on the immensely complex relationship between art and conflict in a surprising and varied manner. The decision to opt for a *longue durée* approach and a study of the representations proves to be highly effective. The book manages to convince the reader that the ravages of war throughout history have been linked to ideological interests, propaganda strategies and a whole series of questions about the restoration, holding and repatriation of damaged and/or stolen works. This is done in a very subtle way, without being in any way boring or overloading the reader with unnecessary details. The catalogue is also richly illustrated with photographs of wartime destruction, as well as of works of art which sometimes show very clearly how the shock of destruction led to the birth of new forms of artistic expression. In short, this is a very inviting book which holds the reader's interest from start to finish and which continually surprises with new accounts.

MATTHIAS MEIRLAEN
Translated by Julian Ross

JO TOLLEBEEK & ELINE VAN ASSCHE (eds.), *Ravaged. Art and Culture in Times of Conflict*, Mercatorfonds, Brussels, 2014, 304 p. (ISBN 978 94 6230 044 6).

Dutch Brazil (1624-1654) and Its Legacy

The central figure in *The Legacy of Dutch Brazil* is Johan Maurits of Nassau-Siegen [1604-1679], a humanist prince in Europe, a statesman and governor of New Holland in Brazil from 1636-1644 and later, after the Peace of Westphalia, governor of Cleves and ruler of the Rhineland. A true Renaissance man, when he went to Brazil he took his court with him, including scholars and artists, who all set about collecting, studying, describing and painting that extraordinary new world out there.

The most exciting article in this volume, edited by historian Michiel van Groesen, is Mariana Françozo's contribution on his culture of wealthy and exotic display of the colonial riches he gathered overseas. He acted this out in The Hague with half naked Tapuya Indians dancing in the Mauritshuis and in 1652 at Cleves too, where he used the Indians in a re-enactment of the Battle of Zama, in which Scipio [read Johan Maurits] defeated Hannibal and Carthage.

As for the colonial side of this short Brazilian episode, the fact is that the Dutch empire was predominantly a maritime and trade affair, spanning the Seven Seas with a network of harbours, islands, fortresses and trading posts dotted around the world, always on or very near to the coast – from New York to Indonesia, the Cape to Japan, along the coasts of India and Ceylon, the Moluccas and the Caribbean.

At the heart of this empire there was always the business imperative: war is bad for business; an army is a drain on finance; and it is more profitable in the long run to have peace. So, in 1661, the Dutch Republic made a lasting peace with the Portuguese in the Treaty of The Hague, a deal whereby the Portuguese paid for the repossession of Brazil with the salt of Setúbal, which the Dutch fishing industry needed much more than all the sugar of Brazil.

The proceedings of a stimulating two-day conference held at Amsterdam University, with participants from the USA, the Netherlands, Spain and Belgium (but no German experts, even though in 2004 it was the German government which placed a bust of Johan Maurits in Recife), the value of this collection is its three-pronged approach to the interlude of Dutch Brazil and its legacy.

In the first part, historians Klooster and Schwarz pursue Dutch Brazil´s geopolitical links to developments elsewhere, in particular the Spanish empire, and its English and French rivals. Also very interesting is Meeuwese's contribution on the Dutch alliances with - and eventually also their abandoning of - the indigenous Indians, who even sent an embassy to the States-General in The Hague to plead for further action against the Portuguese, but to no avail.

In the second part, it is the cultural legacy that takes centre stage, in the Netherlands, Brazil and elsewhere, with contributions on religion e.g. the legacy of religious tolerance as a Dutch element in Brazilian history, but also the Dutch fight with the Jesuits from Antwerp. Another very interesting contribution concerns free trade, in Weststeijn's analysis of Pieter de la Court's ideas on free trade, which eventually inspired the authors (including Diderot) of Raynal's *History of the Two Indies* (1780).

The third and last section brings a number of contributions by leading American art historians on the Brazilian paintings by Post and Eeckhout, and on Johan Maurits's collections and their dispersal around the world, as a result of which Post's paintings are now in the Rijksmuseum and the Amsterdam Maritime Museum, while his drawings are in the British Museum. The closing contribution by

Runies gives a very good critical comparative discussion of historical mentalities and national mythologies concerning this Dutch episode in Brazil's colonial past.

Here we also find editor Michiel van Groesen's own contribution, on the Dutch 17th century cult of naval heroes and their exploits, beginning and ending with Van Haren's poem of 1769 on the proud episode and the missed opportunity of 'Neglected Brazil' (*Verzuimd Brazil*). Who knows, this poem may well have been the reason why Van Haren's grandson, Dirck van Hogendorp – who had enjoyed a long and adventurous career as a Dutch colonial administrator in Java and Bengal, a colonial critic and reformer at home, then as Dutch ambassador to Russia and as a general in the service of Napoleon, before finally being disgraced back in the Netherlands – went in 1817 to Brazil, of all places, where he spent the last years of his life in exile at the Portuguese royal court in Rio de Janeiro.

There is in this volume an interesting footnote on p. 106, pointing to the connection in the 1930s between the Brazilian poet and essayist Paolo Setúbal, who wrote an historical novel with Johan Maurits as its central character, which was co-translated in 1933 by one of Holland's most important writers on the tropics, the poet J.J. Slauerhoff. Instead of a footnote, this modern Dutch-Brazilian connection would have merited a full article.

All in all, the book offers a very rich collection indeed. It has been published to a high standard by Cambridge University Press, with a beautiful picture on the outside jacket of palms, the ruins of a fortress and a rusty canon on the beach. On the inside, too, there are quite a lot of illustrations, maps and figures, but no colour photographs of the beautiful original paintings by Post and Eeckhout.

REINIER SALVERDA

The Legacy of Dutch Brazil, Edited by Michiel van Groesen, Cambridge University Press, 2014, 363 p.

A Failed Political Experiment
The United Kingdom of the Netherlands 1815-1830

2015 marks the bicentenary of the creation of the United Kingdom of the Netherlands. Between 1815 and 1830, Belgium and the Netherlands were briefly joined under William I. How did this come about and what went wrong?

Long before the last remains of the Napoleonic Empire were swept away at Waterloo and the little French emperor was banished to Saint Helena, the European superpowers had already begun to redraw the map of Europe. Great Britain was particularly in favour of creating a buffer state on the northern French border. The idea of merging the Northern and Southern Netherlands and thereby countering French expansionist tendencies actually dates back to 1805. British Prime Minister William Pitt found a willing ear in his Russian ally. In the Eight Articles of London, signed in June 1814, the superpowers secretly agreed to implement the unification, under the leadership of King William I. This agreement was then ratified at the Congress of Vienna. With the appointment of William I, the superpowers sought a return to peace, order and prosperity after two decades of power struggles and upheaval.

William reigned over the United Kingdom of the Netherlands between 1815 and 1830, ruling the land as if it were his own. The 'Functionary King' inundated the people with royal decrees, in the firm belief that he knew the way to prosperity and happiness. He wanted obedient and industrious subjects, and the church, the education system and the press were all expected to serve his government. Only industrialists and merchants were permitted some freedom of movement. He supported these members of society, sometimes even with his own capital.

William saw it as his mission to form the two combined regions into an 'intimate and complete' (*intime et complète*) amalgam, as set out in the first of the Eight Articles of London. His policies provoked misunderstanding and discontent, especially in the South, and led to short-term resistance. The main opposition was in response to his steps regarding religion, language, the education system and the press. His reforms aimed at modernising the economy met with more understanding. He commissioned extensive infrastructure works, earning him nicknames such as the Merchant King and the Canal King, not least because of the Ghent-Terneuzen Canal, which was dug under his rule. He also lent support to entrepreneurs such as John Cockerill, a Briton who modernized the steel industry in Liège. The King managed to raise the funds necessary to finance these activities through the creation of several banks and credit institutions. However, his fiscal policy led to a great deal of protest. Over their many centuries of separation, North and South had developed separate taxation systems, which the King saw it as his job to harmonise. The tax authorities in the United Kingdom acquired the persona of a greedy, interfering official. Opposition to the monarch's fiscal policies was particularly strong in the South, where the population felt exploited and discriminated against. Recent historical research seems to support this perception: there were indeed quite large remittances from the South to the North. When the economic situation worsened, so too did general dissatisfaction.

The establishment of the United Kingdom of the Netherlands put the traditional religious balance under considerable pressure. The South had a large Catholic majority and a church that was organised very much as an established church. In the North, the Reformed Church was traditionally very influential. William I was convinced that the churches would prove an important tool for creating national unity, but they would have to make very large concessions. This led to opposition from the clergy, which Willem interpreted as subversion of his policies. In the South, the King's church politics had a mixed reception. In liberal and anti-clerical circles, there was initially very little protest against curtailment of the power of the church. In church circles, dissatisfaction was high, based on the prevailing impression that 'Dutch' Protestants were imposing their ideas. However, when William introduced

Aula of Ghent University, founded by King William I in 1817. The Aula was completed in 1826. © Michiel Hendryckx

uniform seminary training in 1820, the liberals joined the church in opposing it, describing it as a restriction on freedom of expression and religion. This would eventually lead to an 'unholy alliance' of Catholics and liberals united in opposition.

William I declared Dutch to be the national language of the United Kingdom. The imposition of a single language was another attempt to foster unity and national sentiment, but also to form a barrier against French expansionism. This was no problem in the Northern Netherlands, where Dutch had long been the language of government and education, but not so in the South, where French was the more prestigious language. In 1823, a general 'Dutchification' of education, administration and the judiciary took effect. In Flanders, the policy was largely observed and the switch to Dutch was relatively smooth. In Wallonia, however, where Dutch was almost completely unknown, the changeover was less smooth. William tried all kinds of methods to boost knowledge of the language. He even established a Dutch chair at the University of Liège in 1817. But ultimately the results of all these measures were still very meagre and protests against the introduction of Dutch as the language of government grew. It was perceived as a restriction on the freedom of language and was a source of annoyance in Wallonia in particular.

The authoritarian regime of William I and the series of controversial measures that he issued increased the unrest in the South of the United Kingdom. On August 25 1830, rioting broke out in Brussels after a performance of the opera *La Muette de Portici*. The fact that this led eventually to the independence of Belgium had to do with a number of coincidences, and the revolt was certainly not upheld across the whole country. Although an independent kingdom of Belgium was never really the main issue of the uprising, nevertheless independence was declared on October 4, and a provisional government appointed. In June 1831, Leopold, Prince of Saxe-Coburg and Gotha, took up office as the first King of Belgium. The Netherlands continued to make claims on the lost territory until 1839, when, under pressure from the European powers, King William I was finally forced to recognise the situation.

Was the United Kingdom of the Netherlands a political experiment doomed in advance to failure? Historical writing that has emerged since independence confirms this idea, but there are many counterarguments. The fact remains that King William I and the executors of his policies failed to seize many opportunities to form the United Kingdom into a real nation.

DIRK VAN ASSCHE
Translated by Rebekah Wilson

A book about the United Kingdom of the Netherlands, published by Ons Erfdeel vzw, is due out in 2015. This article is based on a number of texts from this book.

'A Thankless and Vexatious work'
One Hundred and Fiftieth Anniversary of the 'Fat Van Dale'

Language-lovers in the Netherlands and Flanders have been in conspicuous high spirits recently. The year 2014 saw the celebration of the best-known defining dictionary of Dutch: the *Van Dale Groot Woordenboek van de Nederlandse Taal* (Van Dale's Large Dictionary of the Dutch Language), also known as the *Grote Van Dale* (Large Van Dale) or, more fondly, as the 'Fat Van Dale'. Its popularity is apparent from the book *Verhalen over taal* (Stories about Language), a hefty volume of columns, anecdotes and short stories revolving round the Van Dale and Dutch in general[1]. It was published by the Van Dale company which, in addition to the 'Fat Van Dale', also publishes some more slender versions of the same dictionary, as well as translating dictionaries. A poll was also organised, with voting open for almost a month, to find the best of one hundred and fifty so-called 'Van Dale Jubilee Words', Dutch words that first appeared or became common between 1864 and 2014. The most votes went to the word *bolleboos*, which means 'someone who is very gifted, who excels in something'.

The climax is still to come, however. In September 2015 a new paper edition of the 'Fat Van Dale' will be published (including a CD-ROM, of course). The previous paper edition was published in 2005. It has however been updated digitally every six months. By tradition, the editors of the new edition will again be both Dutch and Flemish. One of their most delicate tasks is the choice of words that have never previously appeared in this dictionary, but which now do have the right to an entry. This usually puts them to a severe test and in recent years pressure has been exerted from outside to include certain words.

The Van Dale dictionary owes its name to Johan Hendrik Van Dale (1828-1872), a teacher in Sluis (a small town in Zeeland-Flanders, just north of the Dutch-Belgian border). His parents originated from Meetjesland, a rural area north-west of Ghent, from where they fled at the out-break of a smallpox epidemic. Johan Hendrik soon acquired a taste for language and wrote textbooks on linguistic purity, grammar and parsing. In 1867 he was asked to revise the *Nieuw Woordenboek der Nederlandsche Taal* (New Dictionary of the Dutch Language), which the brothers Isaac Marcus and Nathan Salomon Calisch had published three years previously.

It took Johan Hendrik four years to complete his revision. His work as a teacher was a substantial help in his lexicographical labours. He always tried to keep his pupils in mind and to avoid any form of vagueness. The definition of the meaning of a word had to be as clear and precise as possible. Unfortunately, Johan Hendrik died - from smallpox, would you believe? - just after the first instalments of the revised dictionary were published. In the preface to the 1872 edition he had written: 'Writing a dictionary is a thankless and vexatious work'.

Van Dale's dictionary was written using the De Vries-Te Winkel spelling of Dutch, which was already accepted as the official spelling system in Flanders, but not in the Netherlands[2]. It is apparent from the figures that the later nickname of 'Fat' Van Dale was well deserved. The first two editions contained about 1,400 pages. The third, which appeared in 1884, was a doorstop of almost 1,800 pages. Apart from the Bible, it was just about the thickest book that most Dutch speakers would have in their bookcase. The figures for the most recent edition are of course considerably higher again. This fourteenth edition comes in at about 4,500 pages in three volumes.

Yet the 'Fat Van Dale' is still not the most impressive defining dictionary of Dutch. This honour goes to the *Woordenboek der Nederlandse Taal* (Dictionary of the Dutch language) or WNT for short. The driving force behind what was to become the 'largest dictionary in the world' was the nineteenth-century Dutch language scholar Matthijs de Vries. The first instalment of the WNT

The statue of Johan Hendrik Van Dale in Sluis (Zeeland-Flanders).

was published in 1864, but for the last we had to wait until...1998. Three years later another three volumes of 'Additions' appeared that had not previously been included; these were mostly twentieth-century words. The complete WNT, which is also available on CD-ROM, consists of 43 volumes and has roughly 400,000 headwords. Altogether, this requires about three metres on that already overfull bookcase.

HANS VANACKER
Translated by Gregory Ball

www.vandale.nl and www.vandale.be

1 Compiled by WIM DANIELS and published by Van Dale Uitgevers, Utrecht/Antwerp (ISBN 978 94 60771 7 50).

2 The De Vries-Te Winkel spelling system was officially introduced in the Netherlands in 1883. This was the first time the Netherlands shared the same spelling with Flanders.

Literature

The Emperor Has No Clothes
Sinologist and Essayist Simon Leys (1935-2014)

Simon Leys died on 11 August 2014 in Sydney, Australia, where he lived for the final years of his life. All the major French magazines published articles or dug out old interviews. The New York Review of Books reposted online 'The Man Who Got it Right', a review of Leys' last English publication, The Hall of Uselessness: Collected Essays (Black Inc. Books, 2013), in which Dutch sinologist and commentator Ian Buruma emphasises the originality and honesty of the Belgian sinologist. Most professors at Leiden whose lectures Buruma followed in the early 1970s closed their eyes to the atrocities of Mao's Cultural Revolution in China, events which Leys ruthlessly exposed.

Before he became known as Simon Leys, the man was called Pierre Ryckmans. He was born on 28 September 1935 in Brussels. The young Pierre went to Leuven to study law and history of art. As the editor of a student magazine in 1955 he unexpectedly received the opportunity to take a research trip to China with just nine other students. Fascinated by Chinese culture and frustrated by his inability to converse with ordinary Chinese people in their own language, he subsequently threw himself into the study of Chinese language, art and culture. Ryckmans spent a long time in Singapore, Taiwan and Hongkong.

In his doctorate on Chinese calligraphy (1971) Leys showed that this Chinese art was intrinsically embedded in a cosmology, the aesthetics of the brush stroke forming a component of spirituality. In his introduction to the autobiography (1966) of Shen Fu, the sixteenth-century man of letters, Ryckmans envisages the complex reality surrounding the life story of this artist, husband and father. Serious scholars, in Ryckmans' view, must know the language of the country they were studying and must have thoroughly immersed themselves in the foreign culture. To do otherwise, he felt, was to act like one of the three blind men from the Buddhist fable, each separately feeling a different part of an elephant. The first felt the trunk, the second a leg, and the third the tail, respectively concluding that the elephant was a snake, a pillar or a broom.

In 1971, under the pseudonym Simon Leys, he wrote The Chairman's New Clothes: Mao and the Cultural Revolution (published in English by St. Martin's Press in 1978), an indictment of unseeing European intellectuals such as Sartre and Foucault, and the group based around the French magazine Tel Quel (Barthes, Kristéva, Sollers), who, unhindered by knowledge of the facts, supported the cruel Chinese dictator. The emperor had no clothes, as the child in Andersen's fairy tale knew all too well, but the courtiers refused to see it. The child continued to shout out this simple, honest message in Chinese Shadows (original 1974, English translation published by Viking Press, 1977) and Broken Images (original 1976, English translation published by Allison and Busby, 1979).

It was all in vain, until in 1983 Simon Leys participated in Bernard Pivot's French book programme Apostrophes with an Italian intellectual who had praised the Maoist Cultural Revolution in a book. Leys exploded: 'It is normal for idiots to say stupid things, as it is normal for an apple tree to grow apples and a pear tree pears, but having seen the corpses float past my house on the river day after day, I cannot accept the idyllic story of the Cultural Revolution.'

Pierre Ryckmans thus slowly shed his skin to become Simon Leys. Nomen est omen: Simon is a reference to the first name of the apostle Simon Peter. The name Leys refers to the character René Leys, the hero of Victor Segalen's eponymous novel (1921). When Ryckmans chose his pseudonym in 1971, the novel had been largely forgotten, except among a small group of literature lovers, people who had read a thing or two about China. In Segalen's novel the narrator asks the young René Leys to teach him Chinese. This elegant and mysterious son of a Belgian shipping agent seems to know all about the secrets of the Forbidden City. Leys is also the name of a famous line of painters from Antwerp, the most famous of whom was the

nineteenth-century genre painter Henri Leys. The pseudonym Ryckmans picked reveals what he saw as the constituent parts of his imagined identity: his Catholicism, his curiosity about the highly subtle Chinese civilisation, his Belgian nationality, his Flemish origins and his weakness for painting.

Another of Simon Leys' key works is his essay about the 1629 shipwreck of the Dutch merchant ship the Batavia, *The Wreck of the Batavia: A True Story* (originally published in 2003, English translation by Basic Books in 2005). It is an inspiring reflection on religious and political fanaticism, on terror and the way in which a society must deal with it. The fanatical leader of the mutineers has not committed murder himself. His intelligent rhetoric and moral blackmail sufficed to move others to act. 'The only thing necessary for the triumph of evil is for good men to do nothing,' Edmund Burke would have written. Simon Leys in any case attributes this sentence to him in his collection of worldly wisdom, *Other People's Thoughts*, (original 2005, English translation 2006) dedicated to his Chinese wife Han-fang Chang. The book is also a metaphor for the way in which Leys views the perverse outbreak of violence of the French revolution, in the wake of French historian François Furet or conservative philosopher Burke.

Leys produced pioneering and erudite writing about China (also teaching on the subject at Australian universities). He published wonderful essays about literature in the *New York Review of Books*, and in the French *Magazine Littéraire* he held forth on Nabokov and Victor Hugo, Erasmus and Multatuli, Malraux and George Orwell. He admired Orwell's integrity, commitment and common-sense thinking. He shared with the author of *1984* and *Animal Farm* an aversion to fanaticism, mendacious 'new speak' and the boasting of ostentatious intellectuals.

He loved the liberal commitment of Camus and translated Simone Weil's sharp essay on political democracy into English (*On the Abolition of All Political Parties*, Black Inc. Books, 2013). Perhaps Leys was a liberal conservative socialist in the image of Polish philosopher Leszek Kołakowski. Above all he could not stand a society which systematically bans all beauty and sophistication, his neighbour who cut down a tree because the birds kept on chirping, the pub customers who are not bothered by the noise of the radio but who protest when a Mozart clarinet quintet is played.

The tribute from the French minister of culture Aurélie Filipetti to 'the multilingual Belgian, iconoclast, anticonformist, lover of French literature and intellectual debate' was also Mozart to our ears.

ALEXANDER ROOSE
Translated by Anna Asbury

Guest of Honour 2.0
The Low Countries at Frankfurt Book Fair 2016

On the final day of 2014 I receive a text message from Ine, my right hand on the team for Frankfurt Book Fair 2016, the year in which Flanders and the Netherlands are to be the Guest of Honour. She's staying in Cadzand and writes that she often thinks of Frankfurt there at the seaside.

How can you think of a city of skyscrapers while leaning into the sea wind, you might ask? It makes perfect sense to me.

As with the rest of the team, everything I've heard and seen recently breathes 2016, Frankfurt or the Buchmesse. Everything but everything points towards the vision I'm developing of Flanders and the Netherlands as Guest of Honour.

Ine mentions in passing that water takes a long time to form a wave. Once a wave has been formed, it rises up, gaining strength, only to break immediately afterwards. This observation probably came to her on a beach walk. One wave elicits another. I want to add in my message that it's all beautiful: the approaching end and impending beginning, decline and growth, the peace which sets in, with another movement expanding. Simply put, the game the sea plays with the beach.

All storytellers know they must avoid harmony if they want to keep things interesting. People are far more intrigued by action and reaction than by harmony. Harmony won't have us sitting on the edges of our seats.

My basic idea for the Netherlands and Flanders as Guest of Honour at the Frankfurt Book Fair is the wave, a simple, familiar image, but at the same time rich and sparkling. There's a great deal more significance to a wave than just a bit of foam.

Flemish and Dutch people share a language. That's interesting, but for a foreign country it's hardly the most exciting thought. Sharing a language sounds like being becalmed at sea, and I'm not going to opt for calm when it comes to Frankfurt Book Fair 2016.

Flanders and the Netherlands are the first countries to take their place as European Guest of Honour for the second time, having first shared that honour in 1993. With that first time in mind, the wave metaphor stayed with me when it occurred to me that the Netherlands and Flanders

share not only a language but also the North Sea. We have already made our big entrance together once, and since then a great deal has happened.

Harry Mulish and Hugo Claus have died and new names have entered the scene. The book industry has changed. In 2014 the Frankfurt Book Fair expressly requested that in 2016 we present not just our literature but our entire culture. Flanders and the Netherlands must be the Guest of Honour 2.0. Two point oh.

All well and good. I'll go into details when and where I know them. It's as simple as that.

One wave elicits another.

We might hope that the world has seen the changes in Flanders and the Netherlands since 1993, but we have to ask ourselves whether people have really taken a proper look. If you have an idea about something, you don't necessarily adjust it until someone draws your attention to the changes. If there's no need to adjust what you know, you generally don't.

Hence the wave. A wave takes a long time to come into being. It sweeps along whatever is living, necessary and indispensible – this is a case of directed forces – but once the wave is in motion, it continues to build strength. I know it then breaks, as I was reminded on the last day of the year, but I also know for certain that we won't dwell on the breaking of the wave when it reaches the beach.

No, before you know it we'll have forgotten the breaking.

Instead we'll see the tidemark as a beacon. What we remember are the treasures left behind, the discoveries which make beachcombers happy. A tidemark sounds like the end, but it's really the beginning.

The important thing is what remains after 2016. Observe that significance as you read. Think of everything left to be found after 2016. Observe how happy it makes you.

BART MOEYAERT
Translated by Anna Asbury

'There Is Infinite Enrichment in Perishing'
Leo Vroman (1915-2014)

Leo Vroman was the sort of poet who seemed to have been around forever and promised to go on for just as long. When I learned to read as a child, a volume of his collected poems entitled *Gedichten 1946-1984* (Poems 1946-1984) had recently been published to mark his seventieth birthday. When I first became interested in poetry, he was well into his eighties, but nevertheless still publishing work. In fact, he seemed to become even more productive. Towards the end of his life, a substantial volume appeared almost every two years: 'My prattle pours out perversely' he writes in the poem *Een open kraan* (An open tap), in which he considers his remarkable productivity. His last volumes of poetry often reflect in a superior, ironic way on aging, the corresponding decline of the human body and the impending end of life. In many of these poems, Vroman tries to imagine what happens after death. Is there a heaven? Is there nothing? And what about his eternal love for his wife Tineke? In 'De dood' (Death), from the collection *Nee nog niet dood* (No, not yet dead), Vroman produces an antidote to uncertainty: 'My death will die with my death, / so what's stopping it'. Although his poetry does not lack a sense of perspective, it possesses great vitality: life is wonderful. So despite the realisation that his life is almost over, and the fact that he is at peace with this, he still clings to life nevertheless. How else do you explain the huge urge to write? Even his last two volumes had 216 and 160 pages respectively.

Vroman was born in 1915, the son of Jewish parents. He fled during the Second World War, ending up in the Dutch East Indies, via England and Cape Town, where he was taken as a prisoner of war. After liberation he settled in the United States, where he married and began a career as a haematologist. He carried out pioneering work in the field of blood coagulation; there is even a phenomenon named after him - the Vroman effect – that he described in an article in the respected journal *Nature* in 1962.

He had already made his debut as a poet back in 1933, and during the war he contributed to the legendary surrealist journal *De schone zakdoek* (The clean handkerchief), of which only one copy was made of each issue, and subsequently contributed to various periodicals. His first collection, *Gedichten* (Poems), was published in 1946, and in 1964 he received the P.C. Hooft Award, the highest literary award in the Netherlands.

Vroman's poetry, which was at once surreal and realistic, was perceived as refreshing in the immediate post-war literary climate, which was mainly focused on restoration. In the 1950s, when the experimental generation sought to reinvigorate poetry by breaking all conventions, Vroman was a sort of in-between figure: innovative, but not radical. This typifies his position as a poet: he did not join any particular movement and his work does not belong to any particular school, which of course can partly be explained by his position as a literal outsider. Recurring themes in both his poems and his diaries are memories of his childhood and his experience of the war, his family and his love for his wife and daughters, and his work as a scientist. This in particular led him to believe that, although the world might at first seem chaotic and incoherent, it is actually full of correlations. In volumes such as *Liefde, sterk vergroot* (Love, greatly enlarged) and *Fractaal* (Fractal), he expresses the idea that everything is connected to everything else, a belief that culminates in *Psalmen en andere gedichten* (Psalms and other poems), in which poems written in Dutch and English invoke a 'System'. This is not a secular variation of God, as Vroman makes clear in the opening poem, but the expression of a belief that there is a structure or principle underlying everything.

At a technical level, Vroman represents his idea that all things are connected by means of rhyme: corresponding sounds are used to emphasise the link between words, and by extension between phenomena. In addition, Vroman's poetry is colloquial and straightforward, making it easy to read. Poems such as 'Vrede' (Peace) ('Come this evening with your tales of / how at last the war is finished / then

Leo Vroman (1915-2014)
© Klaas Koppe

repeat them ten times more and / still my tears flow undiminished') and 'Voor wie dit leest' (To whoever reads this) ('My printed words may teach you / but my hot mouth can't speak to you / I can't raise my hot hand from the page to touch you / What can I do? I can't reach you') are classics of Dutch poetry.

Leo Vroman is no more, he died just short of his 100th birthday. He hoped his poetry would survive him for a while, although he was quite realistic about this too. However, he firmly believed that we don't just disappear, but merge into something bigger: 'Although we all must die, / there is infinite enrichment in perishing.'

CARL DE STRYCKER
Translated by Rebekah Wilson

Music

'Too Good to Be Dutch'
Blaudzun

In 2012 Dutch television viewers made their acquaintance with the singer-songwriter Johannes Sigmund, alias Blaudzun (° 1974), through the popular programme *De Wereld Draait Door* (literally The World Goes On or, metaphorically, The World's Going Crazy). He was singing a cover of *Shout*, a 1985 world hit from Tears for Fears, in which he accompanied himself on the banjo. Blaudzun seemed to come from nowhere, but actually he was on his third CD, *Heavy Flowers*. He had already outgrown the alternative club circuit. In the Netherlands *Heavy Flowers* was in the lists of bestselling albums for 63 weeks, 45 weeks in Flanders. Later the remarkable new performer made a fresh impression in *De Wereld Draait Door* with *Waterfall* by Wendy and Lisa, former musical partners of Prince. In the same programme he compiled his ideal TV music evening, spotlighting John Jacob Niles and praising Kurt Cobain as a master song-writer who was as impressive unplugged as on full volume.

Blaudzun owes his importance, among other things, to his original output and presence. He had a definitive breakthrough in 2014, when Dutch public broadcasting used a pregnant passage from his *Promises of No Man's Land* (the text of the chorus: The Heat Is on ...) for the Winter Olympic Games summaries. In the meantime he was willing to co-operate in podia and media events only if their quality was guaranteed.

Johannes Sigmund grew up in a musical family with a variety of instruments in the home. The children were allowed to play them to their heart's content. The Sigmonds were practising members of the Pentecostal Church. In that church the music does not consist of organ tones and solemn hymns in crochets only, but of the modern sound of guitars, drums and whatever resounds and swings to praise the Lord. At an early age Johannes played every possible style of pop music with his brother, at home and in bands. Johannes wrote the songs himself. After studying audiovisual journalism, he invented media formats, produced pilots and made a film about the classic Tour of Lombardy cycle race. It was no accident that he took his artistic name from the sport of cycling: Blaudzun alludes to the Danish racing cyclist, Verner Blaudzun, who was a member of the professional peloton in the 60s and 70s. In 2006 Johannes opted for music. After six years of trial and error he could call himself a professional.

Brother Jacob made a radical break from the Pentecostal Church at an early age, and to this very day is still making music with Johannes. It was only later that the latter cut free from the religious community, and he did so more gradually. The interpretation of his work gains from a knowledge of his background. *Flame on my Head,* for instance, refers to the 'tongues of fire' of the Pentecostal or Whitsun metaphor. But even without this knowledge one can hear that his music strives to go beyond the earthly, with a passionate singing style, inspired texts and equally inspired instrumentation. Moreover, his English sounds as if he is a native speaker. In that respect his music knows no bounds.

Blaudzun's talent was quickly recognized. He won prestigious prizes and became the darling of the Dutch pop critics who showed off their good taste. They gave him the highest compliment possible: 'too good to be Dutch'. By his own admission, he gradually felt the need for more venom in his songs. He also began to devote more space to his autumnal, melancholy side. His music always sounds inspired, whether the lyrics can be understood or not. The gentle warmth and the intelligence that emanate from his stage appearances is partly down to the members of his band, all of them outstanding musicians. They add creative colour to the basic rock sound with violin, accordion, plucked instruments and percussion.

Big words are used for Blaudzun's music, such as stirring, bombastic, euphoric, unruly, ecstatic, but he can also make 'small' music, that makes your flesh creep in a different kind of way. His lyrics are free from romantic clichés and easy doggerel. Although his presentation is somewhat distant,

and at times positively static, the sparks always fly. He is most frequently likened to Arcade Fire and the late Jeff Buckley but, despite this, Blaudzun's music remains distinctive thanks to the individuality of his numbers and his emotionally charged voice. The contrast between the richness of the melodic ideas and arrangements on the one side and, on the other, the relatively boring rhythms (a single pattern is set for each number and is mostly steadfastly adhered to), could be considered as a characteristic of individual style, were it not for the fact that grooves and beats are not usually the forte of Dutch bands in a comparable idiom. In live performances, moreover, what is striking is that many Blaudzun numbers are given a forced ending. As far as form and length go the pop song straitjacket is Sigmond's concession to the conventions. With an interesting originator such as Blaudzun one is naturally curious about his ideas with regard to less predictable forms and tensions.

As a fan of cycle racing, Johannes Sigmond was the obvious choice to write the theme number for the *Grand Départ* of the 2015 Tour de France in Utrecht. That was *Bon Voyage*. The Utrecht animation studio Job, Joris en Marieke - Job Roggeveen, Joris Oprins and Marieke Blaauw, who got to know each other at the Design Academy in Eindhoven and have worked together since - made a clip to go with it. The official première took place on 22 October 2014 in Paris, during the presentation of the circuit for the 2015 Tour de France.

During the 2014-2015 season Blaudzun toured throughout Continental Europe with success. In his own country he was already a universally-known phenomenon, mainly due to the talk-show mentioned earlier on which he was a guest on more than one occasion, but also due to the satirical TV programme *Koefnoen* that honoured Blaudzun with a priceless parody. In Belgium he has already appeared at large events such as the Pukkelpop Festival and in the Ancienne Belgique in Brussels, the Valhalla for alternative bands that take inspiration from a critical and curious public. The German-speaking countries and Scandinavia also regard Blaudzun as a genuine artist. 'Through the Fire I Will Return', he sings, and he promises once more to continue his mature and beautiful interpretation of the art of song writing.

LUTGARD MUTSAERS
Translated by Sheila M. Dale

http://blaudzun.com

Between Darkness and Light
Ghent-New York Rock Singer Trixie Whitley

Timeless. If there were a single adjective to describe the music of Trixie Whitley (born in 1987 in Ghent), then that would be it, but don't confuse 'timeless' with 'retro'. Whitley's music does not aim to transport the listener back to a glorious past. For her it is about writing songs which are not bound to a specific trend or period. Her debut album *Fourth Corner* (2013) may contain echoes of blues, gospel and soul, but it is also unmistakeably a record of the twenty-first century. In addition to the genres already mentioned, dating back half a century or more, contemporary influences such as hip hop and R&B have also made their mark on *Fourth Corner*. Whitley is often considered to be an 'old soul', but of course she is also a young woman who goes to parties with friends in the here and now.

Just as she looks for a musical path between rootsy and contemporary, in her lyrics Whitley swings between darkness and light. In her own words this allows her to follow the cycle of life and nature: creation follows destruction and vice versa, continually repeating. She finds this endlessly fascinating, because she sees parallels with her own personality. While she is highly optimistic by nature, she also has a truly dark, melancholy side. It's difficult to trace precisely where that comes from, but Whitley's unusual family history must have something to do with it.

Her father was American blues singer and guitarist Chris Whitley (1960-2005), an exceptionally talented man from a family of artists who sadly also had self-destructive tendencies. Arriving in Ghent in the 1980s he met Hélène Gevaert, a woman with an artistic and mildly eccentric family background. Whitley and Gevaert not only formed a band together but also had a child, Trixie. She was born in Ghent, spent her childhood in New York and her teenage years in the musical capital of Flanders, and ten years ago opted once again for the American melting pot of The Big Apple.

A background like that had to lead to a life as a performer. Whitley was already singing along with her father on stage as a small child, deejayed at Ghent's S.M.AK. (Municipal Museum of Contemporary Art) at the age of twelve, played in youth theatre performances and toured Europe as a dancer with Les Ballets C de la B and choreographer Sidi Larbi Cherkaoui. Eventually she chose music, or perhaps it would be more accurate to say that music chose her.

She began to express herself through song virtually before she had learnt to walk, completely unaware of the fact that she was singing. The guitar, piano and drum kit similarly 'happened' to her: she picked up the instruments and immediately had an almost physical bond with them, as if her blood flowed through them. She spontaneously found a way of communicating her feelings and thoughts. The artisanal approach, as she calls it, meaning working intuitively and creatively, free of external influences such as other people's music, and with the space to experiment, even if it does not always lead to concrete results.

Trial and error, falling and picking yourself up again. This applies as much to her personal life as to her music. Although Whitley prefers to keep the two separate in interviews, they are inextricably connected. In her lyrics she has worked through the sometimes tragic events of her private life (her parents separated when she was still young; she grew up in two very different countries; she never fitted in at school; her father died in her presence when she was seventeen, felled by a lingering illness), never directly in the form of open-hearted confessional lyrics, but rather in indirect, impressionistic images which often point to overwhelming nature, particularly rivers.

This gives her music an intangible, timeless quality, demanding repeated listening for the power to emerge through the initially positive but superficial impressions of her voice and the sound she produces. Despite, or perhaps

because of, her complex, layered sound and her initially impenetrable lyrics, she has reached a loyal and still growing audience. She has already laid foundations to build on in France, the Netherlands and a handful of other European countries. In her current home, New York, she still has to fight it out with the many other fortune seekers – although Whitley already has a head start thanks to her connections with Daniel Lanois (Canadian songwriter, musician and producer of world stars such as U2 and Peter Gabriel), with whom she worked in the supergroup Black Dub.

But it is mainly in Belgium, where she was born, that she has crowds of loyal fans: here 20,000 copies of her debut *Fourth Corner* have been sold – a very respectable success in times of falling record sales – and she appears at the big festivals, her performances invariably selling out. The Belgian public have also seen her grow up on stage, years before her CD debut came out in 2013, at solo concerts in which she would introduce a number somewhat hesitantly, then suddenly launch into song like a great soul diva; and in performances with a rock band in which she let rip with raw, primitive voodoo blues.

At the end of 2014 she gave a series of small, informal concerts in the Netherlands, Flanders and Switzerland in which she performed songs from *Fourth Corner* in a subtle three-part arrangement and shared a handful of new numbers with the audience from a record to be released in 2015, making the fans a part of the creative process involved in a new album. They heard how Whitley has conquered (or rather accepted) the darkness inside herself, while continuing to extend the boundaries of her sound, integrating North African rhythms into her music, or playing as slowly as possible without it becoming uncomfortable. In one new song she nicely summed up her artistic drive: 'I need to find new frontiers.'

PIETER COUPÉ
Translated by Anna Asbury

www.trixiewhitley.com

Politics

A Senate with Indirect Power
The First Chamber in the Netherlands

In May 2015 the Dutch go to the polls for provincial elections. These are regional elections with a serious national character. Rutte's cabinet anticipates the results with considerable apprehension, as it is through the provinces, rather than directly, that the 75 members of the Senate, or First Chamber, are elected. The Senate in the Netherlands has existed for 200 years. Its task, as a nineteenth century minister put it, lies ˈnot in doing good, but in preventing evilˈ.

At the start of the 19th century, after French rule, when the Netherlands acquired a king, a new constitution was written. There was a political organ, the States General, but there was also a need to divide the power of the States in two, so the House of Representatives (*Tweede Kamer* in Dutch, meaning Second Chamber) was founded to make laws, and the Senate (*Eerste Kamer*, First Chamber) to check them. That Senate was known as the *Chambre de réflexion*, a term still used today.

The Senate currently has 75 members, precisely half that of the House of Representatives. They meet one day a week. The members generally do their work alongside another job, while members of the House of Representatives cannot hold other jobs.

Since the foundation of the bicameral system, the role of the Senate has been debated. Over the last 200 years there have been various proposals to abolish this chamber. Parties arguing for abolition continue to take their seat in the Senate. Relinquishing that right on principle would leave them politically hamstrung, as the power of the First Chamber prevails undiminished. This Chamber cannot directly change laws, nor immediately dismiss a cabinet, but it can do so indirectly. It is therefore a Chamber with indirect power.

The members of the Senate can only reject an entire law; they cannot make amendments. However, the government may still amend a law slightly. This is called a *Novelle*. If this amendment is first approved by the House of Representatives, then it passes to the Senate.

The Dutch cabinets over the last 200 years have always had to give proper consideration to the politicians sitting in the Senate, not only because of the power of the Senate itself, but also because of the individual members, who now tend to be older statesmen and women who have won their spurs in national politics, former party leaders and ministers, a stray captain of industry

© E.-J. Daniels.

or former head of a trade union, and sometimes former high-ranking military officers.

From the foundation of the Senate the members have been 'eminent' people. Two hundred years ago, when the Netherlands and Belgium were still one country, the Southern Netherlands predominantly wanted members of the aristocracy in the Senate. There were fewer aristocrats in the north of the country, so they came to a compromise. Aristocrats were permitted to become members alongside men who 'had rendered services to the State, who by their birth or wealth belong to the most distinguished men in the country'. The king appointed the members of the Senate for life.

When Belgium became independent in 1830, initially little changed in the functioning of the Senate. Over the course of about a century, various changes were implemented. In 1848 it was decided that the members should be elected by the States Provincial. Just forty years later it was decided that the members' personal financial wealth was no longer important. The Senate was also open to citizens (men, that is) who held high office, such as professors. Women became eligible from 1917.

For all these years the core of political decision making in the Netherlands has remained in the House of Representatives, but the Senate can make or break the government, especially at moments when that government does not have a Senate majority. If the cabinet falls, there are new elections for the House of Representatives. The elections for the Senate are fully independent of this. They take place once every four years.

The elections of May 2015 will take place halfway through the term of Rutte's liberal social democratic cabinet. From time immemorial governments able to count on a clear majority in both chambers have had few worries about the result of Senate elections. This government lacks such a majority, so these provincial elections will directly, rather than indirectly, affect national politics.

JORIS VAN DE KERKHOF
Translated by Ana Asbury

Between Myth and Reality
Andreas Vesalius

The year 2014 saw the five hundredth anniversary of the birth, in Brussels, of Andreas Vesalius, the revolutionary anatomist and medical reformer. His work has had enormous repercussions, both on the development of medical science and on the way we look at the body. Vesalius defended the idea that medicine should be founded on the scientific knowledge of the healthy body.

In his masterpiece, *De Humani Corporis Fabrica* (1543), he was the first person in history to produce a description of the human body in minute detail. Not only was the text revolutionary, but the copious illustrations were also of exceptional artistic quality. For centuries Vesalius' 'muscle men' were the model for painters and sculptors. Above all they exemplified the positive manner in which the body was experienced and presented from the time of the Renaissance on.

In this respect the significance of Vesalius goes beyond his direct influence on the medical profession. Vesalius grew to be one of the central figures in early modern science who succeeded in distancing himself from his predecessors and prepared the way for critical and empirical research into nature. But this same veneration provided an appropriate breeding ground for countless myths. As early as the seventeenth century the tale was being spread that, as personal physician to the Spanish court, Vesalius had been condemned to death by the Inquisition, following the autopsy of a nobleman, whose heart, apparently, was still beating. It was only on the intervention of Philip II that Vesalius' punishment could be converted to a pilgrimage to Jerusalem, a journey that eventually proved fatal for him. This myth, which is entirely without historical foundation, developed in the nineteenth century into a more generalised depiction in which Vesalius was the first to defy the ecclesiastical ban on anatomical dissection and so break the taboo on opening up the human body.

However, the reality was something else. Anatomical dissections had been a regular part of medical training in most European universities for centuries already. The religious ban on boiling bones (a practice associated with the transportation of the corpses of crusaders and with the concomitant dealing in relics) had no influence whatsoever on the practice of medical dissections. Vesalius never came into contact with the Inquisition. He adhered strictly to the rules and procedures that applied to dissections. Moreover the Inquisition was after heretics who were turning against the Church of Rome, and there was nothing in the practice of anatomy that in any way gave cause for that. There is absolutely no evidence to suggest that Vesalius had any heretical tendencies. Had that been the case, he would not have been able to continue so long at the court of Emperor Charles and Filip II. However it is historically correct that, as a student, Vesalius would steal corpses from churchyards and gallows sites at all hours of the night. But that was common, and even generally accepted, behaviour for students of medical science – as long as the corpses belonged to criminals or 'reviled' people, no one took the slightest bit of notice.

The myths that have arisen around the figure of Vesalius reflect a particular way of looking at the nature of science. In addition, revolutionary science stands against superstition, obscurantism and irrational traditions. To present Vesalius as a revolutionary pioneer of modern science it was (and still is) useful to present him as someone who came into contention with the religious dogmas and the short-sightedness of society in the times in which he lived. The scientific genius, unrecognised by his contemporaries, could only prevail thanks to his personal courage and perseverance. The myths about Vesalius merely demonstrate what many people still wish to hear, even though that is now out of date and erroneous.

A more discerning view on the figure of Vesalius allows one to see a researcher with exceptional talents, but also huge ambition, and someone marked by the ideas of his time. Vesalius was

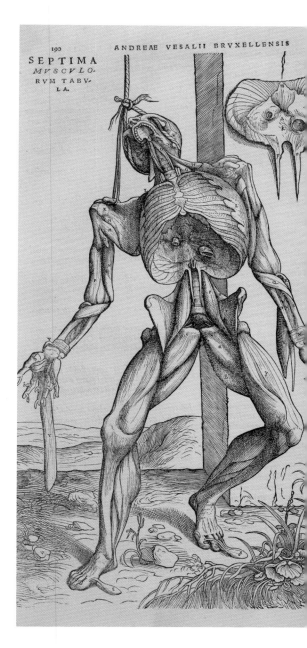

Hanging Corpse in: Andreas Vesalius,
De Humani Corporis Fabrica Libri Septem, Basel, *1543*
© KU Leuven, Universiteitsbibliotheek.

Society

Still Animals & the Workshop
© Liesbeth Peremans (Tuur Marinus@STUK)

not trying to weaken tradition, rather to restore it. As a new Galen he wanted to restore the work of the Greek anatomist to a place of honour, and to improve on it where necessary. Although his work was an important fresh step in the way in which scientific work was undertaken, Vesalius wanted above all to get back to the true knowledge that had existed among the Ancients. His anatomical work fully fitted into the paradigm of the new Galenism that was widespread during the Renaissance. Vesalius met with hardly any resistance.

What really made Vesalius a public icon was the way in which he made the connection between scientific culture and the sensitivities that were coming to be seen in the new ordering of society. More clearly than any other work, the *Fabrica* shows the reborn confidence of Western man, the belief in a better, utopian world. With the *Fabrica* Vesalius set scientific research in a much wider social context, a thought that may provide inspiration again to scientists of the 21st century.

GEERT VANPAEMEL
Translated by Sheila M. Dale

The Gang of Nivelles
Thirty Years on

Thirty years have passed since Belgium was the scene of a series of attacks and cold-blooded murders, mainly carried out at supermarkets. The assailants have never been found. The violent raids took place at branches of the Colruyt chain and (especially) Delhaize supermarkets in 1982, 1983 and 1985, and led to the deaths of 28 people. They culminated in an attack at a Delhaize store in Aalst, in the province of East Flanders, on Saturday, 9 November 1985, in which eight people died. The amount of money stolen in the raids was minimal and certainly out of all proportion to the level of violence used. The case was in danger of expiring, but when the new Belgian government took office it immediately announced that it wished to extend the statute of limitations by ten years.

The impact of the crimes on people's daily lives was enormous, especially in 1985, when a total of 16 people died in attacks in Braine l'Alleud (province of Walloon Brabant), Overijse (Flemish Brabant) and Aalst. All of these attacks took place in Delhaize stores. Following the events in Aalst, the government decided to station armed soldiers in Delhaize stores. According to eyewitnesses, the gang consisted of a tall man ('the Giant'), 'the Killer' (who killed most of the victims) and 'the Old Man', who was usually the driver. There were sometimes several more assailants.

The attacks by the gang coincided with those by the extreme left-wing terrorist group CCC (Cellules Communistes Combattantes). Their attacks cost two people their lives, but the gang members were arrested and sentenced. However, the Gang of Nivelles, named after the Walloon Brabant town that was attacked first, was a puzzle for police. One thing that was clear was that most of the attacks were committed close to motorways, enabling the perpetrators to escape easily out of the country. Some witnesses claim that 'the Killer' died in the final attack in Aalst after being hit by a police bullet. What is certain is that no further attacks took place after this.

Witnesses came forward who claimed to have seen three men in a Volkswagen Golf, the car used in the attacks, in the Bois de la Houssière, a forest in the province of Walloon Brabant, and two sacks containing ammunition and equipment for breaking and entering were found in a nearby canal. The ammunition matched that used in one of the attacks.

All kinds of theories did the rounds, especially given the meagre hauls from the attacks. Were they common criminals or members of an extreme right-wing organisation, whose sole aim was to spread terror? The Nivelles prosecutor, who was in charge of the investigation for many years, did not believe in the extreme right-wing theory and continued to focus the search on the criminal world. The prosecutor's office in Dendermonde achieved some success with the weapons find, but ultimately the case ended up, under great protest, in Charleroi. The authorities there also believed that pure criminality was behind the attacks. The prosecutor indicted a group of criminals from the Borinage area of the Walloon province of Hainaut, but they were ultimately acquitted.

As the years passed, it became increasingly difficult to catch the perpetrators. All manner of books and articles appeared, suggesting a link with the extreme right. It was thought that the gang might be made up of (former) members of the Belgian Gendarmerie, and that their aim was to destabilise the country. This idea was supported by the military precision with which the attacks were carried out. Specific reference was made to the paramilitary Westland New Post organisation. The suspicions grew when it transpired that members of this organisation were very familiar with the La Houssière forest, even holding shooting practice there. But genuinely convincing evidence was lacking.

Even foreign intelligence agencies - the CIA and Mossad - came into the picture. There was also talk of extortion because the attacks mainly targeted Delhaize stores. However, Delhaize denied these rumours categorically. A Senate committee was installed to carry out an inquiry into the investigation. Several irregularities in the overall investigation would lead to the setting up of a standing committee (the Vast Comité I) to oversee the police service.

Public confidence in the functioning of the Belgian judicial system suffered enormously, and was not helped by the inability to solve the puzzle. The brutality of the perpetrators and the choice of the victims - simple shoppers in supermarkets - only served to exacerbate the malaise.

Yet the investigation continues. As recently as 2010, an e-fit of a gang member was published. And recently a man was arrested: a former prisoner who had allegedly divulged all manner of details to a fellow prisoner. He was quickly released again, though.

The Gang of Nivelles continues to occupy people's minds, and has even featured in strip cartoons, novels and a film. The next of kin of the victims, however, have long since given up hope that the perpetrators will ever be found. Each year they are invited to meet the investigators, who bring them up to date on the case. But they have lost their faith in the Belgian justice system. Extending the statute of limitations by ten years will do nothing to change that.

JOS BOUVEROUX
Translated by Julian Ross

Look Up and Plug In
Daan Roosegaarde

Artist and designer Daan Roosegaarde (° 1979) calls himself a 'hippy with a business plan' and a 'technopoet'. The artist was educated at ArtEZ Institute of the Arts in Enschede (in the east of the Netherlands) and at the Berlage Institute in Rotterdam. In recent years he has emerged as a contemporary visionary, melding together new techniques, space, man and nature. His ideas are philosophically, politically, ecologically, socially and artistically inspired. In Roosegaarde's view, old mechanisms from the industrialised world of the 19th and 20th centuries no longer work. Instead we should move towards a society where control plays no role, where the tone is set instead by collaboration, interactive dynamics and empathy for surprising possibilities of all kinds. Roosegaarde believes that technology and social media will increasingly become second nature to us, and that technology and nature have long ceased to be separate worlds.

Daan Roosegaarde has won the Dutch Design Award, the Design for Asia Award and the Innovative Practice Award for his innovative ideas. He leads the multidisciplinary Studio Roosegaarde, which has offices in the Netherlands and China. Trained as an artist and designer, he roams the borders of the two disciplines, revealing himself through his studio in the architecture world, through public spaces and in the art and design world. He also gives lectures and organises master classes, for example in 'meaningful leadership'. One question he often asks is 'Do you know why you can't tickle yourself?' His immediate answer: 'The brain is a system attuned to the avoidance of undesirable situations, so it's constantly predicting what's coming. Before you even move your finger to tickle yourself, you're aware of it - in contrast with someone else tickling you. The same is true of innovation: you need others to break the system open.'[1] His studio is home to the 'yes but' chair, in which he sometimes seats his clients, and for every 'yes but' uttered they receive a small electric shock.

Studio Roosegaarde, *Sustainable Dance Floor*, 2008

'The future is fluid. You can anticipate or design that future, and imagination is crucial for that...,'[2] says Roosegaarde. On the popular television programme *Summer Guests* in 2013 he showed a short film by French designer Philippe Starck, in which he suggests that everyone needs to open their eyes - to look not only downwards to find firm ground, but more importantly upwards - at the world. It is a matter of observation and in particular of being open to amazement. Roosegaarde: 'The world is enormous. ...If we can't fit in in one place, we can just go elsewhere. Making connections strengthens things. If you want something new, the trick is to get people to 'plug in' from different sides. If it works, they strengthen rather than cut into one another.'[3] Daan Roosegaarde is an advocate of combining: 'Experiencing something old differently, and linking it to something new... and eliciting new words – that's what it's all about. (...) It's simply a matter of hacking: shifting the mentality from the old world to the new.'[4]

In *Dune* (2006) Roosegaarde created his first futuristic relationship with urban space. In Rotterdam's Maastunnel and later along the bank of the River Maas (*Dune 4.2.*, 60 metres in length) he created all sorts of stalks (fibre) which sway back and forth as you walk or cycle past. At the same time an LED at the end of each stalk flashes and they produce the sounds of crickets. *Dune* employs advanced technology to bring about a magnificent meeting of public space, man and nature. While *Dune* is surprising and enchanting, at first glance *Marbles* has the appearance of a collection of boulders. The work is located in a square in the new city of Almere (province of Flevoland) where lots of young people meet. The plastic shapes work very interactively, lighting up in different colours when touched, flashing in different rhythms and making noises. The rhythm varies from slightly agitated to rather listless and bored depending on the feedback from the environment.

Roosegaarde and his colleagues conducted research in a laboratory in Eindhoven for the development of *Crystal*. Hundreds of crystal shapes (wireless LEDs charged by magnetic fields) light up when you touch them. They lie strewn across the ground with endless potential for play. There is an open source connection so that they can be programmed democratically. Roosegaarde has nicknamed this work 'Lego from Mars'. *Flow* is an installation with hundreds of ventilators which blow individually when touched, developing an illusory landscape or transparent body in the space. *Lotus Dome* takes the shape of a Renaissance dome made of foil. As you approach the structure a number of aluminium lotus flowers open up, releasing light from the heart of the *Lotus Dome*. The work has been displayed in a 17th century church in the French city of Lille and in the Rijksmuseum in Amsterdam.

Back to Rotterdam for a moment, where dancers in a club generate the energy for everything around them to function optimally. The *Sustainable Dance Floor* sustainably converts the energy of the dancing crowd. Roosegaarde is also developing an

Studio Roosegaarde, *Smart Highway*, 2012

electrostatic vacuum cleaner to 'suck away' stifling smog particles from the sky above Beijing. *The Smog Free Park* works with magnetically charged copper reels to draw the pollution to the ground, where it is filtered. Roosegaarde has succeeded in manufacturing diamonds from the distilled CO_2 by flattening the carbon particles, and then working the diamonds into a piece of jewellery for the future, the *Smog Ring*. Anyone who buys one of these rings is in fact buying 1000 smog particles, thus contributing to a piece of clean sky over Beijing, where a park will be created, supported financially by the profits of the jewellery sales.

The *Smart Highway* is characteristic of the way of working at Studio Roosegaarde. It was developed in collaboration with scientists and a construction company. Since summer 2013 the N329 near Oss (North Brabant) has had colourful light strips instead of streetlights. The paint for this was developed by Roosegaarde in collaboration with the construction company to absorb enough light during the day to shine for eight to ten hours.

The application is based on the glow-in-the-dark principle and inspired by beautiful light-producing jellyfish. There is also paint being developed to change colour when it freezes. Blue snowflakes can then appear on the road surface, warning drivers of slippery conditions. Windmills and solar panels feed the road with its dynamic light patterns. Roosegaarde's dream is to light the Afsluitdijk (the connection between the west and the north of the Netherlands constructed in 1932) in the same way. He has further plans: he is working with Delft University of Technology on a technique for charging electric cars wirelessly while driving along the motorway. Inductive charging through electromagnetic fields in the road surface would allow sustainable drivers of the future to charge their vehicles without having to find a charging station.

Recently six hundred metres of cycle path in Nuenen in Brabant were fitted with glow stones. The thousands of stones recharge during the day to light up together in the evening, transforming the cycle path into the painting *The Starry Night* (1889) by Vincent van Gogh, who lived in Nuenen between 1883 and 1885. It truly creates the feeling of cycling or walking in Van Gogh's sparkling starry night in the south of France.

For Daan Roosegaarde it is clear. He likes to quote the famous media expert Marshall McLuhan: 'There are no passengers on Spaceship Earth. We are all crew.'[5]

DAVID STROBAND
Translated by Anna Asbury

www.studioroosegaarde.net

1 - 5: www. Bindje.nl/laat-je-kietelen-daan-roosegaarde-over-social-design-en-leiderschap .

'The Most Hated Man in America'
The Frick Collection on Show in The Hague

A young New Yorker with a growing taste for art will first find his way to the Museum of Modern Art, for Picasso and van Gogh, then to the Metropolitan Museum of Art for - in my case in the 1950s - the Etruscan warrior and the Cellini cup, the most spectacular works in the museum, both of which were later exposed as forgeries. Eventually, you got wind of a smaller, more exclusive museum with a higher threshold than the Big Two. The Frick Collection, on Seventieth Street at Fifth Avenue, is not a simple walk-in attraction. It is a town palace, built in 1913-1914 as the private home of Henry Clay Frick (1849-1919). When I first visited it, as a student of art history, it was still intimidating, as if Frick himself were about to collar you and ask you what was so special about Turner's *Harbour of Dieppe* or Goya's *Forge*.

Since then, the Frick has bent over backwards to become as accessible as it can, at least online. It was one of the first museums to offer a virtual visit on the Internet, allowing you to go from room to room and to click on any object that you want to see or study in detail. If Frick's original intention was to enable Americans to appreciate great art without crossing the Atlantic, the museum now gives Europeans (and everyone else) access to a great American collection without even getting up from their chairs.

The lover of Dutch and Flemish art finds himself in the company of Frick himself, whose first acquisition of an Old Master, in 1896, was a still life by Jan van Os (1744-1808) and one of whose proudest possessions, bought in 1906, was the magisterial Rembrandt self-portrait of 1658. From 1899 - Frick's 'breakthrough Rembrandt year', as one source has aptly described it - until 1919, the year of his death, Frick would acquire at least 145 paintings, of which more than one-fifth belonged to the Dutch and Flemish schools. None of those paintings, nor the hundreds of objets d'art and sculptures Frick bought in the 1910s, may, under the terms of the donor's will, ever be shown outside the Frick Collection. Therefore, the exhibition organized by the Mauritshuis in The Hague till 10 May 2015 consists exclusively of art that was purchased after Frick's death. This exhibition of 36 works is the largest that the Frick has ever allowed out of its doors. The occasion was a typical museum quid pro quo deal. In 2013-2014, during the renovation of the Mauritshuis, the museum lent 15 of its greatest paintings, crowned by Vermeer's *Girl with a Pearl Earring*, to the Frick for what turned out to be the greatest public success the museum has ever experienced. In exchange the Frick and the Mauritshuis agreed on a selection of mainly non-Netherlandish pieces from the Frick.

As few as they may be, how can one not be thankful for the opportunity to savour a *Virgin and Child* from the studio of Jan van Eyck, a portrait by Hans Memling, *The Three Soldiers* by Pieter Bruegel, a 1652 landscape by Jacob van Ruisdael and a two-sided sheet of studies by Pieter Paul Rubens, in the company of choice works by such as Cimabue, Pisanello, Boucher, Constable and Ingres? The grisaille by Bruegel is perhaps the rarest work in the exhibition. Signed and dated 1568, a year before the artist's death, it is the only grisaille by Bruegel of a secular subject. One soldier, seen in profile, raises a flag; a second, full face, plays a flute, with a horn on his belt; and the third, seen from behind and armed with a sword, beats a drum.

The Frick Collection and the Mauritshuis have a number of things in common. They are both jewel boxes of museums, the secret pride of their respective city-states, New York and the Dutch urban agglomeration called the Randstad. The giants for whom they are named - Johan Maurits van Nassau (1604-1679) and Henry Clay Frick - shared an impassioned love for art that they did not allow to interfere with their effectiveness as leaders, earners and, each in his own way, conquistadors. While Johan Maurits was a notably humane ruler of Dutch Brazil and Cleves

Pieter Bruegel the Elder, *The Three Soldiers*, 1568, oil on oak
© Frick Collection

and the robber baron Frick was called 'the most hated man in America' for his ruthless treatment of labourers in his coal and steel plants, the virtues of the one and the vices of the other have been smoothed level by time and shared patronage of the arts.

GARY SCHWARTZ

http://www.frick.org/

The Frick Collection. Art Treasures from New York: till 10 May 2015 in the Mauritshuis in The Hague (www/mauritshuis.nl).

ESMÉE QUODBACH, ' "I want this collection to be my monument": Henry Clay Frick and the formation of The Frick Collection', *Journal of the History of Collections*, XXI, 2009, pp. 229-240..

Bøkfjord Fyr, Norway
© Stephan Vanfleteren

Shades of Grey and Steely Blue
Two Photo Books about Two Seas

Between 1941 and 1945 a network of bunkers and casemates was built along a coastline stretching more than five thousand kilometres, from the very north of Finland (now Russia) through Norway, Denmark, Germany, the Netherlands, Belgium and France – from a lonely fjord in the far north to the Pyrenees in the south. It was intended to protect German-occupied Western Europe from British-American attack. We know how that ended. General Patton, the hero of manoeuvre warfare, maintained that 'fixed fortifications are a monument to the stupidity of man'. In the end, one long day in Normandy was enough to breach this coastal defence, which has gone down in history as the Atlantic Wall. The work on *Festung Europa* was carried out to the greater glory of invincible Germany using local labour, forced or otherwise, Russian prisoners of war and over 1500 Antwerp Jews even (who were then deported to Auschwitz after just a few months in Northern France).

After the war the bunkers were abandoned. In the meantime some have been demolished, while others, here and there, have actually been protected as heritage. In Raversijde, near Ostend, a complete German battery has been preserved and opened up to the public. The whole evolution of the Atlantic Wall can be deduced from this site which, with its sixty bunkers and several kilometres of trenches, is one of the best preserved sections of the Atlantic Wall.

Flemish photographer Stephan Vanfleteren (1969) was commissioned by the *Atlantic Wall Open Air Museum* Raversijde and the Province of West Flanders to reproduce the entire coastal defence from Norway to Spain in pictures, which he has done in his own inimitable fashion.

Stephan Vanfleteren does not like sun. He prefers grey, mist, starkness. And twilight. In these photos you see nothing but air, sea, rocks, concrete. Greys and blacks. Bunkers float like tankers, like whales in the sea. The tide laps at them, surrounds them, wears them away. Eroding hulks. They slide from the dunes onto the beach, stand or lie there higgledy-piggledy – *Le Temps, ce grand Sculpteur!* – like gigantic toy building blocks scattered on the beaches. Sometimes they look like meteorites that have fallen from the air and bored into the sand. Through the photographer's lens, cliffs, rocks and concrete are often interchangeable, growing toward each other, barely distinguishable from each other: nature and culture. Their noses – like the beaks of birds of prey – stick out above the cliffs, waiting for an enemy that never comes. On land, trees break through the concrete and the bunkers are overrun by woods.

The photographer grew up with these bunkers. His first were in his native village of Oostduinkerke, on the west coast of Belgium. They look like the most humane of structures, stables, sheds. Children play in them. At the other end of the spectrum there are the architectonic constructions of the Channel Islands which – stripped now of any ornament, naked, almost minimalist – are remi-

Saint-Tropez,
France
© Nick Hannes

niscent of the buildings by Frank Lloyd Wright and Le Corbusier. In his introduction Vanfleteren refers to the more than fifteen thousand bunkers that the Germans built as 'pebblestones of history'. It was with a mixture of abhorrence and admiration that he viewed, photographed and immortalized them. Though nature is completely unmoved by history, the history of the Second World War and therefore these structures has not quite faded yet.

The North Sea, the English Channel and the Atlantic Ocean, proliferating in every shade of grey under Vanfleteren's lens, are a far cry from the azure blue of the Mediterranean, *Mare nostrum*, which once washed the shores where European civilisation was born and developed. Flemish photographer Nick Hannes (1974) travelled all around the Mediterranean with a remark made by the historian Ernle Bradford as his motto: 'The Pacific may have the most changeless ageless aspect of any ocean, but the Mediterranean Sea celebrates the continuity of Man.' This sea, which borders the cradle of European civilisation, seems to have become a graveyard for people fleeing from Africa and the Middle East to Fort Europe. So Hannes shows us not idylls, not famous vistas, but pictures of the mass tourism in Benidorm and La Grande Motte, the hedonism of Ibiza (dancing) and Tel Aviv (sunbathing), the luxurious tedium of cruises, the hidden opulence of Monte Carlo and Cannes, the painful cleanliness of Marbella, dingy beaches with their factories in Montenegro; and the walls, borders, demarcation lines and barbed wire of the Spanish (and therefore European) enclaves in Morocco, Ceuta and Melilla,

Nicosia, the Gaza Strip, Bethlehem and Ramallah. You can detect the crisis in Greece in the skeleton of a petrol station without pumps, or a wedding party taking place in a petrol station for lack of a real party venue. Rubbish and urban neglect; war ruins in Libya. Migrants, refugees, fortune-seekers – not to say 'illegals', since that is not a human category (only behaviour or deeds can be 'illegal') – pass before the lens, waving papers at barriers, selling knickknacks on beaches. Metropolises spread far and wide, the apartment buildings of Istanbul march onward, threatening the shepherds crouching in a meadow. The ferries are rusty (Messina) and the wrecked ships on Lampedusa tell nothing of their cargo. The huge, expensive mosque shines, the umbrella seller near the supermarket surreptitiously bends his head on his prayer mat.

The Atlantic Wall is devoid of people; the Mediterranean Sea, sewer and ravishing whore, is awash with them. Black, white and every shade of grey here; steely blue, bright colours and parched soil there. Here impotent, dumb defences; there yearning people in all their guises. We wouldn't be without either of them. The defences, I mean, and the people. And the seas.

LUC DEVOLDERE
Translated by Lindsay Edwards

STEPHAN VANFLETEREN, *Atlantic Wall*,
Uitgeverij Hannibal, Veurne, 2014, 200 pp.
NICK HANNES, *Mediterranean. The Continuity of Man*,
Uitgeverij Hannibal, Veurne, 2014, 192 pp.

Batman in Mons
Saint George and the European Capital of Culture 2015

The historic city of Mons, situated in the French-language region of Belgium, is the European Capital of Culture in 2015. The ambitious programme developed by the city includes numerous exhibitions, all linked in some way to the city and its rich history. An example is the exhibition focusing on Saint George – l'Homme, le Dragon et la Mort – which will be on display from the autumn in MAC's Museum of Contemporary Art at the Grand Hornusite in nearby Boussu.

MAC's is the most important museum of contemporary art in French-speaking Belgium. It is situated in an impressive UNESCO-listed former industrial (mining) facility in the Borinage area. The museum's curator (and founder) is Laurent Busine, one of the most authoritative voices on contemporary art in the world of French and Francophone culture, but also a name of note in Flanders, and to a slightly lesser extent in the Netherlands. So, despite its somewhat eccentric and isolated geographical location, MAC's attracts a large number of Flemish and Dutch visitors.

Busine had for many years been intrigued by the legend of Saint George and the innumerable depictions in European art of this saint whose legendary fight with a dragon is re-enacted every year on Trinity Sunday in Mons. The city's candidacy for European Capital of Culture proved to be the perfect moment to dedicate what is thought to be the first ever exhibition to the way in which Saint George was portrayed from the late Middle Ages up to and including the 17th century. Laurent Busine chose to organise the exhibition in collaboration with the museums in Bruges and with myself – until recently curator there – as co-curator, a result of the intense collaboration that began when Bruges was European Capital of Culture, in 2002. This confirms once again the importance of systematic collaboration across language and geographical boundaries in the cultural sector.

Although he may have faded somewhat into obscurity today, for centuries Saint George was one of the most popular and widely portrayed saints not just throughout Europe, but also in Russia and countries with Orthodox Christian traditions and in regions populated by Coptic Christians. Any number of cities – from Freiburg to Ferrara, from Beirut to Amersfoort –and many countries, such as England, Malta, Lithuania and Portugal, chose Saint George as their patron saint – as did the international scout movement. The appeal is not difficult to explain. The entire mythical account – there is not even a shred of historical reality to the legend – is one of the eternal and heroic struggle between good and evil. The legend did not acquire tangible form until the Middle Ages, in the Legenda aurea, or 'Golden Legend', the famous 13th-century collection of hagiographies. The legend has it that he was a man from a well-to-do family background who served as an officer in the Imperial Roman armies in the Near East in the third century A.D. His conversion to Christianity is said to have led to his death as a martyr. However, George owes his popularity principally to his role as the saviour of a city that was being terrorised by a dragon which continually demanded human sacrifices. When the daughter of the king is about to offer herself for sacrifice due to a lack of other victims, George offers to fight the dragon on condition that the city converts to the Christian faith. And so it went. Good triumphed over evil, naturally. Notable and characteristic here is that an intrinsically traditional theme – think of Perseus and Andromeda, for example – was revived and given new meaning in a Christian context. A clever strategic choice.

It is not hard to understand why the battle between George and the Dragon continues to appeal to the fantasy and imagination to this day. As stated, the battle between good and evil is an eternal one. In reality, George is no different from Batman or Spiderman – a 'human' with superhuman gifts who fights and above all defeats the ever-present evil. The fact that at the same time he rescues a beautiful young woman, a symbol of innocence, is also an eternal theme. But there are more elements that have helped ensure that this theme has been portrayed so often. It is unbelievably attractive for an artist to portray this topic: the battle between good and evil, the drama of a fight, the imagination that is needed to depict the mythical but so threatening subject of a dragon, and the contrast between the beautiful (at least we assume so) princess and the abhorrent monster – Beauty and the Beast. And all that in an open landscape –a theme that was of great significance anyway in the 15th and 16th centuries. It could all be the script for a Walt Disney blockbuster. It is in any event a proven success in the visual arts. And it is precisely this that the exhibition in Mons aims to show: the interaction between and mutual influence of artists in the fields of painting, sculpture, drawing and printmaking, and the sharing of forms and compositions between artists from all regions of Europe.

A nice measure of this appeal is the fact that one of the most recent and most popular attractions in the Efteling theme park in the Netherlands – nominated time and again as the best entertainment park in Europe – is a roller coaster with the name 'George and the Dragon'. Perhaps a harbinger of the appeal that the MAC's exhibition could have?

MANFRED SELLINK
Translated by Julian Ross

The Legend of Saint George (1535-1540) by Lancelot Blondeel
© Musea Brugge. Lukas Art in Flanders. Photo by Hugo Maertens

© Mirjam Devriendt

Subdued Beauty
A Retrospective of Berlinde De Bruyckere's Work

In recent years the work of the Flemish artist Berlinde De Bruyckere (Ghent, 1964) has mainly been on show in international museums and collections. Nevertheless De Bruyckere has remained popular in Belgium. In 2010 she received the Flemish Culture Prize for Visual Arts and she represented Belgium at the Venice Biennale in 2013. But the last solo exhibition De Bruyckere had in her country of origin dates from more than a decade ago. Around that time *The Low Countries* published a portrait of De Bruyckere: 'Innocence Can Be Hell' (2002).[1] Twelve years later the Municipal Museum of Contemporary Art (S.M.A.K.) organised the first ever retrospective of De Bruyckere in her hometown Ghent. A slightly different version of *Sculptures and Drawings 2000-2014* travelled to the Gemeentemuseum in The Hague (28 February – 31 May) and to Kunsthaus Bregenz in Austria (18 April-5 July) in 2015. The exhibition is accompanied by a hefty monograph. [2]

Sculptures and Drawings 2000-2014 begins with De Bruyckere's contribution to the Venice Biennale. The monumental work she created for the Belgian pavilion *Kreupelhout – Cripplewood* (2012-2013) serves both as the exhibition's starting point and its key theme. It was inspired by the city of Venice, the figure of Saint Sebastian and De Bruyckere's interactions with the author John Coetzee, who – incidentally – provided the artwork's title. *Kreupelhout – Cripplewood* shows the remains of a giant elm that lies fallen, bruised and battered on the floor of the museum. Its branches are bandaged. Coloured wax 'bark' peels off it.

This sculpture perfectly encapsulates all of De Bruyckere's themes, motives and sources of inspiration: metamorphosis, duality, the body (human, animal, plant and everything in between), skin (ditto), wounds, fragility which is also strength, defence, melancholy... De Bruyckere, however, never lapses into pessimism or fatalism; her works are of a sublime and subdued beauty.

Trees have always inspired Berlinde De Bruyckere. *Sculptures and Drawings 2000-2014* shows, for instance, an older series of drawings of bleeding trees. It is particularly interesting to see these drawings next to De Bruyckere's more recent work. Every one of her art works inspires another.

Besides *Kreupelhout – Cripplewood* and the drawings, De Bruyckere shows entangled wax stems and branches in a pair of display cases (*019* and *028*, 2007). The two display cases are from a Southern French museum where they were originally used to exhibit pottery. Their patina shows traces of the past, of vulnerability. De Bruyckere does not use these cases simply to hold her sculptures; they are an integral part of the artwork. Their doors remain open. The cases do not offer protection. Case, tree and visitor engage in open dialogue.

It is a small step from trees to antlers. The enormous branches on their heads get many a deer into trouble; antlers can be physically impairing (becoming entangled with other deers' antlers during fights) or attract the attention of hunters. De Bruyckere presents antlers as fragile, hurting bodies of flesh and blood, and attaches them to the walls with heavy meat hooks. The most impressive of antlers, *Actaeon* (2012, which not surprisingly refers to Ovid's *Metamorphoses*), lies on what appears to be an altar or a stake. Again De Bruyckere consciously chooses duality here: antlers are, of course, not flammable, but the new wax skin on the other hand is extremely sensitive to fire.

The material on which the antlers rest wasn't randomly chosen either. The wood and snippets of newspapers and wallpaper all originate from the artist's home. These are traces of an unknown past. Besides the sculptures, the exhibition also includes drawings of human bodies that grow antlers – or are these antlers growing humans?

For Berlinde De Bruyckere models are never simply bodies. This is clear from the titles she bestows on her work: not Mary Magdalene, but *Hanne* (2003), or from the reference she makes to the Portuguese dancer Romeu Runa in her drawing *Romeu my deer* (2010-2011). De Bruyckere approaches her models and sources of inspiration with much respect and she often integrates their personal histories into her work.

She created *The Wound* (2011-2012), for example, after she had seen a series of portraits in Istanbul of Muslim women who show scars on their bodies, apparently without emotion. Their tumours were displayed on separate pictures, exhibited on tables and neatly kept in glass bowls. De Bruyckere's *The Wound* series shows wounds that are at the same time female reproductive organs, symbols of female strength and new life. Horse tackle loosely frames the wounds, referring in turn to the taming of the horse and, simultaneously, its immense natural strength.

Sculptures and Drawings 2000-2014 does not fail to present De Bruyckere's famous horse sculptures. *Lost I* (2006) is exhibited together with two *Schmerzensmannen* (2009), as a counterweight for, firstly, the suffering and entangled human figures in the exhibition and, secondly, the supportive branches and trunks in the display cases *019* and *028* (2007).

The exhibition *Sculptures and Drawings 2000-2014* is clearly not the end point in Berlinde De Bruyckere's oeuvre. It is more of a temporary resting place, a status quaestionis that interconnects the artist's past, present and future.

DOROTHEE CAPPELLE
Translated by Stefanie van Gemert

1 Mark Ruyters, 'Innocence Can Be Hell. The Art of Berlinde De Bruyckere', in: *The Low Countries* 10, 2002, pp. 225-229.
2 Angela Mengoni, Emmanuel Alloa, Gary Carrion-Murayari, Caroline Lamarche, J.M. Coetzee & Philippe Van Cauteren, *Berlinde De Bruyckere*, Mercatorfonds, 2014. Available in English.

© Mirjam Devriendt

Contributors

Maarten Asscher
Writer and Bookseller
m.asscher@wxs.nl

Dirk Van Assche
Deputy Editor *Ons Erfdeel vzw*
dirkvanassche@onserfdeel.be

Mattias Baertsoen
Music Critic
m.baertsoen@gmail.com

Ludo Beheydt
Em. Professor of Dutch
Ludo.Beheydt@skynet.be

Jan Berkouwer
Em. Professor of Economics
robiniafoundation@robiniafoundation.nl

Derek Blyth
Journalist
derekblyth@lycos.com

Jan Blomme
Managing Director Port of Antwerp
International
jan.blomme@portofantwerp.com

Jos Bouveroux
Journalist
jos.bouveroux@telenet.be

Eric Bracke
Art Critic
eric.mc.bracke@gmail.com

Thijs Broer
Journalist
thijs.broer@vn.nl

Vittorio Busato
Psychologist/Author
v.busato1@chello.nl

Dorothee Cappelle
Administrative Secretary *Ons Erfdeel vzw*
adm2@onserfdeel.be

Pieter Coupé
Secretary *Ons Erfdeel.*
Vlaams-Nederlands cultureel tijdschrift
onserfdeel@onserfdeel.be

Luc Devoldere
Chief Editor *Ons Erfdeel vzw*
luc.devoldere@onserfdeel.be

Bernard Dewulf
Writer
dewulfbernard@gmail.com

Harry den Hartog
Architecture Critic
harry.den.hartog@urbanlanguage.org

Frank Hellemans
Literay Critic
hellemans.frank@telenet.be

Wouter Hillaert
Theatre Critic
wouter.hillaert@rektoverso.be

Rick Honings
Post-doctoral Researcher at Leiden
University Centre for the Arts in Society
r.a.m.honings@hum.leidenuniv.nl

Han van der Horst
Historian
horst99@xs4all.nl

Jaap Huisman
Architecture Critic
jaap.huis@planet.nl

Joris van de Kerkhof
Journalist
Joris.van.de.Kerkhof@nos.nl

Petra de Koning
Journalist
P.dekoning@nrc.nl

Anton Korteweg
Poet
antonkorteweg@planet.nl

Bregje Lampe
Fashion Critic
bregjelampe@mac.com

Jonas Lampens
Photographer
jonas.lampens@telenet.be

Annemie Leysen
Literay Critic
annemieleysen@hotmail.com

Matthias Meirlaen
Post-doctoral Researcher at Université
Lille3
matthias.meirlaen@univ-lille3.fr

Bart Moeyaert
Writer
FF16@bartmoeyaert.com

Anne Marie Musschoot
Em. Professor of Dutch Literature
annemarie.musschoot@UGent.be

Lutgard Mutsaers
Music Critic
lut@ision.nl

Alexander Roose
Professor of French Literature at UGent
Alexander.Roose@UGent.be

Tineke Reijnders

Photo Critic

tineker@xs4all.nl

Reinier Salverda

Em. Professor of Dutch

reiniersalverda@yahoo.co.uk

Gary Schwartz

Art Historian

Gary.Schwartz@xs4all.nl

Manfred Sellink

General Director and Head Curator,
Royal Museum of Fine Arts, Antwerp.

manfred.sellink@kmska.be

David Stroband

Art Critic

davidstroband@zonnet.nl

Carl De Strycker

Director Poëziecentrum, Ghent.

carl.destrycker@poeziecentrum.be

Jan Temmerman

Film Critic

jan.temmerman@demorgen be

Jo Tollebeek

Professor of Cultural History at KU
Leuven

jo.tollebeek@arts.kuleuven.be

Nick Trachet

Culinary Journalist

nick.trachet@gmail.com

Hans Vanacker

Secretary *Septentrion. Arts, lettres et
culture de Flandre et des Pays-Bas*

septentrion@onserfdeel.be

Tomas Vanheste

Journalist

t.vanheste@kpnmail.nl

Geert Vanpaemel

Professor Faculty of Economics and
Business at KU Leuven

geert.vanpaemel@wet.kuleuven.be

Jeroen Vullings

Literay Critic

jeroen.vullings@me.com

Jeroen van Zanten

Professor of Dutch History at Amsterdam
University

J.C.vanZanten@uva.nl

Translators

Anna Asbury

Gregory Ball

Pleuke Boyce

James Brockway

David Colmer

Sheila M. Dale

Brian Doyle

Lindsay Edwards

Chris Emery

Peter Flynn

Donald Gardner

Stefanie van Gemert

Yvette Mead

Alison Mouthaan

Leonard Nathan

Julian Ross

Herlinde Spahr

Paul Vincent

Rebekah Wilson

Advisor on English usage

Lindsay Edwards

Colophon

Institution

This twenty-third yearbook is published by the Flemish-Dutch cultural institution 'Ons Erfdeel vzw', with the support of the Dutch Ministry of Education, Culture and Science (The Hague), the Flemish Authorities (Brussels) and the Provinces of West and East Flanders.

'Ons Erfdeel vzw' also publishes the Dutch-language periodical *Ons Erfdeel* and the French-language periodical *Septentrion. Arts, lettres et culture de Flandre et des Pays-Bas*, the bilingual yearbook *De Franse Neder-landen – Les Pays-Bas Français* and a series of books in several languages covering various aspects of the culture of the Low Countries.

The Board of Directors of 'Ons Erfdeel vzw'

President:
Herman Balthazar

Managing Director:
Luc Devoldere

Directors:
Bert De Graeve
Patrick Kindt
Hilde Laga
Mark Leysen
Marita Mathijsen
Frits van Oostrom
Danny De Raymaeker
Paul Schnabel
Adriaan van der Staay
Ludo Verhoeven

Honorary President:
Philip Houben

Address of the Editorial Board and the Administration

'Ons Erfdeel vzw', Murissonstraat 260,
8930 Rekkem, Flanders, Belgium
T +32 56 41 12 01, F +32 56 41 47 07
www.onserfdeel.be, www.onserfdeel.nl
thelowcountriesblog.onserfdeel.be
VAT BE 0410.723.635

Philip Vanwalleghem *Head of Administration*
Dorothee Cappelle *Administrative Secretary*

Aims

With *The Low Countries*, a yearbook founded by Jozef Deleu (Chief Editor from 1993 until 2002), the editors and publisher aim to present to the world the culture and society of the Dutch-speaking area which embraces both the Netherlands and Flanders, the northern part of Belgium.

The articles in this yearbook survey the living, contemporary culture of the Low Countries as well as their cultural heritage. In its words and pictures *The Low Countries* provides information about literature and the arts, but also about broad social and historical developments in Flanders and the Netherlands.

The culture of Flanders and the Netherlands is not an isolated phenomenon; its development over the centuries has been one of continuous interaction with the outside world. In consequence the yearbook also pays due attention to the centuries-old continuing cultural interplay between the Low Countries and the world beyond their borders.

By drawing attention to the diversity, vitality and international dimension of the culture of Flanders and the Netherlands, *The Low Countries* hopes to contribute to a lively dialogue between them and other cultures.

ISSN 0779-5815
ISBN 978-90-79705-191
Statutory deposit no. D/2015/3006/1
NUR 612

Copyright © 2015 'Ons Erfdeel vzw' and SABAM Belgium 2015
Printed by Die Keure, Bruges, Flanders, Belgium
Design by Henk Linskens (Die Keure)

Prices for the yearbook 2015, no. 23

Belgium € 37, The Netherlands € 39, Europe € 39

Other Countries: € 45
All prices inclusive of shipping costs

You can order this book from our webshop at www.onserfdeel.be and pay by credit card

As well as the yearbook
The Low Countries,
the Flemish Netherlands
Institution 'Ons Erfdeel vzw'
publishes a number of books
covering various aspects of
the culture of Flanders and
the Netherlands.

Wim Daniëls
Talking Dutch.
Illustrated; 80 pp.

J.A. Kossmann-Putto &
E.H. Kossmann
*The Low Countries.
History of the Northern
and Southern Netherlands.*
Illustrated; 64 pp.

Isabella Lanz &
Katie Verstockt,
*Contemporary Dance
in the Low Countries.*
Illustrated; 128 pp.

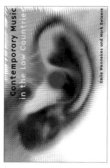

Mark Delaere &
Emile Wennekes,
*Contemporary Music in
the Low Countries.*
Illustrated; 128 pp.

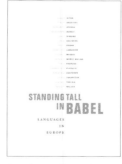

*Standing Tall in Babel.
Languages in Europe.*
Sixteen European writers
about their mother tongues.
Hardcover; 144 pp.

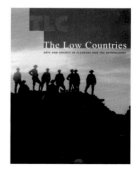

Between 1993 and 2014
twenty two issues of the
yearbook *The Low Countries*
have been published.

EUROPE

NORTH
SEA

Dutch language area

French language area
in Belgium

Brussels bilingual area :
Dutch and French

German language area :
in Belgium

Bilingual area :
Dutch and Frisian

Capital city

Provincial capital

National frontier

Provincial Boundary

FRIESLAND
Leeuwarden
GRONINGEN
Groningen
Assen
DRENTHE
NORTH HOLLAND
FLEVOLAND
Lelystad
Zwolle
Haarlem
OVERIJSSEL
AMSTERDAM
The Hague
Utrecht
UTRECHT
GELDERLAND
Arnhem
SOUTH HOLLAND
ZEELAND
Middelburg
's-Hertogenbosch
NORTH BRABANT
Antwerp
LIMBURG
ANTWERP
Bruges
EAST FLANDERS
Ghent
LIMBURG
WEST FLANDERS
FLANDERS
FLEMISH BRABANT
Hasselt
Maastricht
BRUSSELS
Leuven
GERMANY
Wavre
WALLOON BRABANT
HAINAUT
Mons
Namur
Liège
LIÈGE
FRANCE
NAMUR
LUXEMBOURG
LUX.
Arlon

km

© Carto